MOSES WISDOM,

BIBLE 613 SHAPE US CONSTITUTION AND LAWS

AF691539

CO-AUTHORS:
BEN HAND, J.D.
GEORGE MCCARLEY

ISBN 979-8-9912575-0-3

COPYRIGHT 2024

MOSES WISDOM,

BIBLE 613 SHAPE US CONSTITUTION AND LAWS

How the United States Constitution is fully traceable to The Laws of Moses, as dictated to Moses by God Almighty, fully displayed in The Holy Bible.

Learn God's word on Citizenship and Immigration

Learn how the earliest writer to engage and document God's Law found in the Bible would document 613 laws ordered by God Almighty during The Crusades.

Our book may represent the earliest roots of the United States Constitution.

Those who forget their history are doomed to repeat that history.

May we never forget the history of LIFE, LIBERTY, HAPPINESS

TABLE OF CONTENTS MOSAIC LAW, Bible, US Constitution

Chapter 1 INTRODUCTION

America's Founding Fathers may have been closer to the Bible and possibly greater Theologians than the Church Fathers of today. In their educations, the Founding Fathers studied Religion first and foremost, the three "R's" came next, with all professional studies held for Graduate level. Benjamin Franklin proves this point by opening Constitutional Convention debate one morning saying:

> Benjamin Franklin, in 1788, saw difficulties newly independent American states were having forming a government, and proposed that until new laws could be agreed, they should be governed by "The Laws of Moses", contained in the Old Testament. He explained that the laws had worked in biblical times: "The Supreme Being ... having rescued them from bondage by many miracles, performed by his servant Moses, he personally delivered to that chosen servant, in the presence of the whole nation, a constitution and laws."[1]

Our Founding Fathers understood these lessons as has no one before or since. They studied this vast bibliography in original languages as English translation of the Bible was rare. (see first Harvard college catalogue, "First Fruits").

Cause and effect discoveries gleaned from a full understanding of history, as is proven herein, is that modern legal code along with substantially all of the US Constitution is contained in Biblical Chapter and Verse.

President John Adams stated why he relied on Mosaic Law over Greek philosophy to create the United States Constitution: "As much as I love, esteem, and admire the Greeks, I believe the Hebrews have done more to enlighten and civilize the world. Moses did more than all their legislators and philosophers."

---

[1] Franklin 1834, p. 211. *Franklin, Benjamin (1834), Franklin, William Temple (ed.), Memoirs (eBook), vol. 2, Philadelphia: McCarty & Davis.*

Life, Liberty, and the pursuit of happiness; natural rights, unalienable rights - - those were not just clever words Jefferson created for inclusion in our Declaration of Independence!! These concepts have resided in legal lexicon for millennia. Mankind has for millennia, discussed the impact of God in creation of what we consider sacred philosophies of government in all free nations.

God began to establish his "covenant" (contract) with us in the earliest books of our Holy Bible. Gods' continuing love for his chosen people is a central theme throughout the Bible, in which He shows us many means of His love for us and what he expects in return! An everlasting covenant is introduced in Genesis 9:13. After the flood, God establishes a covenant with Noah and all living creatures, promising never to destroy the earth by flood again. This covenant is marked by the sign of the rainbow.

In chronological order, God strengthens his covenant with the great figures such as Abraham and Moses.

God calls Abraham, and says, "I will establish My covenant as an everlasting covenant between Me and you and your descendants after you for generations to come, to be your God and the God of your descendants after you" (Genesis 17:7).

The Mosaic Covenant, given at Mount Sinai, the primary theme of this book, is an everlasting promise, in moral and ceremonial laws that set Israel apart as Gods' chosen. However, the Davidic Covenant explicitly reiterates the everlasting nature of Gods' promises. "Your house and your kingdom will endure forever before Me; your throne will be established forever" (2 Samuel 7:16).

Jeremiah 31:31-34, foretold a new covenant. This new covenant is inaugurated by Jesus, who, at the Last Supper, declares, "This cup is the new covenant in My blood," (Luke 22:20).

Gods' Everlasting Covenant is a profound testament to His unwavering commitment to His people. It weaves through the biblical narrative, from promises made to the patriarchs to the fulfillment in Christ, offering assurance and hope to all who enter into this divine relationship.

Much education and experience is required to comprehend our Founding Fathers vision aligning the US Constitution with Gods' expectation in The Bible.

They began with Religion, History cause and effect, Wars, Military, Constitutions, Law, Government, Campaigns and Elections, Philosophy, development of civilization, economics, demographics, closing with governance: from tripartite government, military, budgetary, taxation, import/export, education, technology, statesmanship and World Relations. Our Founding Fathers gave us far more than a Constitution and Freedom. Monumental details are missed when those with narrower backgrounds attempt such works.

The Authors of this book share vast academic and professional lives, fully commensurate with the development paths of America's Founding Fathers. It was during a process of many years preaching in "jail ministry" preaching in homeless shelters, plus a lifetime of Corporate Turnaround and Political Campaign activity and Judgeship, that the Authors realized the preponderance of US Constitutional points in our Holy Bible.

Our book will document the entirety with which modern legal codes and the U.S. Constitution were introduced in the Bible, both Old Testament and New, along with important contributions of Iconic figures and countries across millennia that led our Founding Fathers to Development of the United States Constitution.

Moses and Maimonides are the two central figures in this book that expands upon what has for 3500 years been called "MOSAIC LAW." It became clear to the modern author that the vast majority of the United States Constitution was traceable to the Holy Bible. While researching other history, a copy of The 613 MITZVOT, by Maimonides was discovered, a 12th century AD accumulation of 613 commandments that comprise Mosaic Law. The source of the 613 laws is the first five books of our Holy Bible.

The full extent of the Laws of Moses (Mosaic) written by Maimonides is reproduced herein, along with Biblical Chapter and verse for each of the 613 laws. Maimonides identified his 613 laws from the first five books of the Bible ONLY.

The 12th century AD was a tumultuous time in World History, at midpoint of The Crusades. Maimonides may have lived in Spain while writing, although a Jew, he had a residence in Israel and his academic laurels allowed him connections into the Islamic world.

Maimonides may have been the greatest academician /philosopher of his day and was an unsung hero of The Crusades.

While in 15th century BC, there was no requirement for the extensive government forms we see today, The Bible moves far beyond Mosaic Law and introduces most components of the United States Constitution and form of government, along with additional laws over and above those found by Maimonides. We will provide an overview of the chapter and verse of the Bible that "foretell" the coming of The Greatest Treatise on government.

We provide continuous respect to the many Archeologists that continue to dig and result in yet more connections from our modern-day governments to the many scattered remains of ancient knowledge that refine our understanding.

Note the huge number of key historical issues in our Holy Bible. We will feature the chapter and verse which serve as forerunner of our United States Constitution and Legal Code.

HISTORY DEVELOPMENT LEADING TO US CONSTITUTION
KEY LEGAL CODES, PURPOSE OF CHAPTERS

Chapter 1 introduces the fact that while Moses has always been called The Law Giver and The Great Legislator, we rarely hear of Mosaic law beyond the Ten Commandments. While Ten Commandments are important to the legal codes of all peace-loving nations, legal codes and forms of government or constitutions have constantly developed over thousands of years.

Chapter 2 introduces Moses status as The Law Giver, along with historical developments in the life of Moses which lead to some of the strongest leadership challenges throughout history. It is within the life of Moses that God provides expectations for laws and legal codes, with beginning government formats that continue today. You will see constitutional government begin in the day of Moses.

Chapter 3 introduces a remarkable man who may have been the leading academician of his day. Maimonides was a 12th century AD Spanish Hebrew who documented 613 laws found in The Torah or Pentateuch, sometimes called commandments, sometimes called by the Jewish term Mitzvot. We will relate these 613 laws to their uncanny relationship with modern legal codes and constitutions.

Chapter 4 introduces some earliest legal codes - with partial continuation; discovered by Archaeologists after becoming extinct.

Chapter 5 documents the earliest written examples of our modern terms Liberty and Freedom, via Sumerian Cuneiform Clay Tablet.

Chapter 6 delivers a 7000-year chart of Population Growth, as we will learn from population statistics that modern governments or constitutions were not required until the past few hundred years.

Chapter 7 documents knowledge of government prior to Moses.

Chapter 8 serves as an overview of the remarkable Life of Moses, born into slavery, adopted by the daughter of Pharoah, raised as a Prince, ordered back to desert existence, called by God to GET MY PEOPLE OUT of Egyptian slavery.

Chapter 9 overviews the most important Biblical chapter of Exodus

Chapter 10 displays the very first documented organization chart, given to Moses by God, with continuing application in many scalable forms still in use today, across Nations, Governments, Industries, Militaries and Religions. This organization chart seems to be the original concept of government organization.

Chapter 11 expands Moses titles and TEN COMMANDMENTS

Chapter 12 (in this context synonymous with 12th century AD) lists 613 laws identified by Maimonides. Each of the 613 is identified with corresponding Chapter and Verse from which it is derived. The 613 are organized into "bodies of law" consistent with legal code.

Chapter 13 is a brief dictionary to provide definition of so many Hebrew words within the Bible and included in this book.

Chapter 14 reproduces KJV Bible Chapter and Verse Legal Code.

Chapter 15 begins to indicate a greater set of Biblical Chapter and Verse that begins to indicate the need for modern governments and Constitutions.

Chapter 16 may be "THE SHOW YOU HAVE ALL BEEN WAITING FOR." We will commence an exhaustive investigation and relate entirety of our U.S. CONSTITUTION to Bible chapter and verse.

The US Constitution is subdivided into Articles and Sections in the original work of America's Founding Fathers. In our modern day we have categorized the several points contained in each Section into Clauses. Each Article, Section, and Clause will explore the extent to which it conforms to Biblical Chapter and Verse.

Chapter 17 explores the 7000-year practice called Natural Law and Unalienable Rights. These were not just clever words Thomas Jefferson linked together for a strong opening statement in our Declaration of Independence. These words and practices have been fully within legal lexicon since they were first written.

Chapter 18 demonstrates that other modern sources beyond these Authors concur in the Biblical provision of Laws and Constitutions.

Chapter 19 expands upon the Mosaic Organization Chart.
Chapter 20 inserts the U.S. Declaration of Independence
Chapter 21 is the Constitution of the United States
Chapter 22 is Cross Reference to authorities for the 613 Mitzvot
Chapter 23 Founding Fathers Compliance With Orders of God
Chapter 24 Author Bio's
Chapter 25 Index and Illustrations
Cross Reference, Constitution Clauses found in Holy Bible

Chapter 2. Moses Overview as Law Giver

Moses[1] (moʊzɪz, -zɪs)[2] is considered the leading prophet in Judaism[3][4] and a most important prophet in Christianity, Islam, the Druze faith,[5][6] and other Abrahamic religions. According to the Bible and Quran,[7] Moses was leader of the Israelites and lawgiver to whom the "acquisition from heaven", of the Torah (first five books of the Bible) is attributed.[8]

Moses is called "The Lawgiver, and The Great Legislator."

According to Exodus, Moses was born in a time when his people, the Israelites, were increasing in population and, Pharaoh worried they might ally with Egypt's enemies.[9] Moses' Hebrew mother, Jochebed, secretly hid him when Pharaoh ordered all newborn Hebrew boys to be killed to reduce the Israelites population. Through Pharaoh's daughter (identified as Queen Bithia in the Midrash), the child was adopted as a foundling from the Nile and grew up with the Egyptian royal family. After killing an Egyptian slave-master who was beating a Hebrew, Moses fled across the Red Sea to Midian, where he encountered the Angel of the Lord,[10] speaking to him from a burning bush on Mount Horeb, which he regarded as the Mountain of God.

God sent Moses to Egypt to demand the release of the Israelites from slavery. Moses said that he could not speak eloquently,[11] so God allowed Aaron, his elder brother,[12] to become his spokesperson. After the Ten Plagues, Moses led the Exodus out of Egypt and across the Red Sea, after which they camped at Mount Sinai, where Moses received the Ten Commandments. After 40 years of wandering in the desert, Moses died on Mount Nebo at the age of 120, within sight of the Promised Land.[13]

Scholars say Moses lived in 15th century BC.[14][15][16][17][18] Jerome suggested 1592 BC,[20] James Ussher suggested 1571 BC as his birth year.[21]

The Exodus, Moses the Prophet and Deliverer of Israel

The Israelites settled in the Land of Goshen in the time of Joseph and Jacob, but a new Pharaoh arose who oppressed the children of Israel. At this time Moses was born to his father Amram, son (or descendant) of Kehath the Levite, who entered Egypt with Jacob's household; his mother was Jochebed (Yocheved), who was kin to Kehath. Moses had one older (by seven years) sister, Miriam, and one older (by three years) brother, Aaron.[44] Pharaoh had commanded that all male Hebrew children born would be drowned in the Nile, but Moses' mother placed him in an ark and concealed the ark in bulrushes by the riverbank, where the baby was discovered and adopted by Pharaoh's daughter, and raised as an Egyptian. After Moses reached adulthood, he killed an Egyptian who was beating a Hebrew. Attempting escape from Pharaoh's death penalty, he fled to Midian (south of Judah), where he married Zipporah.[45]

At Mount Horeb, God appeared to Moses as a burning bush, revealed to Moses His name YHWH (Yahweh)[46] and commanded him to return to Egypt and bring His people out of bondage, into the Promised Land (Canaan).[47][48]

During the journey,[49]; Moses returned to carry out God's command, but God caused Pharaoh to refuse, and after God subjected Egypt to ten plagues did Pharaoh relent. Moses led the Israelites to the border of Egypt, but God hardened Pharaoh's heart once more, so that he could destroy Pharaoh and his army at the Red Sea Crossing as a sign of his power to Israel and the nations.[50]

After defeat of the Amalekites in Rephidim,[51] Moses led Israel to Mount Sinai, where he was given the Ten Commandments from God, carved into stone tablets. Since Moses remained a long time on the mountain, some of the people feared that he might be dead, so they made a statue of a golden calf and worshipped it, thus disobeying and angering God and Moses. Moses, out of anger, broke the tablets, and later ordered the elimination of those who had worshiped the golden statue, which was melted down and fed to the idolaters.[52]

He also wrote the ten commandments on a new set of tablets. Later at Mount Sinai, Moses and the elders entered a covenant, by which Israel became the people of YHWH, obeying His laws, and YHWH would be their God. Moses delivered the laws of God to Israel, instituted the priesthood under Moses' brother Aaron, and destroyed those Israelites who fell away from his worship. In his final act at Sinai, God gave Moses instructions for the Tabernacle, the mobile shrine by which he traveled to the Promised Land.[53]

From Sinai, Moses led the Israelites to the Desert of Paran on the border of Canaan. From there he sent twelve spies into the land. The spies returned with samples of the land's fertility but warned them that its inhabitants were giants. The people were afraid and wanted to return to Egypt, and some rebelled against Moses and against God. Moses told the Israelites they were not worthy to inherit the land, and would wander the wilderness for forty years until the generation who refused to enter Canaan died, so it would be their children to possess the land.[54] Later, Korah was punished for leading a revolt against Moses.

When forty years had passed, Moses led the Israelites around the Dead Sea to Edom and Moab. There they escaped the temptation of idolatry, conquered the lands of Og and Sihon in Transjordan, received God's blessing, and massacred the Midianites, who by the end of the Exodus journey had become enemies of the Israelites due to their notorious role in enticing the Israelites to sin against God. Moses was twice told he would die before reentry into the Promised Land: in Numbers 27:13,[55] once he had seen the Promised Land from Mount Abarim, and again in Numbers 31:1[56] once battle with the Midianites had been won.

On the banks of the Jordan River, in sight of the land, Moses assembled the tribes. After recalling their wanderings, he delivered God's laws by which they must live in the land, sang a song of praise, and pronounced a blessing on the people, and passed his authority to Joshua, under whom they would possess the land. Moses then went up Mount Nebo, looked over the Promised Land spread out before him, and died, at the age of one hundred and twenty.

Moses is honored among Jews as the "lawgiver of Israel", and he delivers several sets of laws in the course of the four books. The first is the Covenant Code,[57] the terms of the covenant which God offers to the Israelites at Mount Sinai. Embedded in the covenant are the Decalogue (the Ten Commandments, Exodus 20:1–17),[58] and the Book of the Covenant (Exodus 20:22–23:19).[59][60] The entire Book of Leviticus constitutes a second body of law, the Book of Numbers begins with yet another set, and the Book of Deuteronomy another.

Moses is traditionally regarded as author of those four books and the Book of Genesis, which comprise the Torah, the first section of the Hebrew Bible.[61]

References

1. *Filler, Elad.* "Moses and the Kushite Woman: Classic Interpretations and Philo's Allegory". *TheTorah.com.*
2. "Moses." Random House Webster's Unabridged Dictionary.
3. Deuteronomy 34:10
4. Maimonides, 13 principles of faith, *7th principle.*
5. *Hitti, Philip K. (1928). The Origins of the Druze People and Religion: With Extracts from Their Sacred Writings. Library of Alexandria. p. 37.* ISBN 9781465546623.
6. *Dana, Nissim (2008). The Druze in the Middle East: Their Faith, Leadership, Identity and Status. Michigan University press. p. 17.* ISBN 9781903900369.
7. "Moses". *Oxford Islamic Studies.* Retrieved 6 December 2020.
8. Dever, William G. *(2001).* "Getting at the "History behind the History"". What Did Biblical Writers Know and When Did They Know It? What Archeology Can Tell Us About the Reality of Ancient Israel. Grand Rapids, Michigan *and* Cambridge, U.K.*:* Wm. B. Eerdmans*. pp. 97–102.* ISBN 978-0-8028-2126-3. OCLC 46394298.
9. Exodus 1:10
10. *Douglas Stuart (2006). Exodus: Exegetical Theological Exposition Holy Scripture. B&H Pub Group.p110–113*
11. Exodus 4:10
12. Exodus 7:7
13. *Kugler, Gili (December 2018). Shepherd, David; Tiemeyer, Lena-Sofia (eds.). "Moses died the people moved on: A hidden narrative in Deuteronomy".* Journal for the Study of the Old Testament. SAGE Publications. ***43** (2): 191–204.* doi:10.1177/0309089217711030. ISSN 1476-6728. S2CID 171688935.
14. *Nigosian, S.(1993)."Moses as They Saw Him". 43(3): 339-350.* doi:10.1163/156853393X00160.
15. *William G. Dever (2001).* What Did Biblical Writers Know and When Did They Know It? What Archeology Can Tell Us About Reality of Ancient Israel. *Wm. B. Eerdmans Publishing. p. 99.* ISBN 978-0-8028-2126-3.
16. *Beegle, Dewey (5 July 2023).* "Moses"*. Encyclopædia Britannica.*
17. "Moses"*. Oxford Biblical Studies Online.*

18. *Miller II, Robert D. (25 Nov 2013).* Illuminating Moses: History of Reception from Exodus to Renaissance. *BRILL. pp. 21, 24.* ISBN 978-90-04-25854-9.
19. Seder Olam Rabbah
20. Jerome's Chronicon (4th century) gives 1592 for the birth of Moses
21. 17th-century Ussher chronology calculates 1571 BC (Annals of the World, 1658 paragraph 164)
22. St Augustine. The City of God. Book XVIII. Chapter 8 - Who Were Kings When Moses Was Born, And What Gods Began To Be Worshipped Then.
23. *Hoeh, Herman L (1967),* Compendium of World History *(dissertation), vol. 1, The Faculty of the Ambassador College, Graduate School of Theology, 1962.*
24. Ushi. (2023). Let's Hear It From The Pharaohs: The Egyptian Story of Moses. Museum of the Jewish People. https://www.anumuseum.org.il/blog/lets-hear-it-from-the-pharaohs-the-egyptian-story-of-moses/
25. Exodus history behind -Torah.com. (n.d.). /www.thetorah.com/article/exodus-the-history-behind-the-story
26. Gruen, E. S. (1998). Use Abuse Exodus Story. Jewish Hist, 12(1), 93–122. http://www.jstor.org/stable/20101326
27. Feldman, L. H. (1998). Responses: Did Jews Reshape the Tale of the Exodus?. Jewish History, 123-127.
28. Newman, S.(2016). Moses cured of leprosy. Jewish Bible Quarterly, 44(3),166-170
29. Hays, Christopher B. 2014. Hidden Riches: Sourcebook for Comparative Study of the Hebrew Bible and Ancient Near East. Presbyterian Publishing. p. 116.
30. Kenneth A. Kitchen, On the Reliability of the Old Testament (2003), pp. 296–97:
31. Ulmer, Rivka. 2009. Egyptian Cultural Icons in Midrash. de Gruyter. p. 269.
32. Naomi E. Pasachoff, Robert Littman (2005), Concise History of Jewish People, Rowman & Littlefield, p. 5.
33. Exodus 2:10
34. Maciá, Lorena Miralles. 2014. "Judaizing a Gentile Biblical Character through Fictive Biographical Reports: The Case of Bityah, Pharaoh's Daughter, Moses' Mother, according to Rabbinic Interpretations". pp. 145–175 in C. Cordoni and G. Langer (eds.), Narratology, Hermeneutics, and Midrash: Jewish, Christian, and Muslim Narratives, Late Antiquity to Modern Times. Vandenhoeck & Ruprecht.
35. Dozeman 2009, pp. 81–82.
36. "Riva on Torah, Exodus 2:10:1". *Sefaria.* Retrieved 2021-03-14.
37. Greifenhagen, Franz V. 2003. Egypt on the Pentateuch's Ideological Map: Constructing Biblical Israel's Identity. Bloomsbury. pp. 60ff [62] n.65. [63].
38. Scolnic, Benjamin Edidin. 2005. p. 82.
39. Salkin, Jeffrey K. (2008). Righteous Gentiles in the Hebrew Bible: Ancient Role Models for Sacred Relationships. Jewish Lights. pp. 47ff [54].
40. Harris, Maurice D. 2012. Moses: Stranger Among Us. Wipf and Stock. pp. 22–24.
41. "Did Pharaoh's Daughter Name Moses? In Hebrew?". *TheTorah.com.* Retr 4/18/22
42. *Danzinger, Y. Eliezer (2008-01-20)* "What Was Moshe's Real Name?" *Chabad.org.* Retr 5 May 2022.
43. McClintock, John*;* James, Strong *(1882). "Moses".* Cyclopaedia of Biblical, Theological Ecclesiastical Literature. *Vol. VI. ME-NEV. New York: Harper & Brothers. pp. 677–87.*
44. According to Manetho the place of his birth was at the ancient city of Heliopolis.[43]

45. Exodus 2:21
46. Exodus 3:14
47. Exodus 8:1
48. Schmidt, Nathaniel *(Feb 1896). "Moses: His Age and His Work II". The Biblical World. 7 (2):105–19 [108].* doi:10.1086/471808. S2CID 222445896. *It was the prophet's call; like David under the baka-tree, Elijah on the mountain, Isaiah in the temple, Ezekiel on the Khebar, Jesus in the Jordan, Paul on Damascus road.*
49. Exodus 4:24–26
50. Ginzberg, Louis (1909). The Legends of the Jews Vol III : Chapter I (Translated by Henrietta Szold) Philadelphia: Jewish Publication Society.
51. *Trimm, Charlie (Sept 2019). Shepherd, David; Tiemeyer, Lena-Sofia (eds.).* "God's staff and Moses' hand(s): The battle against the Amalekites as a turning point in the role of the divine warrior". Journal for the Study of the Old Testament. SAGE Publications. ***44** (1): 198–214.* doi:10.1177/0309089218778588. ISSN 1476-6728.
52. *Rad, Gerhard von; Hanson, KC.; Neill, Stephen (2012).* Moses *Cambridge:JClarke.* ISBN978-0-227-17379-4
53. *Ginzberg, Louis (1909).* The Legends of the Jews (PDF). *Vol. III: The Symbolical Significance of the Tabernacle. Translated by Szold, Henrietta. Philadelphia: Jewish Publication Society.*
54. *Ginzberg, Louis (1909).* Legends of Jews (PDF). *Vol. III: Ingratitude Punished. Translated by Szold, Henrietta. Philadelphia: Jewish Publication Society.*
55. Numbers 27:13
56. Numbers 31:1
57. Exodus 20:19–23:33
58. Exodus 20:1–17
59. Exodus 20:22–23:19
60. Hamilton 2011, p. xxv.
61. *Robinson, George (2008).* Essential Torah: A Complete Guide to the Five Books of Moses. *Knopf Doubleday Publishing Group. p. 97.* ISBN 978-0-307-48437-6.

Chapter 3. Maimonides Introduced

Moses ben Maimon (1138–1204), known as Maimonides (/maɪˈmɒnɪdiːz/ *my-MON-ih-deez*) referred to by the Hebrew acronym Rambam (Hebrew: רמב״ם), was a Sephardic rabbi and philosopher who became one of the most prolific and influential Torah scholars of the Middle Ages.

An oft-cited legal maxim from his pen is: "It is better and more satisfactory to acquit a thousand guilty persons than to put a single innocent one to death." He argued that executing a defendant on anything less than absolute certainty would lead to a slippery slope of decreasing burdens of proof, until defendants would be convicted merely according to the judge's caprice. He was also a preeminent astronomer and physician, serving as the personal physician of Saladin. He was born and lived in Córdoba within the Almoravid Empire (present-day Spain), on Passover eve, 1138 (or 1135), until his family was expelled for refusing to convert to Islam.[9][10][11] Later, he lived in Morocco and Egypt and worked as a rabbi, physician, and philosopher.

During his lifetime, most Jews greeted Maimonides' writings on Jewish law and ethics with acclaim and gratitude, even as far away as Iraq and Yemen. Maimonides rose to become the revered head of the Jewish community in Egypt.

Early Years

Maimonides was born 1138 or 1135 in Córdoba, Andalusia, in Muslim-ruled Almoravid Empire, during what some scholars consider the end of the golden age of Jewish culture in the Iberian Peninsula, after the first centuries of Moorish rule. His father Maimon ben Joseph was a Spanish dayyan (Jewish judge). Aaron ha-Kohen wrote that he traced Maimonides' descent back to Simeon ben Judah ha-Nasi from the Davidic line.[13] His ancestry, of four generations, is given in his Iggeret Teiman (Epistle to Yemen), as Moses son of Maimon the Judge, son of Joseph the Wise, son of Isaac the Rabbi, son of Obadiah the Judge.[14]

Dominion of the Almohad Caliphate at its greatest extent, c. 1200

Exile

Almohads, a Berber dynasty, conquered Córdoba (1148), abolishing *dhimmi* status (i.e., state protection of non-Muslims ensured through payment of a tax, the *jizya*). Loss of this status forced the Jewish and Christian communities to choose conversion to Islam, death, or exile.[16] Many Jews were forced to convert, but due to suspicion of fake conversions, new converts had to wear identifying clothing that set them apart and made them subject to public scrutiny.[18]

Maimonides' family, along with most other Jews, chose exile. For the next ten years, Maimonides moved about in southern Spain and North Africa, settling in Fez, Morocco. Some say that his teacher in Fez was Rabbi Yehuda Ha-Cohen Ibn Susan, until the latter was killed in 1165.[19]

He composed his commentary on the Mishnah, during 1166–1168.

Following this sojourn in Morocco, he lived in Palestine with his father, before settling in Fustat in Fatimid Caliphate-controlled Egypt by 1168.[20] There is mention that Maimonides first settled in Alexandria, and moved to Fustat in 1171. While in Cairo, he studied in a yeshiva at a small synagogue, which bears his name.[21] In Palestine, he prayed at the Temple Mount. He wrote that this day of visiting the Temple Mount was a day of holiness for him and his descendants.[22]

Maimonides was instrumental in helping rescue Jews taken captive during Christian Amalric of Jerusalem's siege of the Nile Delta town of Bilbies. He sent five letters to the Jewish communities of Lower Egypt asking them to pool money to pay the ransom. The money was collected and then given to two judges sent to Palestine to negotiate with the Crusaders. The captives were eventually released.[23]

Maimonides, in 1171 AD, was appointed *Nagid* of the Egyptian Jewish community.[21] Arabist Shelomo Dov Goitein believes the leadership he displayed ransoming Crusader captives led to this appointment.[25] He was replaced by Sar Shalom ben Moses in 1173. Sar Shalom was accused of tax farming. Maimonides excommunicated and fought with him until Maimonides was appointed Nagid in 1195. A work known as "Megillat Zutta" was written by Abraham ben Hillel, a scathing description of Sar Shalom while praising Maimonides as "the light of east and west and unique master and marvel of the generation."[26][27]

Maimonides THIRTEEN PRINCIPLES OF FAITH

In his commentary on the Mishnah (Tractate Sanhedrin, chapter 10), Maimonides formulates his "13 principles of faith"; and that these principles summarized what he viewed as the required beliefs of Judaism:

1. The existence of God.
2. God's unity and indivisibility into elements.
3. God's spirituality and incorporeality.
4. God's eternity.
5. God alone should be the object of worship.
6. Revelation through God's prophets.
7. The preeminence of Moses among the prophets.
8. The entire Torah (both Written and Oral law) are of Divine origin and were dictated to Moses by God on Mt. Sinai.
9. Torah given by Moses is permanent, not be changed.
10. God's awareness of all human actions and thoughts.
11. Reward of righteousness and punishment of evil.
12. The coming of the Jewish Messiah.
13. The resurrection of the dead.

Resurrection

Religious Jews believed in immortality in a spiritual sense, most believed that future would include a messianic era and resurrection of the dead. Thus the subject of Jewish eschatology. Maimonides wrote on this topic, but in most cases he wrote about immortality of the soul for people of perfected intellect; his writings were usually *not* about the resurrection of dead bodies. Rabbis of his day were critical of this thought, with controversy over his views.

Eventually, Maimonides felt pressured to write "The Treatise on Resurrection." In it, he wrote that those who claimed he believed the verses of the Hebrew Bible referring to the resurrection were only allegorical were spreading falsehoods.

Maimonides asserts belief in resurrection is a fundamental truth of Judaism about which there is no disagreement.

Footnote Citations

1. Schwartz, Yitzhack (31 July 2011). "The Maimonides Portrait: An Appraisal of One of the World's Most Famous Pictures". Rambam Maimonides Medical Journal. 2 (3). doi:10.5041/RMMJ.10052.
2. "Moses Maimonides | Bio, Philosophy, Teachings". Encyclopedia Britannica. Arch 20/12/16. Retr 8/12/16
3. "Hebrew Date Converter 14 Nisan, 4895". Hebcal Jewish Calendar. Arch 7 March 2021.
4. "Hebrew Date Converter–14 Nisan, 4898". Hebcal Jewish Calendar. Arch 7 March 2021.
5. "H-Net". Archived from the original on 9 October 2007. Retrieved 6 May 2007.
6. "The Influence of Islamic Thought on Maimonides". Maimonides Islamic Influences. Stanford. 2016. Archived from the original on 9 December 2014. Retrieved 6 May 2007.
7. "Isaac Newton: "Judaic monotheist of school of Maimonides"". Achgut.com. 19 June 2007. Archived from the original on 28 April 2015. Retrieved 13 March 2010.
8. Commentary of the Mishnah, Maimonides (1967), s.v. Uktzin 3:12
9. Joel E. Kramer, "Moses Maimonides: An Intellectual Portrait", p. 47 note 1. In Kenneth Seeskin, ed. (Sept 2005). Cambridge Companion to Maimonides. Cambridge U Press. ISBN 9780521525787.
10. 1138 in Stroumsa, Maimonides in His World: Portrait of Mediterranean Thinker, Princeton U Press, 2009, p8
11. Sherwin B. Nuland (2008), Maimonides, Random House LLC, p. 38
12. Marder, Michael (11 Nov 2014). The Philosopher's Plant: An Intellectual Herbarium. New York: Columbia Univ Press. p. 97. ISBN 978-0-231-53813-8. Archived on 17 July 2021.
13. Joel L. Kraemer, Maimonides: The Life and World of One of Civilization's Greatest Minds, Crown Publishing Group 2008 ISBN 978-0-385-52851-1 p.486 n.6.
14. "Iggerot HaRambam, Iggeret Teiman". sefaria.org Arch 23 April 2021.
15. Stroumsa, Maimonides in His World: Portrait of Mediterranean Thinker, Princeton UPress,2009,p65
16. 1954 Encyclopedia Americana, vol. 18, p. 140.
17. Touri, Abdelaziz; Benaboud, Mohammad; Boujibar El-Khatib, Naïma; Lakhdar, Kamal; Mezzine, Mohamed (2010). Andalusian Morocco: Discovery in Living Art(2 ed.). Ministry of Cultural Affairs Kingdom of Morocco& Museum With No Frontiers. ISBN 978-3902782311.
18. Y. K. Stillman, ed. (1984). "Libās". Encyclopaedia of Islam. Vol. 5 (2nd ed.). Brill Academic Publishers. p. 744. ISBN 978-90-04-09419-2.
19. See for example: Solomon Zeitlin, "MAIMONIDES", The American Jewish Yearbook, Vol. 37, pp 65 – 66. Archived 25 December 2021 at the Wayback Machine
20. Davidson, p. 28.
21. Goitein, S.D. Letters Medieval Jewish Traders, Princeton U Press,1973 (ISBN 0-691-05212-3)p208
22. Magazine, rambam_temple_mount, Jewish. "No Jew had been permitted to enter holy city which has become a Christian bastion since Crusaders conquered in 1096". jewishmag.com. Archived 3 Nov 2018. Retr 9 Feb 2018.

23. Cohen, Mark R. Poverty and Charity in the Jewish Community of Medieval Egypt. Princeton University Press, 2005 (ISBN 0-691-09272-9), pp. 115–116
24. Goitein, Letters of Medieval Jewish Traders, p. 207
25. Cohen, Poverty and Charity in the Jewish Community of Medieval Egypt, p. 115
26. Baron, Salo Wittmayer (1952). A Social and Religious History of the Jews: High Middle Ages, 500–1200. Columbia University Press. p. 215. ISBN 978-0-231-08843-5. Archived 25 Dec 2021. Retrieved 16 Nov 2020.
27. Rustow, Marina (1 October 2010). "Sar Shalom ben Moses ha-Levi". Encyclopedia of Jews in Islamic World.

Bibliography

- This article incorporates text from a publication now in the public domain: Joseph Jacobs; Isaac Broydé *(1901–1906).* "Moses Ben Maimon". *In* Singer, Isidore*; et al. (eds.).* The Jewish Encyclopedia. *The Executive Committee of the Editorial Board, and* Jacob Zallel Lauterbach.
- *Barzel, Uriel (1992).* Maimonides' Medical Writings: The Art of Cure Extracts. *Vol. 5. Galen: Maimonides Research Institute.* Archived *from the original on 17 June 2016.*
- *Bos, Gerrit (2002). Maimonides. On Asthma (vol.1, vol.2). Provo, Utah: BYU Press.*
- *Bos, Gerrit (2007). Maimonides. Medical Aphorisms Treatise 1–5 (6–9, 10–15, 16–21, 22–25). Provo, Utah: BYU*
- *Davidson, Herbert A. (2005). Moses Maimonides: The Man and his Works. Oxford University Press.*
- *Feldman, Rabbi Yaakov (2008). Shemonah Perakim: Eight Chapters of Rambam.* Targum Press.

Chapter 4. EARLY SO-CALLED LEGAL CODES

Archaeologists continue to discover more and more ancient artifacts, and we continue to learn mankind was not well established and was poorly organized at best, during ancient days. The following is a list of ancient legal codes in chronological order, some are recent discoveries and attempts at translation. All discovered in the region of Mesopotamia:

- Code of Urukagina (2380–2360 BCE)
- Code of Ur-Nammu, king of Ur (c. 2050 BCE). Copies with slight variations found in Nippur, Sippar, and Ur
- Laws of Eshnunna (c. 1930 BCE)
- Codex of Lipit-Ishtar of Isin (c. 1870 BCE)
- Code of Hammurabi (1750 BC, disappeared 1150BC)
- Mosaic Law (c. 1500 BC)
- First Demokratia in Greece (c. 1200 BC)
- Laws of the Twelve Tables (Rome c. 449 BC)
- Many Roman Updates

These civilizations and their codes appear to have been short-lived. Please see the chapter, ANCIENT GOVERNMENT EMERGES for an expanded discussion of these most ancient foundations of FREEDOM and LIBERTY. The following legal codes continue to serve as the basis for all societies who follow the "law of peace."

- Mosaic Law 1550 BC
- Twelve Tables of Roman Law 600 BC
- Justinian Code (c. 500 AD)
- Magna Carta (c. 1200 AD)
- United States Constitution (1789 AD)

Chapter 5. FREEDOM AND LIBERTY FIRST WRITTEN, URAKAGINA (Clan or City, Near Babylon/Baghdad – Iran/Iraq) *ama-gi₄* written in Classical Sumerian cuneiform.

The diagram is believed to be the earliest written form of the word FREEDOM and can also be translated as LIBERTY. A possible date of this written word has been discovered by archaeologists, written on clay tablets, and dated as early as 2500 BC. *Ama-gi* translates as "freedom", as well as "manumission", "exemption from debts or obligations",[1] and "the restoration of persons and property to their original status" including remission of debts.[2] Other interpretations are "reversion to a previous state"[3] release from debt, slavery, taxation or punishment.[4][5][6] Earliest known usage of the word was the reforms of Urukagina.[7] By Third Dynasty of Ur, it was a term for manumission of individuals,[7] related to the Akkadian word *anduraāru(m)*, or "freedom", "exemption"(debt) release, slavery".[3][8][9]

Libertarian organizations adopted this cuneiform glyph as a symbol as it is "earliest-known written appearance of the word 'freedom'".[10] It is a logo of *Instituto Político para la Libertad of* Peru,[11] the *New Economic School – Georgia*,[12] Libertarian publishing firm Liberty Fund,[13] and was the name and logo of the journal of the London School of Economics' *Hayek Society*.[14]

1. John Alan Halloran (2006). Sumerian Lexicon: A Dictionary Guide to the Ancient Sumerian Language. David Brown Book Company. p. 19. ISBN 978-0978642907.
2. Karen Radner, Eleanor Robson, ed. (2011). The Oxford Handbook of Cuneiform Culture. Oxford University Press. pp. 208–209. ISBN 978-0199557301.
3. "amargi". Electronic Pennsylvania Sumerian Dictionary.
4. Åke W. Sjöberg, ed. (1998). The Sumerian Dictionary of the University of Pennsylvania Museum. Philadelphia. pp. 200–201, 208–210.
5. A Descriptive Grammar of Sumerian
6. Kramer, Samuel Noah (1963). The Sumerians: Their History, Culture, and Character. University of Chicago Press. p. 79. ISBN 0226452387.
7. Niels Peter Lemche (2014). Biblical Studies and the Failure of History: Changing Perspectives 3. Taylor & Francis. pp. 72–. ISBN 978-1317544944.
8. Niels Peter Lemche (January 1979). "Andurārum and Mīšarum: Comments on the Problem of Social Edicts and Their Application in the Ancient near East". Journal of Near Eastern Studies. 38 (1): 11–22. doi:10.1086/372688. JSTOR 544568. S2CID 162196494.
9. Jeremy A. Black; Andrew George; J. N. Postgate (2000). A Concise Dictionary of Akkadian. Otto Harrassowitz Verlag. p. 17. ISBN 978-3447042642.
10. "Our Logo | Liberty Fund". libertyfund.org. Retrieved 2019-05-03.
11. "Instituto Politico para la Libertad – Inicio". iplperu.com. Archived on 31 March 2009.
12. New Economic School – Georgia
13. "Trademark Electronic Search System". US Patent, Trademark Office. Retr 2012-11-16
14. "Trademark Electronic Search System". US Patent, Trademark Office. Arch 10-06-2011

Uru-ka-gina, Iri-ka-gina *URU-KA-gi.na*; (24th century BC,)

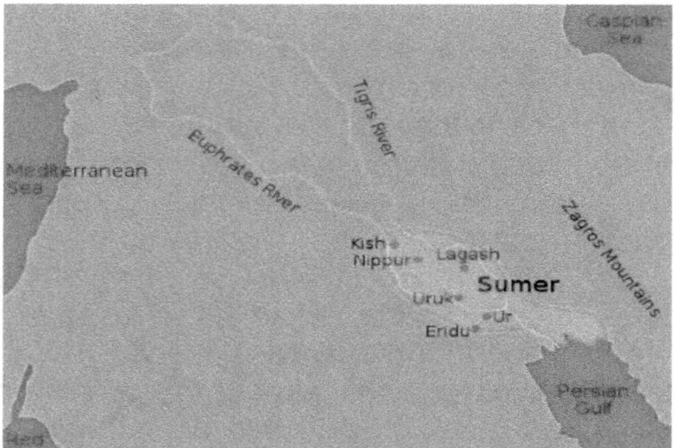

Urukagina was King of city-states of Lagash and Girsu in Mesopotamia, and the last ruler of the 1st Dynasty of Lagash.[3] He assumed the title of king, claiming to be divinely appointed, upon the downfall of his corrupt predecessor, Lugalanda.

He is best known for his reforms to combat corruption, which are sometimes cited as the first example of a legal code in recorded history. Although the actual text has not been discovered, much of its content may be surmised from other references to it that have been found. In it, he exempted widows and orphans from taxes; compelled the city to pay funeral expenses (including the ritual food and drink libations for the journey of the dead into the lower world); and decreed that the rich must use silver when purchasing from the poor, and if the poor does not wish to sell, the powerful man (the rich man or the priest) cannot force him to do so.[4]

He also took part in several conflicts, notably a losing conflict with Uruk. In the seventh year of his reign, Uruk fell under leadership of Lugal-Zage-Si, *énsi* of Umma, who ultimately annexed most of the territory of Lagash and established the first reliably documented kingdom to encompass all of Sumer. The destruction of Lagash was described in a lament (possibly the earliest recorded example of what would become a prolific Sumerian literary genre), which stressed that "the men of Umma ... committed a sin against Ningirsu. ... Offence there was none in Urukagina, king of Girsu, but as for Lugal-Zage-Si, governor of Umma, may his goddess Nisaba make him carry his sin upon his neck" (alternatively – "may she carry his sin upon her neck").[5]

Reforms of Urukagina

Urukagina's code is hailed as the first recorded example of government reform, seeking higher freedom and equality.[6] It limited power of the priesthood and large property owners, took measures against usury, burdensome controls, hunger, theft, murder, and seizure (of people's property and persons); as he states, "The widow and orphan were no longer at the mercy of the powerful man". Here, the word "freedom" ("ama-gi"), appears for the first time in recorded history.[7]

Despite apparent attempts to curb excesses of the elite class, it seems elite or royal women enjoyed greater influence and prestige in his reign than previously. Urukagina greatly expanded the royal "Household of Women" from about 50 persons to about 1500 persons, renamed it the "Household of goddess Bau", gave it ownership of vast amounts of land confiscated from the former priesthood, and placed it under supervision of his wife, Shasha (or Shagshag).[8] In his second year, Shasha presided the lavish funeral of his predecessor's queen.

In addition to such changes, two of his other surviving decrees, first published and translated by Samuel Kramer in 1964, have attracted controversy in recent decades. First, he seems to have abolished the former custom of polyandry in his country, on pain of the woman taking multiple husbands being stoned with rocks upon which her crime is written.[9] Second is a statute stating that "if a woman says [text illegible...] to a man, her mouth is crushed with burnt bricks." No comparable laws from Urukagina addressing penalties for adultery by men survived. The discovery of these fragments has led some modern critics to assert that they provide "the first written evidence of the degradation of women".[10]

Excerpt of some regulations from the Reform document. (These regulations do not resemble our concept of legal code, yet such an early Freedom and Liberty should be reviewed):

- From border territory of Ningirsu to the sea, no person shall serve as officers.
- For a corpse being brought to the grave, his beer shall be 3 jugs and his bread 80 loaves. One bed and one lead goat shall the undertaker take away, and 3 *ban* (18 l.) of barley shall the person(s) take away.
- When to the reeds of Enki a person has been brought, his beer will be 4 jugs, and his bread 420 loaves. One *barig* (36 l.) of barley shall the undertaker take away, and 3 *ban* of barley shall the persons of ... take away. One woman's headband, and one *sila* (1 l.) of regal fragrance shall the *eresh-dingir* priestess take away. 420 loaves of bread that have sat are the bread duty, 40 loaves of hot bread are for eating, and 10 loaves of hot bread are the bread of the table. 5 loaves of bread are for the persons of the levy, 2 mud vessels and 1 *sadug* vessel of beer are for the lamentation singers of Girsu. 490 loaves of bread, 2

mud vessels and 1 *sadug* vessel of beer are for the lamentation singers of Lagash. 406 loaves of bread, 2 mud vessels, and 1 *sadug* vessel of beer are for the other lamentation singers. 250 loaves of bread and one mud vessel of beer are for the old wailing women. 180 loaves of bread and 1 mud vessel of beer are for the men of Nigin.

- The blind one who stands in ..., his bread for eating is one loaf, 5 loaves of bread are his at midnight, one loaf at midday, and 6 loaves are his bread in the evening.
- 60 loaves of bread, 1 mud vessel of beer, and 3 *ban* of barley for the person who performs as the *sagbur* priest, king, or God.

1. "Site officiel du musée du Louvre". cartelfr.louvre.fr.
2. THUREAU-DANGIN, F. (1904). "La Ruine de Shirpourla (Lagash): Sous le Règne d'Ouroukagina". Revue d'Assyriologie et d'archéologie orientale. **6** (1): 26–32. ISSN 0373-6032. JSTOR 23275695.
3. Finegan, Jack (2019). Archaeology History, Ancient Middle East. Routledge. p 46. ISBN 978-0-429-72638-5.
4. "The Reforms of Urukagina". History-world.org. Arch 2018-11-17. Retr 2019-12-03.
5. "Site officiel du musée du Louvre". cartelfr.louvre.fr.
6. "Social Reform in Mesopotamia", Benjamin R. Foster, Social Justice in Ancient World, K. Irani and M. Silver eds., 1995, p. 169.
7. Finegan, Jack (2019). Archaeology History, Ancient Middle East. Routledge. p 46. ISBN 978-0-429-72638-5.
8. Katherine I. Wright, Archaeology and Women, 2007, p. 206.
9. The Powers p. 40 by Walter Wink, 1992
10. Marilyn French, From Eve to Dawn: A History of Women, 2008, p. 100.

The foregoing bullet points illustrate these earliest codes were written to establish standard practices for existing moral codes, including marriage and burial. No complete codes from the period survived. A study of history of the day indicates these early attempts at governance were short lived, often destroyed by the next conquering king. Practice of the Code of Hammurabi would have been destroyed no later than Nebuchadnezzar.

Several additional documented yet forgotten governments that preached freedom and liberty have been discovered in the past 200 years, from Sumer and Mesopotamia. Again, the context of this book is to produce all those historical instances recognized to influence America's Founding Fathers.

Chapter 6 Population Development and Growth [2]

Period	Population
4000 BC	7,000,000
3000 BC	14,000,000
2000 BC	27,000,000
1000 BC	50,000,000
500 BC	162,000,000
0 to 500 AD	185,000,000
500 1000	220,000,000
1000- 1500	400,000,000
1500- 1750	575,000,000
1750- 1800	710,000,000
1800- 1850	1,000,000,000 (first reaches 1 billion)
1850- 1900	1,310,000,000
1900- 1920	1,750,000,000
1920- 1950	2,300,000,000
1950- 2000	4,750,000,000
2000- 2010	7,000,000,000
2010- 2020	7,800,000,000

The earliest civilizations and societies developing in the era of 2000 BC were so very widely scattered that there was no requirement for government or law. However, as multi-family communities became cities, we first began to realize the need for organization of many types. It can only be debated which came first; was military style security the element of government to emerge first, or was it legal/moral rules for behavior. You will see in the story of Moses guiding the Hebrews across a barren desert for 40 years; Hebrew population of that desert trek reached 1.5 million. The book of Exodus states the census of male population alone was 600,000.

---

[2] Bureau of the United States Census and many other sources make this information available and provide many academic and math studies in support. Until the modern period, these numbers are World Population estimates.

Scholars of religion are satisfied that the total population of Hebrews on that trek was 1.5 million, yet other history and census demographers establish that population as high as 2.7 million. Moses provided rules for a military organization, guidelines for the establishment of leaders, judges, and a legal code that extended far beyond the 10 Commandments, fully documented in Books of Exodus, Leviticus, Numbers, and Deuteronomy. In the population statistics above, you will see a possible worldwide population of 35 million, thus the Hebrews neared 8% of worldwide population.

Philosophers have, since the time of Socrates and Aristotle, debated the proper form of government and law. We find the first human documentation of government and law deep within the pages of our Biblical Old Testament, preceding the great philosophers by 1000 years, typically with the greatest Biblical leaders. (Torah, Books of The Law, First Five Books of the Bible).

America's Founding Fathers began their development of this vast continent called North America beginning in the early 1600's, continuing until today, although those we consider the Founders were that group of 55 who authored first The Declaration of Independence, then, The Articles of Confederation, then our United States Constitution. All these precious documents were written between 1776 and 1789. The actual development of our form of government began its roots millennia ago. The vast library of knowledge in this book is intended as a demonstration of the preparation of philosophical thought, as that thought advanced through several thousand years of trial and error with government.

Many chapters of this book provide a discussion of the philosophy involved in our development. This chapter will provide a review of the most successful ancient leaders, primarily Biblical leaders along with a few others from whom our Founders gleaned many valuable lessons on leadership and defense of vast territories.

Chapter 7.
GOVERNMENT PRIOR TO MOSES, HEBREW ENSLAVEMENT

In the 19th Century BC, our Bible tells us the Hebrew people were faced with a devastating famine in the land of Israel. The famine continued for so many decades that the people were in the process of dying out.

One Hebrew named Joseph had been illegally sold into slavery in Egypt. His older brothers had been jealous of the love their father had shown to the youngest sibling. Thus the sale.

The brilliance of Joseph caused him to be moved upward into higher levels of "ownership" and to be given work activities and responsibility. Many historians believe this Joseph may have been the architect of the first pyramid, while directing the world's very first "supply-chain" development which was a system for stockpiling grain in Egypt to be stored in good times to provide food in bad agricultural years.

Modern Archaeologists who continue the excavation of Pyramids in Egypt gave the Judeo Christian world a great gift early in the 21st century, when they located an Architect cornerstone at possibly the very first pyramid, then ultimately translated the names contained on that cornerstone, and there in the prominent location of the Architect of that Pyramid, was the name of JOSEPH.

Genesis 41 Joseph Interprets Pharaoh's Dreams

14Then Pharaoh sent and called Joseph, and they brought him hastily out of the dungeon: and he shaved *himself*, and changed his raiment, and came in unto Pharaoh.
15And Pharaoh said unto Joseph, I have dreamed a dream, and *there is* none that can interpret it: and I have heard say of thee, *that* thou canst understand a dream to interpret it.
16And Joseph answered Pharaoh, saying, *It is* not in me: God shall give Pharaoh an answer of peace.
17And Pharaoh said unto Joseph, In my dream, behold, I stood upon the bank of the river:
18And, behold, there came up out of the river seven kine, fat fleshed and well favoured; and they fed in a meadow:

19And, behold, seven other kine came up after them, poor and very
ill favoured and lean fleshed, such as I never saw in all the land of
Egypt for badness: 20And the lean and the ill favoured kine did eat
up the first seven fat kine: 21And when they had eaten them up, it
could not be known that they had eaten them; but they *were* still ill
favoured, as at the beginning. So I awoke. 22And I saw in my
dream, and behold, seven ears came up in one stalk, full and
good: 23And, behold, seven ears, withered, thin, *and* blasted with
the east wind, sprung up after them: 24And the thin ears devoured
the seven good ears: and I told *this* unto the magicians; but *there
was* none that could declare *it* to me.
25And Joseph said unto Pharaoh, The dream of Pharaoh *is* one:
God hath shewed Pharaoh what he *is* about to do. 26The seven
good kine *are* seven years; and the seven good ears *are* seven
years: the dream *is* one. 27And the seven thin and ill favoured kine
that came up after them *are* seven years; and the seven empty
ears blasted with the east wind shall be seven years of
famine. 28This *is* the thing which I have spoken unto Pharaoh:
What God *is* about to do he sheweth unto Pharaoh. 29Behold,
there come seven years of great plenty throughout all the land of
Egypt: 30And there shall arise after them seven years of famine;
and all the plenty shall be forgotten in the land of Egypt; and the
famine shall consume the land; 31And the plenty shall not be
known in the land by reason of that famine following; for it *shall
be* very grievous. 32And for that the dream was doubled unto
Pharaoh twice; *it is* because the thing *is* established by God, and
God will shortly bring it to pass. 33Now therefore let Pharaoh look
out a man discreet and wise, and set him over the land of
Egypt. 34Let Pharaoh do *this*, and let him appoint officers over the
land, and take up the fifth part of the land of Egypt in the seven
plenteous years. 35And let them gather all the food of those good
years that come, and lay up corn under the hand of Pharaoh, and
let them keep food in the cities. 36And that food shall be for store
to the land against the seven years of famine, which shall be in the
land of Egypt; that the land perish not through the famine.

Joseph Given Charge of Egypt

37And the thing was good in the eyes of Pharaoh, and in the eyes
of all his servants.
38And Pharaoh said unto his servants, Can we find *such a one* as
this *is*, a man in whom the Spirit of God *is*? 39And Pharaoh said
unto Joseph, Forasmuch as God hath shewed thee all this, *there*
is none so discreet and wise as thou *art*: 40Thou shalt be over my
house, and according unto thy word shall all my people be ruled:
only in the throne will I be greater than thou.
41And Pharaoh said unto Joseph, See, I have set thee over all the
land of Egypt. 42And Pharaoh took off his ring from his hand, and
put it upon Joseph's hand, and arrayed him in vestures of fine linen,
and put a gold chain about his neck; 43And he made him to ride in
the second chariot which he had; and they cried before him, Bow
the knee: and he made him *ruler* over all the land of Egypt. 44And
Pharaoh said unto Joseph, I *am* Pharaoh, and without thee shall
no man lift up his hand or foot in all the land of Egypt. 45And
Pharaoh called Joseph's name Zaphnathpaaneah; and he gave
him to wife Asenath the daughter of Potipherah priest of On. And
Joseph went out over *all* the land of Egypt.

The Seven Years of Plenty

46And Joseph *was* thirty years old when he stood before Pharaoh
king of Egypt. And Joseph went out from the presence of Pharaoh,
and went throughout all the land of Egypt. 47And in the seven
plenteous years the earth brought forth by handfuls. 48And he
gathered up all the food of the seven years, which were in the land
of Egypt, and laid up the food in the cities: the food of the field,
which *was* round about every city, laid he up in the same. 49And
Joseph gathered corn as the sand of the sea, very much, until he
left numbering; for *it was* without number.

The Sons of Joseph

50And unto Joseph were born two sons before the years of famine
came, which Asenath the daughter of Potipherah priest of On bare
unto him. 51And Joseph called the name of the firstborn
Manasseh: For God, *said he*, hath made me forget all my toil, and
all my father's house. 52And the name of the second called he
Ephraim: For God hath caused me to be fruitful in the land of my
affliction.

The Famine Begins

53And the seven years of plenteousness, that was in the land of
Egypt, were ended. 54And the seven years of dearth began to
come, according as Joseph had said: and the dearth was in all
lands; but in all the land of Egypt there was bread. 55And when all
the land of Egypt was famished, the people cried to Pharaoh for
bread: and Pharaoh said unto all the Egyptians, Go unto Joseph;
what he saith to you, do. 56And the famine was over all the face of
the earth: And Joseph opened all the storehouses, and sold unto
the Egyptians; and the famine waxed sore in the land of
Egypt. 57And all countries came into Egypt to Joseph for to
buy *corn*; because of the famine.

Genesis 45 Joseph Reveals his Identity

1Then Joseph could not refrain himself before all of them that stood
by him; and he cried, Cause every man to go out from me. And
there stood no man with him, while Joseph made himself known
unto his brethren. 2And he wept aloud: and the Egyptians and the
house of Pharaoh heard. 3And Joseph said unto his brethren,
I *am* Joseph; doth my father yet live? And his brethren could not
answer him; for they were troubled at his presence. 4And Joseph
said unto his brethren, Come near to me, I pray you. And they
came near. And he said, I *am* Joseph your brother, whom ye sold
into Egypt. 5Now therefore be not grieved, nor angry with
yourselves, that ye sold me hither: for God did send me before you
to preserve life. 6For these two years *hath* the famine *been* in the

land: and yet *there are* five years in the which *there shall* neither *be* earing nor harvest. 7And God sent me before you to preserve you a posterity in the earth, and to save your lives by a great deliverance. 8So now *it was* not you *that* sent me hither, but God: and he hath made me a father to Pharaoh, and lord of all his house, and a ruler throughout Egypt.

Joseph Sends for his Father

9Haste ye, and go up to my father, and say unto him, Thus saith thy son Joseph, God hath made me lord of all Egypt: come down unto me, tarry not: 10And thou shalt dwell in the land of Goshen, and thou shalt be near unto me, thou, and thy children, and thy children's children, and thy flocks, and thy herds, and all that thou hast: 11And there will I nourish thee; for yet *there are* five years of famine; lest thou, and thy household, and all that thou hast, come to poverty. 12And, behold, your eyes see, and the eyes of my brother Benjamin, that *it is* my mouth that speaketh unto you. 13And ye shall tell my father of all my glory in Egypt, and of all that ye have seen; and ye shall haste and bring down my father hither. 14And he fell upon his brother Benjamin's neck, and wept; and Benjamin wept.

Pharaoh Invites Jacob to Egypt

16And the fame thereof was heard in Pharaoh's house, saying, Joseph's brethren are come: and it pleased Pharaoh well, and his servants. 17And Pharaoh said unto Joseph, Say unto thy brethren, This do ye; lade your beasts, and go, get you unto the land of Canaan; 18And take your father and your households, and come unto me: and I will give you the good of the land of Egypt, and ye shall eat the fat of the land. 19Now thou art commanded, this do ye; take you wagons out of the land of Egypt for your little ones, and for your wives, and bring your father, and come. 20Also regard not your stuff; for the good of all the land of Egypt *is* yours. 21And the children of Israel did so: and Joseph gave them wagons, according to the commandment of Pharaoh, and gave them provision for the way. 22To all of them he gave each man changes of raiment; but to Benjamin he gave three hundred *pieces* of silver,

and five changes of raiment. 23And to his father he sent; ten asses
laden with the good things of Egypt, and ten she asses laden with
corn and bread and meat for his father by the way. 24He sent his
brethren away, they departed: he said to them, See that ye fall not
out.

The Revival of Jacob

25They went up out of Egypt, and came into the land of Canaan
unto Jacob their father, 26And told him, saying, Joseph *is* yet alive,
and he *is* governor over all Egypt. And Jacob's heart fainted, for he
believed them not. 27And they told him all the words of Joseph,
which he had said unto them: when he saw the wagons which
Joseph had sent to carry him, the spirit of Jacob their father
revived: 28And Israel said, *It is* enough; Joseph my son *is* yet
alive: I will go and see him before I die.

GET MY PEOPLE OUT

Recognizing the Hebrew race was at deaths doorstep, the leaders began to migrate into Egypt where they could produce a strong society along the Nile River. Pharoah of that day recognized the strong wisdom and work ethic of the Hebrew and invited them into Egypt in friendship. Then the successor to Pharoah took census and learned there were more Hebrews then living in Egypt than there existed Native Egyptians. Recognizing the possible problem if the Hebrews learned of their superior numbers, Pharoah ordered them into Slavery, where they remained 430 years. Ultimately God had enough, finds Moses in the wilderness east of the Jordan River and at the Burning Bush, orders Moses to "GET MY PEOPLE OUT."

Chapter 8. LIFE OF MOSES

Born at a time when Pharoah had ordered the slaughter of all the infants, Moses' mother placed Moses in a reed basket in river just upstream from a spot she knew the daughter of Pharoah would be bathing. Pharoah's daughter took Moses as her own and he was raised in the palace of Pharoah. Moses became the equal of Pharoah's oldest son until they reached adulthood. Moses seems the superior of the two and then Pharoah had a problem. He could not allow Moses to supplant his eldest son. Moses was declared a General and dispatched to fight two wars considered impossible to win, and Moses won both. (see Josephus recitation) Upon his return to Egypt, he came upon an Egyptian Pyramid supervisor beating a Hebrew slave to death. Moses killed the supervisor and Pharoah banished Moses.

Moses goes into hiding in the Mountains of Jordan for the next 40 years. Ultimately, God has had enough with Egyptian oppression and in the incident at the Burning Bush, God orders Moses to return to Egypt and "get my people out."

Exodus 3 – Burning Bush and Great I am.

1Now Moses kept the flock of Jethro his father in law, the priest of
Midian: he led the flock to the backside of the desert, and came to
the mountain of God, *even* to Horeb.
2And the angel of the LORD appeared unto him in a flame of fire
out of the midst of a bush: and he looked, the bush burned with
fire, and the bush *was* not consumed.
3And Moses said, I will now turn aside, and see this great sight,
the bush is not burnt.
4And when the LORD saw that he turned aside to see, God called
unto him out of the midst of the bush, and said, Moses, Moses. And
he said, here *am* I.
5And he said, draw not nigh hither: put off thy shoes from off thy
feet, for the place whereon thou standest *is* holy ground.

6Moreover he said, I *am* the God of thy father, the God of
Abraham, the God of Isaac, and the God of Jacob. Moses hid his
face; he was afraid to look upon God.
7And the LORD said, I have surely seen the affliction of my
people in Egypt, and have heard their cry by reason of their
taskmasters; for I know their sorrows;
8And I am come down to deliver them out of the hand of the
Egyptians, and to bring them up out of that land unto a good land
and a large, unto a land flowing with milk and honey; unto the place
of the Canaanites, and the Hittites, and the Amorites, and the
Perizzites, and the Hivites, and the Jebusites.
9Now therefore, behold, the cry of the children of Israel is come
unto me: and I have also seen the oppression where with the
Egyptians oppress them.
10Come now, and I will send thee unto Pharaoh, that thou mayest
bring forth my people the children of Israel out of Egypt.
11And Moses said unto God, who *am* I, that I should go unto
Pharaoh, that I should bring the children of Israel out of Egypt?
12And he said, Certainly I will be with thee; and this *shall be* a
token to thee, that I have sent thee: When thou hast brought forth
the people out of Egypt, ye shall serve God on this mountain.
13And Moses said unto God, Behold, *when* I come unto the
children of Israel, and shall say unto them, The God of your fathers
hath sent me unto you; and they shall say to me, what *is* his name?
what shall I say unto them?
14And God said unto Moses, I AM THAT I AM: and he said, thus
shalt thou say unto the children of Israel, I AM hath sent me to you.
15God said to Moses, Thus shalt thou say to the children of Israel,
The LORD God of your fathers, the God of Abraham, the God of
Isaac, and the God of Jacob, hath sent me unto you: this *is* my
name for ever, and this *is* my memorial unto all generations.
16Go, and gather the elders of Israel together, and say unto them,
The LORD God of your fathers, the God of Abraham, of Isaac, and
of Jacob, appeared unto me, saying, I have surely visited you,
and *seen* that which is done to you in Egypt:

17And I have said, I will bring you up out of the affliction of Egypt
unto the land of the Canaanites, and the Hittites, and the Amorites,
and the Perizzites, and the Hivites, and the Jebusites, unto a land
flowing with milk and honey.
18And they shall hearken to thy voice: and thou shalt come, thou
and the elders of Israel, unto the king of Egypt, and ye shall say
unto him, The LORD God of the Hebrews hath met with us: and
now let us go, we beseech thee, three days' journey into the
wilderness, that we may sacrifice to the LORD our God.
19And I am sure that the king of Egypt will not let you go, no, not
by a mighty hand.
20And I will stretch out my hand and smite Egypt with all my
wonders which I will do in the midst thereof: and after that he will
let you go.

Moses returns to Egypt, negotiates with Pharoah, but just as God said, Pharoah had a hard heart and did not cooperate. God strikes Egypt with 10 plagues, ending with death of the first-born children of Egypt. God ordered the Hebrews to paint their door posts with blood, thus the Hebrews were spared THE PASSOVER.

Chapter 9. MOSES AND THE EXODUS (15TH Century BC)

Now Pharoah allows Moses to take the Hebrew people out of Egypt. They cross the Red Sea to escape the Egyptians, God "parts the Red Sea," the Hebrews make a safe crossing and the sea closes and drowns the Egyptian Army.

Moses must now accomplish the most impossible leadership, governance, and security objective of any leader recorded throughout history. It is not the intent of this book to convert the reader to another religion. However, it is essential to record for you the Biblical narrative that documents Moses extreme task. Forty years would be required to return the Hebrew people to Israel and The Promised Land. The population would grow to at least 1.5 million plus their livestock. They had to live in what is the most forbidding wilderness on this Earth.

Modern explorers documented the path followed by Moses in the Exodus can be traversed by men in as little as 11 days. Moses population of 1.5 million included infants and octogenarians. Earths history includes many groups of Nomadic travelers, yet never have 1.5 million remained nomadic and together for 40 years.

Please read the following summary of Moses beyond the Red Sea.

Exodus 14 God parts the Red Sea, and the Israelites escape the Egyptians; The Egyptian soldiers are drowned in the sea.

Exodus 15 Moses and Miriam sing songs of joy and praise to God for rescuing the Israelites; they complain for water; God provides water at Marah and Elim.

Exodus 16 Israelites complain, lack of food; God provides Manna and Quail

10 And it came to pass, as Aaron spake unto the congregation of Israel, they looked toward the wilderness, the glory of the LORD appeared in the cloud.

11 And the LORD spake unto Moses, saying,
12 I have heard murmurings of children of Israel: say to them
At even ye shall eat flesh, and in the morning ye shall be filled
with bread; and ye shall know that I am the JORD your God.
13 And it came to pass, that at even the quails came up, and
covered the camp: and in the morning the dew lay round about
the morning the dew lay round about the host.
14 And when the dew was gone, behold, upon
the wilderness there lay a small round thing, as small as the hoar
(Hebrew for color gray) frost on the ground.
15 When the children of Israel saw it, they said one to another, It
is manna. Moses said unto them, This is the bread which
the LORD hath given you to eat.
16 This is the thing which the LORD hath commanded, Gather of
it every man according to his eating, an omer for
every man, according to the number of your persons; take ye
every man for them which are in his tents.
31 And the house of Israel called the name thereof Manna: and it
was like coriander seed, white; and the taste of it was
like wafers made with honey.
35 And the children of Israel ate manna forty years, until
they came to a land inhabited; they ate manna, until
they came unto the borders of the land of Canaan.

The Bible gives us many remarkable examples of God's work. An explanation of "quail" is necessary to your understanding. The small bird called Quail has been recorded for as long as mankind has inhabited this earth. Quail are in the same family as Chicken, Duck, Geese, Pheasant, Poultry. There are hieroglyphics existing in the Pyramids that memorialize quail. Pharaoh's enjoyed Quail hunting which has been referred to as The Sport of Kings. A Quail is a smaller bird. Two or three quail would provide a meal for a grown man. Do the math and recognize that with a human population up to 1.5 million, 2-3 million quail were required to feed the population daily. The Hebrews are in the middle of a terrible desert location, not at all conducive to a Quail population. Only God could produce such a miracle daily for 40 years.

Equally miraculous is the nutrition provided by Quail. Many nutrition tables exist on our modern internet and show that ounce for ounce, Quail provide more protein and stronger total nutrition than any other meat, fish, or poultry source.

As for MANNA, it is described as something like a sweet bread. Manna has no other example in our acknowledged food tables or food descriptions at any time in history. Verse 31 tells us that Manna was like Coriander Seed, and coriander seed is available at well supplied grocery store Spice shelves. Coriander has a pleasant taste and could be blended to produce a sweet bread or sweet cake.

Exodus 17 The Israelites quarrel with Moses about a lack of water and long to go back to Egypt; God provides water through a rock at Horeb (Mount Sinai). The Israelites led by Joshua defeat the Amalekites.

Exodus 18 Moses father-in-law Jethro teaches Moses to delegate responsibility.

In Exodus Chapter 18 we have the earliest iteration of an Organization Chart, all organizations since that instance have followed some form of this organization chart. This will include Corporations large and small, Military structures, Government organizations, educational organizations, Organizations that enforce Rule of Law, Medical organizations, Legislative organizations. U.S. and Western European organizations have become bloated. Japanese systems remained with a 4-tier organization structure. Catholic Church follows a three-tier structure. Bible verses herein indicate God liked the 4-tier structure.

The organization chart described in Exodus 18:20-26 is consistent with modern management expectations for "scalability."

At this time, Moses is leading over one million Hebrews through the desert on what will become a 40-year trek through a forbidding desert wilderness in the Hebrew return to THE PROMISED LAND. Moses oversees all requirements. There is no established organization beyond family Elders and Captains of military forces.

Near the end of each day, Moses established a practice of finding a small hill that was broad enough that he could walk up a few paces and all the people could see Moses. Anyone who had a problem or grievance that they could not solve themselves would seek Moses help with the issue. Moses was more than 80 years old. Moses was taking great wear and tear on his mind and body.

Jethro the father-in-law of Moses came to visit the Hebrews. Observing Moses actions, Jethro recommended an organization to Moses, inspired by the word of God. Many times in the Old Testament, God would tell the Hebrew leaders to take certain levels of the organization and complete certain projects.

The "Organization Chart" commonly derived from the words given to Moses, continue to serve as a method of organization for all organizations, both large and small, business, government, military, medical, educational, church, civic organizations.

Chapter 10. FIRST ORGANIZATION CHART

The Author was first introduced to Organization Charts in a University Junior level Management Class at Jacksonville State University. The Biblical chapter and verse is referred to as the Law of Ones, Tens, and Thousands. (Exodus Chapter 18)

6 And he said unto Moses, I thy father
in law Jethro am come unto thee, and thy wife, and
her two sons with her.
7 And Moses went out to meet his father in law, and
did obeisance, and kissed him; and they asked each other of
their welfare; and they came into the tent.
8 Moses told his father in law all the LORD had done to Pharaoh
and to the Egyptians for Israel's sake, and all the travail that had
come upon them by the way, and how the LORD delivered them.
9 And Jethro rejoiced for all the goodness which the Lord had
done to Israel, whom he had delivered out of the hand of
the Egyptians.
10 Jethro said, Blessed be the LORD, who hath delivered you out
of the hand of the Egyptians, and out of the hand of Pharaoh, who
hath delivered the people from the hand of the Egyptians
11 Now I know that the LORD is greater than all God's: for in
the thing wherein they dealt proudly he was above them.
12 Jethro, Moses' father in law, took a burnt offering and
sacrifices for God: Aaron came, and all elders to eat bread with
Moses father in law before God.
13 It came to pass on the morrow, Moses sat to judge
the people: they stood by Moses from morning unto the evening.
14 And when Moses' father in law saw all that he did to the people,
he said, What is this thing that thou doest to the people?
Why sittest thou thyself alone, and all the people stand by thee
from morning unto even?
15 Moses said to his father in law, Because the people come to
me to enquire of God:
16 When they have a matter, they come unto me; and judge
between one and another, and I do make them know the statutes
of God, and his laws.

17 And Moses' father in law said unto him, The thing that thou
doest is not good.
18 Thou wilt surely wear away, both thou, and this people that is
with thee: for this thing is too heavy for thee; thou art
not able to perform it thyself alone.
19 Hearken now unto my voice, I will give thee counsel, and God
shall be with thee: Be thou for the people to God-ward*, that thou
mayest bring the causes unto God:
20 And thou shalt teach them ordinances and laws, and shalt
shew them the way wherein they must walk, and the work they
must do.
21 Moreover thou shalt provide out of all the people able men,
such as fear God, men of truth, hating covetousness; and place
over them, to be rulers of thousands, and rulers of hundreds, and
rulers of fifties, and rulers of tens:
22 And let them judge the people at all seasons: and it shall be,
that every great matter they shall bring unto thee, but every small
matter they shall judge: so shall it be easier for thyself, and they
shall bear the burden with thee.
23 If thou shalt do this thing, and God command thee so, then
thou shalt be able to endure, and all this people shall also go to
their place in peace.
24 Moses hearkened to the voice of his father in law, and did all
that he had said.
25 Moses chose able men out of all Israel, and made them heads
over all Israel, and made them heads over the people, rulers
of thousands, rulers of hundreds, rulers of fifties, rulers of tens.
26 They judged the people at all seasons: the hard causes they
brought to Moses, but every small matter they judged themselves.
27 And Moses let his father in law depart; and he went his way
into his own land.

In the verses above, you see the first example of courts and appeals court, along with Gods guidance for organization of large bodies of people.

In Exodus Chapter 18, we see the first system of election. Follow the math represented in the organization chart. If Moses had to establish an organization of over 100,000 leaders, no single human could know 100,000 people. We can be sure the system of Elders remained in place. Moses required extreme assistance to establish proper leaders. The Bible does not foretell the process utilized although it gives a view of recommendations for Elder nomination and approval by the people.

Also in Exodus Chapter 18, we see elements stated that are a preview of what is called "tripartite" government and "separation of powers." A Judiciary format and "Appeal to Higher Judiciary" is introduced, although it is not clearly identified in those terms. The reader must remember the tiny footprint of human population in this day. Vast government as we know it today will not be needed for another 3500 years, commencing, continuing to develop in 1600's AD.

Exodus 19 God fulfills his promise to Moses (Exodus 4) to bring him back to Mt. Sinai; Moses meets God on the mountain; God gives instructions for the Israelites to consecrate themselves before giving the Ten Commandments.

Chapter 11.MOSES THE LAWGIVER AND GREAT LEGISLATOR

Exodus 20 God gives the Israelites his Ten Commandments; The people are frightened by God's presence and ask Moses to be their mediator. God reiterates his command not to worship idols or erect altars to other God's.

Moses is called THE LAW GIVER and GREAT LEGISLATOR. God dictates the 10 commandments to Moses atop the mountain. God later dictates the books of The Law to Moses, called THE PENTATEUCH. These laws became governance for all RULE OF LAW statutes and codes for many thousand years. All too often, governments established laws that conflict with God. As documented herein, The Founding Fathers US Constitution is fully traceable to The Bible.

Moses, influenced by the Word of God, gave us far more than THE TEN COMMANDMENTS. The Pentateuch presents a complete legal code, along with the forerunner of our modern US Constitution. However, little of the chapter and verse that provides legal code or constitutional material shows appearance of codes or constitutions. It is necessary to "drill down" on ancient definitions and apply a multi-disciplined view to fully comprehend our Founding Fathers, who began with Religion, History cause and effect, Wars, Military, Constitutions, Law, Government, Campaigns and Elections, Philosophy, development of civilization, economics, demographics, closing with governance: from tripartite government, military, budgetary, taxation, import/export, education, technology, statesmanship and World Relations. Our Founding Fathers gave us more than a Constitution and Freedom. Key details are missed when academicians with narrow backgrounds attempt these works.

The Authors of this book share vast academic and professional lives, fully commensurate with the development paths of America's Founding Fathers. It was during a process of many years preaching in "jail ministry" along with preaching in homeless shelters, plus a lifetime of Corporate Turnaround and Political Campaign activity and Judgeship, that the Authors realized the preponderance of US Constitutional points contained in our Bible.

Few would argue THE TEN COMMANDMENTS importance as a key element of all freedom-centric legal codes.

Exodus Chapter 20

THE TEN COMMANDMENTS

1st Thou shalt have no other God's before me.

2nd Thou shalt not make unto thee
Any graven image.

3rd Thou shalt not take the name of the LORD
thy God in vain.

4th Remember the sabbath day, keep it holy.

5th Honor thy father and thy mother.

6th Thou shalt not kill.

7th Thou shalt not commit adultery.

8th Thou shalt not steal.

9th Thou shalt not bear false witness.

10th Thou shalt not covet thy neighbor's house,
nor his wife.

Exodus Chapter 20

1 And God spake all these words, saying,
2 I am the LORD thy God, which have brought thee out of the land
of Egypt, out of the house of bondage.
3 Thou shalt have no other God's before me.
4 Thou shalt not make unto thee any graven image, or any
likeness of anything That is in heaven above, or that is in the
earth beneath, or in the water under the earth:
5 Thou shalt not bow down thyself to them, nor serve them: for I,
the LORD thy God am a jealous God, visiting the iniquity of
the fathers upon the children unto the third and fourth generation
of them hat hate me;
6 shewing mercy to thousands of them that love me, and keep my
commandments
7 Thou shalt not take the name of the LORD thy God in vain;
For the LORD will not hold him guiltless that taketh his name in
in vain.
8 Remember the sabbath day, keep it holy.
9 Six days shalt thou labor, and do all thy work:
10 But the seventh day is the sabbath of the LORD thy God: in it
thou shalt not do any work, thou, nor thy son, nor thy daughter,
thy manservant, maidservant, nor thy cattle, nor thy stranger that
is within thy gates:
11 In six days the LORD made heaven and earth, the sea, and all
that is in them and rested the seventh day: wherefore the LORD
blessed the sabbath, and hallowed it.
12 Honor thy father and thy mother: that thy days may be long
upon the land which the LORD thy God giveth thee.
13 Thou shalt not kill.
14 Thou shalt not commit adultery.
15 Thou shalt not steal.
16 Thou shalt not bear false witness against thy neighbor
17 Thou shalt not covet thy neighbor's house, thy
neighbor's wife, his manservant
his maidservant, his ox, his ass, nor any thing that is
thy neighbor's.

18 All the people saw the thundering's and lightning, noise of the
trumpet, and the mountain smoking: and when the people saw it,
they stood afar off.
19 And they said unto Moses, Speak thou with us, and we
will hear: but let not God speak with us, lest we die.
20 Moses said unto the people, Fear not: God is come to prove
you, that his fear may be before your faces, that ye sin not.

Exodus 21
God gives instructions on servants (Israelites who become slaves); God gives instructions on incidents of personal injury (eye for eye, tooth for tooth).

Exodus 22
God instructs us to protect property and social responsibility.

Exodus 23
God gives instructions about justice and mercy; God gives instructions about the day of rest (or the Sabbath day); God gives instructions about three annual festivals; God places his angel in front of the Israelites to lead the way to the Promised Land.

Exodus 24
God confirms his covenant with Israel; Moses explains the laws; consecrates the people by sprinkling blood. Moses takes Aaron, his two sons, and 70 elders up to see God. Moses takes Joshua up the mountain to meet God 40 days and nights.

Exodus 25
God instructs Moses to make the Tabernacle. Instructions about the making of The Ark of the Covenant; about making a special table; and about making the lampstand.

Exodus 26
Instructions concerning the making of the Tabernacle itself

Exodus 27
Instructions about making the Altar of Burnt Offering; about making the Courtyard; about making the oil for the lampstand.

Exodus 28
Instructions about Priestly Garments; about making the Ephod; about making the Breastplate; making other Priestly Garments.

Exodus 29
God gives instructions about the consecration of the Priests.

Exodus 30
God gives instructions about making The Altar of Incense; instructions about an atonement tax; about making a wash basin; making Anointing Oil; making incense.

Exodus 31
God gives instructions to Moses about two special craftsmen to lead the construction project - Bezalel of the tribe of Judah and Oholiab from the tribe of Dan. God reiterates his command about the Sabbath Day of rest.

Exodus 32
Moses is gone too long; Israelite people force Aaron to make an idol; Aaron makes a Golden Calf. Moses descends the mountain. Moses broke the two tablets of the Testimony. Levites side with Moses and kill three thousand of those worshipping the Golden Calf. Moses goes back up the mountain to intercede for the Israelites.

Exodus 33
God tells Moses the people can travel to the Promised Land by themselves. Moses prepares The Tent of Meeting (special tent Moses used to meet with God); Moses sees God's glory.

Exodus 34
God gives Moses new stone tablets with the ten commandments on them. Moses pleads with God to fulfill His promise to take Israel to Canaan. God reiterates his covenant with Moses. Moses must veil his face after meeting with God.

Exodus 35
Moses shares Sabbath regulations with the Israelites; Moses calls on the people to gather materials to make the Tabernacle and all its articles. Bezaleel and Oholiab are chosen to be the general contractors for the Tabernacle project.

Exodus 36
The construction of the Tabernacle begins

Exodus 37
Craftsmen make The Ark of the Covenant; The Table; Lampstand; Altar of Incense

Exodus 38
The making of the Altar of Burnt Offering; the Basin of Washing; and the Courtyard; a list of materials used to construct the tabernacle.

Exodus 39
The making of the Priestly Garments including the Ephod, Breastpiece; and other priestly garments; Moses inspects the parts of the Tabernacle.

Exodus 40
Tabernacle is set up; The Glory of the Lord filled the Tabernacle. (Shekinah Glory)

Deuteronomy Chapter 34

And Moses went up from the plains of Moab unto the mountain of Nebo, to the top of Pisgah, that *is* over against Jericho. And the LORD shewed him all the land of Gilead, unto Dan,

2 And all Naphtali, and the land of Ephraim, and Manasseh, and all the land of Judah, unto the utmost sea,
3 And south, the plain of the valley of Jericho, the city of palm trees, unto Zoar.
4 And the LORD said unto him, This *is* the land which I sware unto Abraham, unto Isaac, and unto Jacob, saying, I will give it unto thy seed: I have caused thee to see *it* with thine eyes, but thou shalt not go over thither.
5 So Moses, servant of the LORD died in the land of Moab, according to the word of the LORD.
6 And he buried him in a valley in the land of Moab, over against Bethpeor: but no man knoweth of his sepulchre unto this day.
7 And Moses *was* an hundred and twenty years old when he died: his eye was not dim, nor his natural force abated.
8 And the children of Israel wept for Moses in the plains of Moab thirty days: so the days of weeping *and* mourning for Moses were ended.
9 And Joshua the son of Nun was full of the spirit of wisdom; for Moses had laid his hands upon him: and the children of Israel hearkened unto him, and did as the LORD commanded Moses.
10 There arose not a prophet since in Israel like Moses, whom the LORD knew,

Moses became the next great leader to provide a perfect example of the type of leadership, vision, and guiding hand required to govern and lead a people through such impossible conditions safely and effectively. No other leader recorded in history would complete such an impossible task as leading 1.5 million people for 40 years, in tent dwelling, living off the land, providing the vision to establish government and laws first initiated 7000 years ago, that have governed our world 3500 years.

The forbidding terrain of the region traversed by Moses has rarely ever been traveled afoot by multi-generations numbering 1.5 million people as did Moses. Our Founding Fathers would realize this as another perfect example of how America could be colonized from sea to shining sea. Additionally, Moses of necessity proved a perfect example of effective international relations, as he found it necessary to intermingle and negotiate safe passage through tribal areas that became home turf of many of the most dangerous and murderous people named throughout history. Moses would also provide us with the very first "books of the law," upon which our United States Constitution finds it foundation. In addition to legal foundations documented in EXODUS, those books are found in our Holy Bible under the names LEVITICUS, NUMBERS, DEUTERONOMY.

TRANSITION TO MAIMONIDES

The continuing development of issues that ultimately yielded the United States Constitution will transition through many iterations of activity. A period of some 2700 years will transpire between the life of Moses and Maimonides. During those many centuries, we will see a collection of Iconic individuals that will all take part in the process of development of the ultimate form of Democracy we practice today.

We will see the Greco-Roman world become involved, albeit not associated with the Word of God. We will see philosophers such as Socrates, Plato, and Aristotle lend their visionary skills. We will see Jesus Christ and the Apostles further develop our practice of Gods' word. We will see Roman leaders and Dictators take actions pro and con. Then Roman Emperor Constantine will declare Christianity the official religion of Rome, followed by Emperor Justinian who will further develop churches.

Next great government development will be Magna Carta.

Then, the first visionary to move beyond Moses in development of government and constitutions consistent with the Word of God, will be Maimonides.

Chapter 12. Maimonides identifies 613 Mitzvot Commandments

- Jewish tradition teaches there are 613 commandments.
- This is the list of 613 identified by Rambam/Maimonides.
- The order stated below is modern organization.

God	Employees	The Firstborn
Torah	Vows	Priests & Levites
Signs & Symbols	Sabbatical & Jubilee	Tithes & Taxes
Prayer & Blessings	Court	The Temple
Love & Brotherhood	Injuries & Damages	Sacrifice
&Offerings		
The Poor	Property	Ritual Purity
Gentiles	Criminal Laws	Leprosy
Family	Punishment& Restitution	The King
Forbidden Sex	Prophecy	Wars
Times	Idolatry	Business Practices
Dietary Laws	Agriculture	Clothing

Below is a list of the 613 mitzvot (commandments). It is based on the list compiled by Maimonides/Rambam in the Mishnah Torah (first five books of the Holy Bible, but I have consulted other sources as well. Rambam's list is a most widely accepted. The order herein is the authors, as are explanations of how some rules are derived from biblical passages.

613 Mitzvot located by Book of The Bible

Genesis	2 Laws
Exodus	109 Laws
Leviticus	243 Laws
Numbers	56 Laws
Deuteronomy	203 Laws

Jewish tradition says, the Torah holds 613 commandments (Hebrew: תרי״ג מצוות, romanized: taryag mitzvot). This tradition is first recorded in 3rd century CE, when Rabbi Simlai states so in a sermon recorded in Talmud Makkot 23b.[1]

Other "sages" holding this view are Rabbi Simeon ben Azzai[2] and Rabbi Eleazar ben Yose the Galilean.[3] It is quoted in Midrash Exodus Rabbah 33:7, Numbers Rabbah 13:15–16; 18:21 and Talmud Yevamot 47b.[4]

The 613 include "positive commandments", to perform an act, "negative commandments", to abstain.

For each Biblical law or commandment, we have provided a citation to the biblical passage or passages from which it is derived. We added an addendum following the Index that provides much information beyond the actual Verse. For commandments that can be observed today, we have also provided citations to the Chafetz Chayim's Concise Book of Mitzvot (CCA refers to affirmative commandments; CCN refers to negative commandments; CCI refers to commandments that only apply in Israel).[5] Commandments that cannot be observed relate to the Temple, its sacrifices, and services (because the Temple does not exist) and criminal procedures (the theocratic state of Israel does not exist).[6]

Although the 613 is mentioned in the Talmud, its significance increased in medieval rabbinic literature, including works listing or arranged by the *mitzvot*. The most famous of these was an enumeration of the 613 commandments by Maimonides.

The Vilna Gaon suggested there exists more than 613 commandments (otherwise much of the Pentateuch would be without commandments - considered difficult), the count of 613 refers to "roots" (*shorashim*) of the other commandments.[7]

Footnote Citations

1. Israel Drazi (2009). Maimonides and the Biblical Prophets. Gefen Publishing House Ltd. p. 209.
2. Sifre, Deuteronomy 76
3. Midrash Aggadah to Genesis 15:1
4. Babylonian Talmud, Makkot 23b-24a
5. Chofetz Chaim (1990). Sefer HaMitzvot HaKatzar (in Hebrew). Jerusalem: Feldheim. pp. 9, 16, 17.
6. Yisrael Meir Kagan, The Concise Book of Mitzvoth: The Commandments which can be Observed Today, Trans., Charles Wengrov. Feldheim, 1990.
7. Avraham of Vilna, Maalot haTorah (print in Nachmanides,Sefer haEmunah vehaBitachon, Warsaw: 1877, p.1

- Moses Maimonides, translation, Charles Ber Chavel and Moses ibn Tibbon. Book of divine commandments (the Sefer Ha-mitzvoth of Moses Maimonides) London: Soncino Press, 1940.HEBREW DICTIONARY

THE 613 MITZVOT

End of book appendix cross-references many of these verses to Jewish meanings, plus Bible Chapter and Verse for each Mitzvot.

God

1. To know that God exists (Ex. 20:2; Deut. 5:6).
2. Not entertain idea there is any god but the Eternal (Ex. 20:3).
3. Not blaspheme (Ex. 22:27; Ex. 22:28), penalty is death.
4. To hallow God's name (Lev. 22:32). See The Name of God.
5. Not to profane God's name (Lev . 22:32). See Name of God.
6. To know that God is One, a complete Unity (Deut. 6:4).
7. To love God (Deut. 6:5) (CCA3).
8. To fear Him reverently (Deut. 6:13; 10:20).
9. Not to put the word of God to the test (Deut. 6:16)
10. To imitate His good and upright ways (Deut. 28:9).

Torah

11. To honor the old and the wise (Lev. 19:32).
12. To learn Torah and to teach it (Deut. 6:7)..
13. To cleave to those who know Him (Deut. 10:20) (the Talmud states cleaving to scholars is equivalent to cleaving to Him).
14. Not to add to commandments of the Torah, whether in Written Law or in its interpretation received by tradition (Deut. 13:1).
15. Not to take away from commandments of Torah (Deut. 13:1).
16. That every person shall write a scroll of the Torah for himself.

Signs and Symbols

17. To circumcise the male offspring (Gen. 17:12; Lev. 12:3)
18. To put tzitzit on corners of clothing (Num. 15:38). (fringe)
19. To bind tefillin on the head (Deut. 6:8).
20. To bind tefillin on the arm (Deut. 6:8).
21. To affix mezuzah to the doorposts and gates of your house.

Prayer and Blessings

22. To pray to God (Ex. 23:25; Deut. 6:13).
23. To read the Shema in the morning and at night (Deut. 6:7).
24. To recite grace after meals (Deut. 8:10).
25. Not to lay down a stone for worship (Lev. 26:1).

Love and Brotherhood

26. To love all human beings of the covenant (Lev. 19:18).
27. Not to stand idly when a human life is in danger (Lev. 19:16).
28. Not to wrong any one in speech (Lev. 25:17).
29. Not to carry tales (Lev. 19:16).
30. Not to cherish hatred in one's heart (Lev. 19:17).
31. Not to take revenge (Lev. 19:18).
32. Not to bear a grudge (Lev. 19:18).
33. Not to put any Jew to shame (Lev. 19:17).
34. Not to curse any other Israelite (Lev. 19:14) (by implication: if you may not curse those who cannot hear, you certainly may not curse those who can).
35. Not give occasion to simple-minded to stumble (Lev. 19:14) (this includes doing anything that will cause another to sin).
36. To rebuke the sinner (Lev. 19:17).
37. To relieve a neighbor of his burden and help unload his beast.
38. To assist replacing the load on neighbor's beast (Deut. 22:4).
39. Not leave beast, fallen beneath burden, unaided (Deut. 22:4).

The Poor and Unfortunate

40. Not to afflict an orphan or a widow (Ex. 22:21
41. Not to reap the entire field (Lev. 19:9; Lev. 23:22).
42. To leave unreaped corner of the field or orchard for the poor.
43. Not gather gleanings (ears that fell to ground while reaping).
44. To leave the gleanings for the poor (Lev. 19:9)
45. Not to gather ol'loth (the imperfect clusters) of the vineyard.
46. To leave ol'loth (imperfect clusters) for the poor (Lev. 19:10;).
47. Not to gather the peret (grapes) that have fallen to the ground.

48. To leave peret (single grapes) of the vineyard for the poor.
49. Not return to take a forgotten sheaf (Deut. 24:19) fruit trees.
50. To leave the forgotten sheaves for the poor (Deut. 24:19-20).
51. Not refrain maintaining a poor man and giving him his needs.
52. To give charity according to one's means (Deut. 15:11).

Treatment of Gentiles

53. To love the stranger (Deut. 10:19).
54. Not to wrong the stranger in speech (Ex. 22:20).
55. Not to wrong the stranger in buying or selling (Ex. 22:20).
56. Not to intermarry with gentiles (Deut. 7:3).
57. To exact the debt of an alien (Deut. 15:3).
58. To lend to an alien at interest (Deut. 23:21)

Marriage, Divorce and Family

59. To honor father and mother (Ex. 20:12).
60. Not to smite a father or a mother (Ex. 21:15).
61. Not to curse a father or mother (Ex. 21:17).
62. To reverently fear father and mother (Lev. 19:3).
63. To be fruitful and multiply (Gen. 1:28).
64. A eunuch shall not marry a daughter of Israel (Deut. 23:2).
65. A mamzer shall not marry daughter of a Jew (Deut. 23:3).
66. Ammonite or Moabite shall never marry daughter Israelite.
67. Not exclude descendant of Esau from Israel for 3 generations.
68. Not exclude an Egyptian from of Israel for three generations.
69. Shall be no harlot (in Israel); no intercourse, without marriage, deed of marriage, formal declaration marriage (Deut. 23:18).
70. Take wife by kiddushin, sacrament of marriage (Deut. 24:1).
71. New married husband (be free) one year to rejoice with wife.
72. Bridegroom exempt a whole year from public labor, such as military service, guarding the wall, etc. (Deut. 24:5).
73. Not withhold food, clothing, or conjugal rights from wife.
74. A woman suspected of adultery shall be dealt with per Torah.
75. If defame wife honor before marriage, live with her for life.
76. Man may not divorce his wife whom he has publish evil report.

77. To divorce by a formal written document (Deut. 24:1).
78. One who divorced his wife shall not remarry her, if after the divorce she had been married to another man (Deut. 24:4).
79. Widow whose husband died childless must only marry deceased husband's brother (Deut. 25:5).
80. To marry the widow of a brother who has died childless
81. Widow formally release brother-in-law (if refuses to marry her.

Forbidden Sexual Relations

82. Not indulge in familiarities with relatives, such as kissing, embracing, winking, skipping, may lead to incest (Lev. 18:6).
83. Not to commit incest with one's mother (Lev. 18:7
84. Not to commit sodomy with one's father (Lev. 18:7).
85. Not to commit incest with one's father's wife (Lev. 18:8).
86. Not to commit incest with one's sister (Lev. 18:9).
87. Not to commit incest with father's wife's daughter (Lev. 18:11).
88. Not to commit incest with one's son's daughter (Lev. 18:10).
89. Not commit incest with one's daughter's daughter (Lev. 18:10)
90. Not commit incest with one's daughter (not explicitly in Torah, inferred from other explicit commands that would include it).
91. Not to commit incest with one's fathers sister (Lev. 18:12).
92. Not to commit incest with one's mother's sister (Lev. 18:13).
93. Not commit incest with father's brothers wife (Lev. 18:14).
94. Not to commit sodomy with one's father's brother (Lev. 18:14).
95. Not to commit incest with one's son's wife (Lev. 18:15).
96. Not to commit incest with one's brother's wife (Lev. 18:16).
97. Not to commit incest with one's wife's daughter (Lev. 18:17).
98. Not commit incest with daughter of one's wife's son.
99. Not commit incest with daughter of one's wife's daughter.
100. Not to commit incest with one's wife's sister (Lev. 18:18).
101. Not have intercourse with a woman, in menstrual period.
102. Not have intercourse with another man's wife (Lev. 18:20).
103. Not to commit sodomy with a male (Lev. 18:22).
104. Not to have intercourse with a beast (Lev. 18:23).
105. Woman shall not have intercourse with beast (Lev. 18:23).
106. No castrate male; not man, domestic/wild beast/fowl.

Times and Seasons

107. New month shall be solemnly proclaimed as holy, months and years to be calculated by Supreme Court only. Not travel on Shabbat outside limits of place of residence.
108. To sanctify Shabbat (Ex. 20:8).
109. Not to do work on Shabbat (Ex. 20:10).
110. To rest on Shabbat (Ex. 23:12; 34:21).
111. Celebrate the festivals [Passover, Shavu'ot and Sukkot].
112. To rejoice on the festivals (Deut. 16:14).
113. To appear in the Sanctuary on the festivals (Deut. 16:16).
114. To remove chametz on the Eve of Passover (Ex. 12:15).
115. To rest on the first day of Passover (Ex. 12:16; Lev. 23:7).
116. Not work on first day of Passover (Ex.12:16; Lev. 23:6-7).
117. Rest on seventh day Passover (Ex. 12:16; Lev. 23:8).
118. Not to do work on the seventh day of Passover.
119. Eat matzah on first night of Passover (Ex. 12:18).
120. No chametz in Israelite possession during Passover.
121. Not eat food containing chametz on Passover (Ex. 12:20).
122. Not to eat chametz on Passover (Ex. 13:3).
123. Chametz not be seen in Israelite homes during Passover.
124. Discuss departure from Egypt, first night Passover.
125. Not to eat chametz after mid-day on fourteenth of Nissan.
126. Count forty-nine days from time of the cutting of the Omer (first sheaves of the barley harvest) (Lev. 23:15).
127. To rest on Shavu'ot (Lev. 23:21).
128. Not to do work on the Shavu'ot (Lev. 23:21).
129. To rest on Rosh Hashanah (Lev. 23:24).
130. Not to do work on Rosh Hashanah (Lev. 23:25).
131. To hear sound of shofar on Rosh Hashanah (Num. 29:1).
132. To fast on Yom Kippur (Lev. 23:27).
133. Not to eat or drink on Yom Kippur (Lev. 23:29).
134. Not to do work on Yom Kippur (Lev. 23:31).
135. To rest on the Yom Kippur (Lev. 23:32).
136. To rest on the first day of Sukkot (Lev. 23:35)..
137. Not to do work on the first day of Sukkot (Lev. 23:35).

138. To rest on the eighth day of Sukkot (Lev. 23:36).
139. Not to work on eighth day of Sukkot (Lev. 23:36).
140. Take during Sukkot a palm branch and other three plants.
141. To dwell in booths seven days during Sukkot (Lev. 23:42).

Dietary Laws (See Animals that MAY NOT be eaten)

143. Examine marks in cattle (distinguish clean from unclean)
144. Not to eat the flesh of unclean beasts (Lev. 11:4).
145. Examine marks in fishes (distinguish clean from unclean.
146. Not to eat unclean fish (Lev. 11:11).
147. Examine marks in fowl, distinguish clean from unclean.
148. Not to eat unclean fowl (Lev. 11:13).
149. Examine marks in locusts, distinguish clean from unclean.
150. Not to eat a worm found in fruit (Lev. 11:41).
151. Not eat things that creep upon the earth (Lev. 11:41-42).
152. Not to eat any vermin of the earth (Lev. 11:44).
153. Not eat things that swarm in water (Lev. 11:43 and 46).
154. Not to eat of winged insects (Deut. 14:19).
155. Not eat flesh of a beast that is terefah (lit torn) (Ex. 22:30).

See Kosher slaughtering.

156. Not eat flesh of a beast that died of itself (Deut. 14:21).
157. Slay cattle, deer, fowl by shechitah law if to be eaten.
158. Not eat a limb removed from a living beast (Deut. 12:23).
159. Not slaughter animal and its young on same day.
160. Not to take the mother-bird with the young (Deut. 22:6).
161. Set the mother-bird free when taking nest (Deut. 22:6-7).
162. Not eat flesh of ox condemned to be stoned (Ex. 21:28).
163. Not to boil meat with milk (Ex. 23:19).
164. Not eat flesh with milk (Ex. 34:26) (according to Talmud, passage is distinct prohibition from (Ex. 23:19).
165. Not to eat of the thigh-vein which shrank (Gen. 32:33).
166. Not to eat chelev (tallow-fat) (Lev. 7:23).
167. Not to eat blood (Lev. 7:26).
168. Cover blood of undomesticated animals& fowl after killed.
169. Not to eat or drink like glutton or drunkard,

Business Practices

170. Not to do wrong in buying or selling (Lev. 25:14).
171. Not to make a loan to an Israelite on interest (Lev. 25:37).
172. Not borrow on interest (would cause lender to sin).
173. Not to take part in any usurious transaction between borrower and lender, neither as surety, nor as witness, nor as a writer of the bond (Ex. 22:24).
174. To lend to a poor person (Ex. 22:24) (though passage says "if you lend" it is understood as obligatory).
175. Not demand from a poor man repayment of his debt, when creditor knows that he cannot pay, nor press him.
176. Not take pledge utensils used prepare food (Deut. 24:6).
177. Not exact a pledge from a debtor by force (Deut. 24:10).
178. Not keep pledge from owner if he needs(Deut. 24:12)
179. To return a pledge to its owner (Deut. 24:13).
180. Not to take a pledge from a widow (Deut. 24:17).
181. Not to commit fraud in measuring (Lev. 19:35).
182. To ensure scales and weights are correct (Lev. 19:36).
183. Not to possess inaccurate measures and weights.

Employees, Servants, and Slaves

184. Not to delay payment of a hired man's wages (Lev. 19:13).
185. Hired laborer shall be permitted to eat produce he reaps.
186. That the hired laborer shall not take more than he can eat.
187. Hired laborer shall not eat produce not being harvested.
188. To pay wages to the hired man at the due time.
189. Deal judicially with Hebrew bondman in accord with law.
190. Not compel the Hebrew servant to do work of a slave.
191. Not to sell a Hebrew servant as a slave (Lev. 25:42).
192. Not to treat a Hebrew servant rigorously (Lev. 25:43)).
193. No gentile bad treatment, Hebrew bondman sold him.
194. Not send away Hebrew bondman empty handed, if freed.
195. To bestow liberal gifts upon Hebrew bondsman (at end of term of service), do same to a Hebrew bondwoman
196. To redeem a Hebrew maid-servant (Ex. 21:8).

197. Not to sell a Hebrew maid-servant to another person.
198. To espouse a Hebrew maid-servant (Ex. 21:8-9).
199. To keep the Canaanite slave forever (Lev. 25:46).
200. Slave not escape to Israel, owner live Palestine(Dt23:16)
201. Not to wrong such a slave (Deut. 23:17).
202. Not to muzzle beast, while it works in produce it can eat.

Vows, Oaths and Swearing

203. That a man should fulfill whatever he has uttered.
204. Not to swear needlessly (Ex. 20:7).
205. Not to violate an oath or swear falsely (Lev. 19:12).
206. To decide annulment of vows, according to rules in Torah.
207. Not to break a vow (Num. 30:3).
208. To swear by His name truly (Deut. 10:20).
209. Not to delay fulfill vows or bring vowed free-will offerings.

Sabbatical and Jubilee Years

210. To let the land lie fallow in the Sabbatical year.
211. To cease from tilling the land in the Sabbatical year.
212. Not to till the ground in the Sabbatical year (Lev. 25:4).
213. Not to do any work on the trees in the Sabbatical year.
214. Not reap aftermath that grows in Sabbatical year, same way as it is reaped in other years (Lev. 25:5).
215. Not gather fruit in Sabbatical year same as other years.
216. To sound the Ram's horn in the Sabbatical year.
217. To release debts in the seventh year (Deut. 15:2).
218. Not demand return of loan after Sabbatical year passed.
219. Not deny loan to poor, due to release in Sabbatical year
220. Assemble people to hear Torah at close of seventh year.
221. Count years of Jubilee by years and by cycles of seven.
222. Keep Jubilee year holy by resting and let land lie fallow.
223. Not cultivate soil nor do work on trees, in the Jubilee Year.
224. Not reap aftermath of field that grew of itself in Jubilee Year, in same way as in other years (Lev. 25:11).
225. Not gather tree fruit in Jubilee Year, same as other years.
226. To grant redemption to the land in the Jubilee year.

The Court and Judicial Procedure

227. Appoint judges and officers in every community of Israel.
228. Not appoint as judge, a person who is not well versed in laws of the Torah, even if he is expert in other knowledge.
229. To adjudicate cases of purchase and sale (Lev. 25:14).
230. To judge cases of liability of a paid depositary (Ex. 22:9).
231. Adjudicate loss for which gratuitous borrower is liable.
232. To adjudicate cases of inheritances (Num. 27:8-11).
233. To judge cases of damage caused by an uncovered pit.
234. Judge cases of injuries caused by beasts (Ex. 21:35-36).
235. Judge cases of damage caused by trespass of cattle.
236. To adjudicate cases of damage caused by fire (Ex. 22:5).
237. To adjudicate damage caused by gratuitous depositary.
238. Adjudicate other cases between plaintiff and defendant.
239. Not to curse a judge (Ex. 22:27).
240. That one who possesses evidence shall testify in Court.
241. Not to testify falsely (Ex. 20:13).
242. Witness in capital case, shall not state law in the case.
243. That a transgressor shall not testify (Ex. 23:1).
244. Court no take testimony of relatives in capital punishment.
245. Not to hear one party to a suit in absence of other party.
246. To examine witnesses thoroughly (Deut. 13:15).
247. Not to decide a case on the evidence of a single witness.
248. To give decision according to majority when there is a difference of opinion among Sanhedrin on law (Ex. 23:2).
249. Not decide capital cases, by view of majority, if those for condemnation exceed by one, those for acquittal (Ex. 23:2).
250. In capital cases, if argued acquittal, shall not argue guilt.
251. To treat parties in a litigation with equal impartiality.
252. Not to render iniquitous decisions (Lev. 19:15).
253. Not to favor a great man when trying a case (Lev. 19:15).
254. Not to take a bribe (Ex. 23:8).
255. Not to be afraid of a bad man, when trying a case.
256. Not to be moved in trying case, by poverty of parties.
257. Not to pervert the judgment of strangers or orphans.
258. Not pervert judgment of sinner or poor.

259. To render a decision only on evidence of two witnesses.
260. Not execute one guilty of a capital offense before his trial).
261. To accept the rulings of every Supreme Court in Israel.
262. Not to rebel against the orders of the Court (Deut. 17:11)

Injuries and Damages (See Love and Brotherhood)

263. To make a parapet for your roof (Deut. 22:8).
264. Not to leave something that might cause hurt (Deut. 22:8).
265. Save the pursued even at cost of life of the pursuer.
266. Not spare pursuer, but he is to be slain before he reaches the pursued and slays latter, or uncovers nakedness.

Property and Property Rights

267. Not to sell a field in the land of Israel in perpetuity.
268. Not change character of open land of Levites or their fields; not sell it in perpetuity; may be redeemed any time.
269. Houses sold within walled city may be redeemed in year.
270. Not to remove landmarks (property boundaries).
271. Not to swear falsely in denial of another's property rights.
272. Not to deny falsely another's property rights (Lev. 19:11).
273. Never to settle in the land of Egypt (Deut. 17:16).
274. Not to steal personal property (Lev. 19:11).
275. To restore that which one took by robbery (Lev. 5:23).
276. To return lost property (Deut. 22:1).
277. No pretend not to see lost property - obligation to return

Criminal Laws

278. Not to slay an innocent person (Ex. 20:13).
279. Not to kidnap a person of Israel (Ex. 20:13) a person distinguished from Lev. 19:11, regarding taking property).
280. Not to rob by violence (Lev. 19:13).
281. Not to defraud (Lev. 19:13).
282. Not to covet what belongs to another (Ex. 20:14).
283. Not to crave something that belongs to another.
284. Not to indulge in evil thoughts and sights (Num. 15:39).

Punishment and Restitution

285. Court shall pass sentence of death by decapitation.
286. That Court shall pass sentence of death by strangulation.
287. That Court shall pass death sentence by burning with fire.
288. That the Court shall pass sentence of death by stoning.
289. Hang the dead body of one who has incurred that penalty.
290. An executed criminal shall not remain hanging over night.
291. To inter the executed on the day of execution.
292. Not to accept ransom from a murderer (Num. 35:31).
293. To exile one who committed accidental homicide.
294. Establish six cities of refuge (for accidental homicide).
295. No accept ransom for accidental homicide, to relieve exile.
296. Decapitate heifer in manner prescribed (in expiation of murder on road, perpetrator not discovered) (Deut. 21:4).
297. Not plow or sow rough valley (where heifer's neck broken)
298. Adjudge thief to pay compensation or suffer death.
299. He who inflicts bodily injury shall pay compensation.
300. To impose penalty of fifty shekels upon seducer (of an unbetrothed virgin) enforce other rules connected to case
301. That violator (of an unbetrothed virgin) shall marry her.
302. If raped a damsel and (per law) married her, not to divorce
303. Not to inflict punishment on Shabbat (Ex.35:3).
304. To punish the wicked by the infliction of stripes.
305. No exceed statutory number stripes laid on (Deut. 25:3).
306. Not spare offender, on guilty penalty (Deut.19:13).
307. Do unto false witnesses as they purposed (to accused).
308. Not to punish one who committed offense under duress.

Prophecy

309. Heed the call of every prophet in each generation, provided that he Neither adds, nor takes away from Torah.
310. Not to prophesy falsely (Deut. 18:20).
311. Not refrain putting false prophet to death nor be in fear of.

Idolatry, Idolaters, Idolatrous Practices

312. Not make a graven image; neither by oneself nor by others.
313. Not make figures for ornament, even if not worshipped.
314. Not to make idols even for others (Ex. 34:17; Lev. 19:4).
315. Not to use the ornament of any object of idolatrous worship.
316. Not use idol or accessory objects, offerings, libations.
317. Not to drink wine of idolaters (Deut. 32:38).
318. Not worship an idol in the way it is usually worshipped.
319. Not bow down to idol, even if that is not its mode of worship.
320. Not to prophesy in the name of an idol.
321. Not hearken to one who prophesies in the name of an idol.
322. Not to lead the children of Israel astray to idolatry
323. Not to entice an Israelite to idolatry (Deut. 13:12).
324. To destroy idolatry and its appurtenances (Deut. 12:2-3).
325. Not to love the enticer to idolatry (Deut. 13:9).
326. Not to give up hating the enticer to idolatry (Deut. 13:9).
327. Not save enticer from capital punishment,
stand by at execution (Deut. 13:9).
328. Person he attempted to entice to idolatry not urge acquittal.
329. A person he attempted to entice shall not refrain from giving evidence of enticer's guilt if he has such evidence.
330. Not swear by idol to worshipers, nor cause them to swear.
331. Not to turn one's attention to idolatry (Lev. 19:4).
332. Not adopt institutions of idolaters nor their customs.
333. Not to pass a child through the fire to Molech (Lev. 18:21).
334. Not suffer any one practicing witchcraft to live (Ex. 22:17).
335. Not practice onein (observing times-seasons).
336. No practice nachesh (signs, charms, incantations).
337. Not to consult ovoth (ghosts) (Lev. 19:31).
338. Not to consult yid'onim (wizards) (Lev. 19:31).
339. Not to practice kisuf (magic).
340. Not to practice kessem (general term for magical practices)
341. Not practice chover chaver (cast spells on snakes).
342. Not to enquire of an ob (a ghost) (Deut. 18:11).
343. Not to seek the maytim (dead) (Deut. 18:11).
344. Not to enquire of a yid'oni (wizard) (Deut. 18:11).

345. Not to remove the entire beard, like the idolaters.
346. Not round corners of the head, as the idolatrous priests do.
347. Not cut oneself or incise flesh in grief, like idolater.
348. Not to tattoo the body like the idolaters (Lev. 19:28).
349. Not to make a bald spot for the dead (Deut. 14:1).
350. Not to plant a tree for worship (Deut. 16:21).
351. Not to set up a pillar (for worship) (Deut. 16:22).
352. Not to show favor to idolaters (Deut. 7:2).
353. No covenant with 7 (Canaanite, idolatrous) nations.
354. Not to settle idolaters in our land (Ex. 23:33).
355. Slay inhabitants of a city becoming idolatrous, burn city.
356. Not to rebuild a city that has been led astray to idolatry.
357. Not make use of property of city that has been led astray.

Agriculture and Animal Husbandry

358. Not to cross-breed cattle of different species (Lev. 19:19)).
359. Not to sow different kinds of seed together in one field
360. Not to eat fruit of a tree for three years from its planting.
361. Fruit of fruit-bearing trees in fourth year planting shall be sacred like the second tithe and eaten in Jerusalem.
362. Not to sow grain or herbs in a vineyard (Deut. 22:9).
363. Not eat produce of diverse seeds sown in a vineyard.
364. Not work with beasts of different species, yoked together.

Clothing

365. That a man shall not wear women's clothing (Deut. 22:5).
366. Woman should not wear men's clothing (Deut. 22:5).
367. Not wear garments of wool and linen mixed together.

The Firstborn

368. To redeem the firstborn human male
369. To redeem the firstling of an ass (Ex. 13:13; Ex. 34:20).
370. To break neck of firstling of an ass if it not redeemed
371. Not to redeem the firstling of a clean beast (Num. 18:17).

Kohanim and Levites, (Care for the Dead, Mourning, Prohibited Marriages and Illegitimate Children, Levi)

372. Kohanim shall put on priestly vestments for the service.
373. Not to tear the High Kohein's robe (Ex. 28:32).
374. Kohein not enter Sanctuary (unless performing service) .
375. Kohein not defile self by contact with dead except relative
376. Kohanim defile selves by attending burial of deceased relatives, mourn commanded to mourn for relatives
377. Kohein who had immersion during day (to cleanse from uncleanness) not serve in Sanctuary until after sunset.
378. That a kohein shall not marry a divorced
379. That a kohein shall not marry a harlot (Lev. 21:7).
380. That a kohein shall not marry a profaned woman
381. Show honor to kohein, give precedence in all things holy.
382. High Kohein shall not defile self with dead, even relatives
383. High Kohein shall not go (under roof) with a dead body.
384. That the High Kohein shall marry a virgin (Lev. 21:13).
385. High Kohein shall not marry a widow (Lev. 21:14).
386. High Kohein not cohabit widow, even without marriage, he profanes (Lev. 21:15).
387. Person with physical blemish shall not serve (Sanctuary)
388. That a kohein with a temporary blemish shall not serve
389. Person with physical blemish not pass Sanctuary altar.
390. kohein who is unclean shall not serve (in Sanctuary).
391. Send unclean out of Camp of Shechinah, out of Sanctuary
392. Unclean kohein not to enter courtyard (Num. 5:2-3) In Camp of Shechinah.
393. That the kohanim shall bless Israel (Num. 6:23).
394. To set apart a portion of the dough for the kohein.
395. Levites not provide kohanim service, nor vice versa.
396. Only descendant of male line of Aaron serve Sanctuary
397. That the Levite shall serve in the Sanctuary (Num. 18:23).
398. To give Levites cities to dwell in, serve as cities of refuge.
399. None of tribe of Levi shall take territory in land (of Israel).
400. Tribe of Levi not share spoil (conquest Promised Land)
401. Kohanim serve in Sanctuary in divisions, on festivals.

T'rumah, Tithes and Taxes

402. Uncircumcised shall not eat t'rumah (heave offering),
403. Not alter order of separating t'rumah and tithes;
404. Give half a shekel every year (to Sanctuary
405. That a kohein who is unclean shall not eat of the t'rumah
406. If no kohein or wife or unmarried daughter not eat t'rumah.
407. Sojourner with kohein or hired servant not eat the t'rumah
408. Not eat tevel (from which t'rumah and tithe not separated)
409. To set apart tithe of the produce for the Levites
410. To tithe cattle
411. Not to sell the tithe of the herd (Lev. 27:32-33).
412. Levites set apart tenth of tithes, received from Israelites,
413. Not to eat the second tithe of cereals outside Jerusalem
414. Not consume second tithe of vintage outside of Jerusalem
415. Not consume second tithe of the oil outside of Jerusalem
416. Not to forsake Levites (Deut. 12:19);
417. Set apart second tithe in first, second, fourth, fifth years of sabbatical
418. Set apart second tithe in third and sixth year of sabbatical cycle for poor
419. To give the kohein due portions of the carcass of cattle
420. Give first of fleece to kohein (Deut. 18:4)
421. Set apart t'rumah g'dolah (great heave-offering, for kohein
422. Not expend second tithe on anything but food and drink.
423. Not eat Second Tithe, even in Jerusalem, in uncleanness,)
424. Not to eat Second Tithe, when mourning (Deut. 26:14).
425. Make declaration, bringing second tithe to Sanctuary

The Temple, The Sanctuary and Sacred Objects

426. Not to build an altar of hewn stone (Ex. 20:22).
427. Not to mount the altar by steps (Ex. 20:23).
428. To build the Sanctuary (Ex. 25:8).
429. Not to remove the staves from the Ark (Ex. 25:15).
430. Set showbread, frankincense before the Lord on Shabbat.

431. To kindle lights in the Sanctuary (Ex. 27:21).
432. That the breastplate shall not be loosened from the ephod.
433. To offer up incense twice daily (Ex. 30:7).
434. Not offer strange incense or any sacrifice upon golden altar.
435. Kohein shall wash hands and feet at the time of service.
436. Prepare anointing oil to anoint high kohanim and kings.
437. Not compound oil for lay use after formula of anointing oil.
438. Not to anoint a stranger with the anointing oil (Ex. 30:32).
439. Not to compound anything after the formula of the incense.
440. Make restitution if makes unlawful use of sacred things,
441. To remove the ashes from the altar (Lev. 6:3).
442. To keep fire always burning on altar of burnt-offering.
443. Not to extinguish the fire on the altar (Lev. 6:6).
444. A kohein shall not enter Sanctuary with disheveled hair.
445. That a kohein shall not enter Sanctuary with torn garments.
446. Kohein shall not leave Sanctuary Courtyard during service.
447. Intoxicated not enter Sanctuary, not give Law decisions.
448. To revere Sanctuary (today, applies to synagogues).
449. That when Ark is carried, should be carried on the shoulder.
450. To observe the second Passover (Num. 9:11).
451. Eat flesh Paschal lamb, with unleavened bread, bitter herb
452. Not leave flesh of Paschal lamb on 2nd Passover
453. Not break bone of Paschal lamb brought second Passover.
454. Sound trumpets, offering sacrifices and times of trouble.
455. To watch over the edifice continually (Num. 18:2).
456. Not to allow Sanctuary to remain unwatched (Num. 18:5).
457. Offering shall be brought by one who in error committed trespass against sacred things, or robbed, or lain carnally with a bond-maid betrothed to a man, or denied what was deposited with him and swore falsely to support his denial.
458. Not to destroy anything of the Sanctuary, synagogues, houses of study, nor holy names (of God); nor sacred scriptures

459. To sanctify the firstling of clean cattle and offer it up.
460. To slay the Paschal lamb (Ex. 12:6).
461. Eat flesh of Paschal sacrifice night of fifteenth of Nissan.
462. Not to eat the flesh of the Paschal lamb raw or sodden.
463. Not to leave flesh of Paschal sacrifice until the morning.
464. Not give flesh of Paschal lamb to Israelite who is apostate.
465. No give flesh of Paschal lamb to stranger among you.
466. No take flesh of Paschal lamb from place of assembly.
467. Not to break a bone of the Paschal lamb (Ex. 12:46).
468. Uncircumcised shall not eat flesh of the Paschal lamb.
469. Not slaughter Paschal lamb with chametz in home.
470. No leave Paschal lamb that should be burnt until morning,
471. Not go to Sanctuary for festival without bringing offering
472. To bring the first fruits to the Sanctuary (Ex. 23:19).
473. Flesh of a sin-offering and guilt-offering shall be eaten.
474. One not of seed of Aaron, not eat flesh of holy sacrifices.
475. To observe the procedure of the burnt-offering (Lev. 1:3).
476. To observe the procedure of the meal-offering (Lev. 2:1).
477. Not to offer up leaven or honey (Lev. 2:11).
478. That every sacrifice be salted (Lev. 2:13).
479. Not to offer up any offering unsalted (Lev. 2:13).
480. Court of Judgment to offer sacrifice if erred in judgement.
481. Shall bring a sin-offering if he sinned by transgression.
482. Offer sacrifice of varying value in accord with one's means
483. Not sever completely, head of fowl brought as sin-offering.
484. Not to put olive oil in a sin-offering made of flour (Lev. 5:11).
485. Not to put frankincense on a sin-offering made of flour.
486. Individual shall bring offering if in doubt if committed a sin calling for a sin-offering. Called guilt-offering for doubtful sins.
487. That the remainder of the meal offerings shall be eaten.
488. Not allow remainder of meal offerings to be leavened.
489. That the High Kohein shall offer a meal offering daily.
490. Not to eat of the meal offering brought by the kohanim.
491. To observe the procedure of the sin-offering (Lev. 6:18).
492. Not eat flesh of sin offerings, blood brought in Sanctuary.
493. To observe the procedure of the guilt-offering (Lev. 7:1).

494. Observe the procedure of peace-offering (Lev. 7:11).
495. To burn meat of the holy sacrifice that has remained over.
496. Not to eat sacrifices beyond appointed time.
497. Not to eat of holy things that have become unclean.
498. Burn meat of the holy sacrifice that has become unclean.
499. Person who is unclean shall not eat of things that are holy.
500. Kohein's daughter who profaned not to eat of holy things.
501. After childbirth, she shall bring offering when she is clean.
502. That the leper shall bring a sacrifice after he is cleansed.
503. Man having an issue shall bring sacrifice after he cleansed.
504. Woman having an issue to bring sacrifice after cleansed.
505. Observe, Yom Kippur, service appointed, sacrifice, etc.
506. Not to slaughter beasts for sacrifices outside (Sanctuary)
507. Not eat flesh of sacrifice left over (beyond time appointed).
508. Not sanctify blemished cattle for sacrifice on altar.
509. That every animal offered up shall be without blemish.
510. Not to inflict a blemish on cattle set apart for sacrifice.
511. Not slaughter blemished cattle as sacrifices (Lev. 22:22).
512. Not to burn the limbs of blemished cattle upon the altar.
513. Not to sprinkle blood of blemished cattle upon the altar.
514. Not offer blemished beast that comes from non-Israelites.
515. Cattle Sacrifices can only take place, aged eight days old
516. Not leave any flesh of thanksgiving offering until morning.
517. Offer meal-offering of Omer after the first day of Passover.
518. Not eat new grain bread before Omer of barley, Passover.
519. Not eat roasted grain of the new produce before that time.
520. Not to eat fresh ears of new grain before that time.
521. On Shavu'ot, bring bread with sacrifices offered.
522. To offer up an additional sacrifice on Passover.
523. One who vows to the Lord monetary value of person pay amount appointed in the Scriptural portion.
524. Beast swapped for one set apart as offering, both sacred
525. Not to exchange a beast set aside for sacrifice.
526. He who vows to the Lord, value of unclean beast will pay.
527. He who vows value of house shall pay kohein appraisal.
528. One who sanctifies to the Lord a portion of field shall pay according to estimation appointed in the Scriptural portion.
529. Not transfer beast set apart from one sacrifice to another.

530. To decide in regard to dedicated property as to which is sacred to the Lord and which belongs to the kohein.
531. Not to sell a field devoted to the Lord (Lev. 27:28).
532. Not to redeem a field devoted to the Lord (Lev. 27:28).
533. Make confession before the Lord of any sin committed.
534. No olive oil in meal-offering-woman suspected of adultery.
535. Not to put frankincense on it (Num. 5:15) (negative).
536. Offer regular sacrifices daily (two lambs as burnt offerings).
537. Offer an additional sacrifice every Shabbat (two lambs).
538. To offer up an additional sacrifice every New Moon.
539. Bring an additional offering on Shavu'ot (Num. 28:26-27).
540. To offer up an additional sacrifice on Rosh Hashanah.
541. To offer up an additional sacrifice on Yom Kippur.
542. To offer up an additional sacrifice on Sukkot.
543. Offer additional on Shemini Atzeret, festival by itself.
544. Bring offerings, obligatory or freewill, 1st festival after incur.
545. Not to offer up sacrifices outside (the Sanctuary).
546. To offer all sacrifices in the Sanctuary (Deut. 12:14).
547. Redeem cattle set for sacrifice with disqualifying blemish.
548. Not to eat of the unblemished firstling outside Jerusalem.
549. Not eat burnt-offering, Prohibition applying to trespasser.
550. Kohanim not eat the sin-offering outside the Courtyard.
551. Not eat sacrifices that are holy, before blood sprinkled.
552. Kohein not eat first-fruits before set in Courtyard.
553. Bring sacrifices to Sanctuary from outside Israel.
554. Not eat flesh of beasts set apart as sacrifices, that are rendered unfit by deliberately inflicted blemish.
555. Not to do work with cattle set apart for sacrifice.
556. Not to shear beasts set apart for sacrifice (Deut. 15:19).
557. Not leave festival offering brought 14th Nissan unto day.
558. Not to offer up a beast that has a temporary.
559. Not bring sacrifices out of hire of harlot or price of a dog.
560. To read the portion prescribed on bringing the first fruits.

Ritual and Impurity

561. That eight species of creeping things defile by contact.
562. That foods become defiled by contact with unclean things.
563. One touching carcass of beast that died of itself unclean.
564. A lying-in woman is unclean like a menstruating woman.
565. That a leper is unclean and defiles (Lev. 13:2-46).
566. Leper universally recognized by prescribed marks.
567. That a leprous garment is unclean and defiles.
568. That a leprous house defiles (Lev. 14:34-46).
569. That a man, having a running issue, defiles (Lev. 15:1-15).
570. That the seed of copulation defiles (Lev. 15:16).
571. Purify from defilement by immersion in waters of mikvah.
572. That a menstruating woman is unclean and defiles others.
573. That a woman, having a running issue, is unclean.
574. Carry out ordinance of Red Heifer so ashes available.
575. That a corpse defiles (Num. 19:11-16).
576. That the waters of separation defile one who is clean, and cleanse the unclean from pollution by a dead body.

Lepers and Leprosy

577. Not to drove off the hair of the scall (Lev. 13:33).
578. Procedure to cleanse leprosy, of man or house, requires cedar-wood, hyssop, scarlet thread, two birds, running water.
579. That the leper shall shave all his hair (Lev. 14:9).
580. Not to pluck out the marks of leprosy (Deut. 24:8).

The King

581. Not curse ruler, King, head of the College in land of Israel.
582. To appoint a king (Deut. 17:15).
583. Not appoint ruler over Israel who is non-Israelites.
584. King shall not acquire an excessive number of horses.
585. That King shall not take an excessive number of wives.
586. King shall not accumulate excessive gold and silver.
587. King shall write a Torah scroll for himself, in addition to one that every person should write, so he writes two scrolls.

Nazarites

588. Nazarite not drink wine, or mixed wine, it is prohibited.
589. That he shall not eat fresh grapes (Num. 6:3).
590. That he shall not eat dried grapes (raisins) (Num. 6:3).
591. That he shall not eat the kernels of the grapes (Num. 6:4).
592. That he shall not eat of the skins of the grapes (Num. 6:4).
593. That the Nazarite shall permit his hair to grow (Num. 6:5).
594. That the Nazarite shall not cut his hair (Num. 6:5).
595. Not to enter covered structure where there is a dead body.
596. Nazarite not defile himself (being in presence of corpse).
597. Shave hair when bring offerings, completion Nazariteship.

Wars

598. In warfare, do not fear enemies nor panic.
599. To anoint special kohein (to speak to soldiers) in a war.
600. In permissive war (not obligatory), follow Torah procedure.
601. Not keep alive any individual of seven Canaanite nations.
602. Exterminate seven Canaanite nations from land of Israel.
603. Not to destroy fruit trees (wantonly or in warfare).
604. Deal with beautiful woman taken captive in war per Torah.
605. Not to sell a beautiful woman, (taken captive in war).
606. No degrade beautiful woman taken in war as bondwoman.
607. Not offer peace to Ammonites and Moabites before war.
608. Anyone unclean shall not enter Camp of Levites
609. To have a place outside the camp for sanitary purposes.
610. To keep that place sanitary (Deut. 23:14-15).
611. Always to remember what Amalek did (Deut. 25:17).
612. The evil done to us by Amalek shall not be.
613. To destroy the seed of Amalek (Deut. 25:19).

Chapter 13. Hebrew Dictionary for Reference

Many Jewish words are embedded in the 613 laws above. We introduce a brief dictionary to assist the readers understanding. This method saves much space.

Tzitzit and Tallit. The word tzitzit (צִיצִית) is literally defined as " fringes ," and refers to the strings attached to the corners of the tallit, the Jewish prayer shawl.

Tefillin The Torah commands Jewish men to bind tefillin onto their head and upper arm every weekday, in fulfillment of the verse, "You shall bind them as a sign upon your hand, and they shall be for a reminder between your eyes. (Deut. 6:8)

Mezuzah A mezuzah (Hebrew: מְזוּזָה "doorpost"; plural: מְזוּזוֹת mezuzot) is a piece of parchment inscribed with specific Hebrew verses from the Torah, which Jewish followers of Rabbinical Judaism fix to the doorposts of their homes.

The word "serve" in these verses refers to prayer

Shema = Jewish Liturgy

See Birkat Ha-Mazon: Grace After Meals

See Speech and Lashon Ha-Ra

ol'loth (the imperfect clusters) of the vineyard

Interfaith Marriages
Mamzer = See Prohibited Marriages and Illegitimate Children.

Kiddushin and Nisuin, two elements of Jewish marriage.
Kiddushin is the Betrothal, Nisuin is the Nuptials.

Ammonite – a tribal group, non Hebrew, occupants of east and west bank of Jordan River near Jerusalem.

Moabite = Jordanian

Shabbat (shah-BAHT; SHAH-bis) Lit. end, cease, rest. The Jewish Sabbath, a day of rest and spiritual enrichment. See also Shabbat Evening Home Ritual Havdalah Home Ritual.

The Festivals [Passover, Shavu'ot and Sukkot]

Chametz on the Eve of Passover UNLEAVENED BREAD

MATZAH UNLEAVENED BREAD

Passover seder = the family home for Passover

See The Counting of the Omer unit of measure = sheaf

Shavu'ot (shuh-VOO-oht; shah-VOO-uhs) Lit. weeks. One of the Shalosh R'galim (three pilgrimage festivals), commemorating the giving of the Torah and the harvest of the first fruits.

"Rosh Hashanah" means, literally, "head of the year" or "first of the year." Rosh Hashanah is commonly known as the Jewish New Year. This name is somewhat deceptive, because there is little similarity between Rosh Hashanah, one of the holiest days of the year, and the American midnight drinking bash and daytime football game.

Yom Kippur (YOHM ki-PAWR) Lit. Day of Atonement. A day set aside for fasting, depriving oneself of pleasures, and repenting from the sins of the previous year.

Sukkot (soo-KOHT; SUK-uhs) Lit. booths. One of the Shalosh R'galim (three pilgrimage festivals). A festival commemorating the wandering in the desert and the final harvest. Also known as the Feast of Tabernacles or the Festival of Ingathering.

See also Sukkot Blessings.

To rest on the eighth day of Sukkot (Shemini Atzeret)

Unclean beasts = animals that may not be eaten

Terefah (literally torn)
See Separation of Meat and Dairy. Many rules like this were established while the Hebrews were in 40 year desert exodus. To do this practice could make one sick.

Not eat chelev (tallow-fat) (Lev. 7:23) (CCN88). See Forbidden Fats and Nerves.

tu B'Shevat (TOO bish-VAHT) Lit. 15th of Shevat. The new year is for purpose of counting the age of trees for purposes of tithing.

Pidyon Ha-Ben (peed-YOHN hah-BEHN) Lit. redemption of the son. A ritual redeeming the firstborn son from his obligation to serve in the Temple.
See Qorbanot: Sacrifices and Offerings
See Olah: Burnt Offering.
See Food and Drink Offerings.
Chatat: Sin Offering.
Asham: Guilt Offering.
Zebach Sh'lamim: Peace Offering.
Parah Adumah: Red Heifer, Shabbat Parah
See Care for the Dead.

Nazirite - Nazarite (Hebrew: נָזִיר *Nāzīr*)[1] is a man or woman[2] who voluntarily took a vow which described in Numbers 6:1–21. This vow required the Nazirite to:

- Abstain from wine and other grape products, such as vinegar[3]
- Refrain from cutting the hair on his head[4]
- Not to become ritually impure by contact with corpses or graves, even those of family members.[5]

After following these requirements for a designated time period (which would be specified in the individual's vow), the Nazirite would offer a specific animal sacrifice; along with it, the Nazirite's hair was to be shorn and burned.

The Nazirite is described as being "holy" and "holy unto God";[6] yet at the same time, he or she must bring a sin offering. This has led to divergent approaches to the Nazirite in the Talmud, and later authorities, with some viewing the Nazirite as an ideal, and others viewing as a sinner.

Levi (LAY-vee); Levite A descendant of the tribe of Levim. set aside to perform duties in connection with Temple; 2) Son of Jacob (Israel). Ancestor of tribe of Levi.

The Seven Nations (Hebrew: שבעת העמים, romanized: *Shivat Ha'amim*) according to the Hebrew Bible lived in the Land of Canaan prior to the arrival of the Israelites. God instructed Israelites to destroy these seven nations upon entering Canaan.[1][2]

The seven nations are all descendants of Canaan, son of Ham and grandson of Noah, from whom they derive their collective name Canaanites. Enumerated separately, one of the seven nations is called Canaanites, while the others are called Amorites, Girgashites, Hittites, Hivites, Jebusites and Perizzites.[3]

Ammonites Throughout the early history of Israel, we find references to the Ammonite people. Who were they, where did they come from, and what happened to them? The Ammonites were a Semitic people, closely related to the Israelites. Despite that relationship, they were more often counted enemies than friends.

Lot, Abraham's nephew, was the progenitor of the Ammonites. After Abraham and Lot separated (Genesis 13), Lot settled in the city of Sodom. When God destroyed Sodom and Gomorrah because of their wickedness, Lot and his daughters fled to the hill country on the southern end of the Dead Sea. Probably thinking they were the only people left on the earth, Lot's daughters got him drunk and had incestuous relations with him to produce children (Genesis 19:37-38).

The older daughter had a son named Moab ("from father"), and the younger gave birth to Ben-Ammi ("son of my people"). The Ammonites, descendants of Ben-Ammi, were nomadic people who lived in the territory of modern-day Jordan, and the name of the capital city, Amman, reflects the name of those ancient inhabitants.

In the time of Moses, the Amorites, Ammonites and Moabites occupied the fertile plains of the Jordan River valley. When Israel left Egypt, the Ammonites refused to assist them in any way, and God punished them for their lack of support (Deuteronomy 23:3-4). Later, however, as the Israelites entered the Promised Land, God instructed them, "When you approach the territory of the people of Ammon, do not harass them or contend with them, for I will not give you any of the land of the people of Ammon as a possession, because I have given it to the sons of Lot for a possession" (Deut. 2:19). The Israelite tribes of Gad, Reuben, and half of Manasseh claimed the Amorite territory bordering that of the Ammonites.

Moabites were a tribe descended from Moab, the son of Lot, born of an incestuous relationship with his oldest daughter (Genesis 19:37). From Zoar, the cradle of this tribe, on the southeastern border of the Dead Sea, they gradually spread over the region on the east of Jordan. Shortly before the Exodus, warlike Amorites crossed the Jordan under Sihon their king and drove the Moabites out of the region between the Arnon River Valley and the Jabbok River, and occupied it, making Heshbon their capital. The Moabites were then confined to the territory south of the Arnon Valley (Numbers 21:26–30).

During the Exodus, the Israelites did not pass through Moab, but through the "wilderness" to the east, eventually reaching the north of Arnon. The Moabites were alarmed, and king, Balak, sought aid from the Midianites (Numbers 22:2–4). This was the occasion the visit of Balaam to Balak took place (Num22:2–6).

In the Plains of Moab, which was in the possession of the Amorites, the children of Israel had their last encampment before they entered the land of Canaan (Numbers 22:1; Joshua 13:32).

If we had nothing else to interest us in the land of Moab, it was from the top of Pisgah that Moses, the mightiest of prophets, looked upon the Promised Land; it was here on Nebo that he died his solitary death; it was here in the valley against Beth-peor where he was buried (Deuteronomy 34:5–6).

The Amalekites were a formidable tribe of nomads living in the area south of Canaan, between Mount Seir and the Egyptian border. The Amalekites are not listed in the table of nations in Genesis 10, as they did not originate until after Esau's time. In Numbers 24:20 Balaam refers to the Amalekites as "first among the nations," but he most likely meant only that the Amalekites were the first ones to attack the Israelites upon their exodus from Egypt or that the Amalekites were "first" in power at that time. Genesis 36 refers to the descendants of Amalek, the son of Eliphaz and grandson of Esau, as Amalekites (verses 12 and 16). Amalekites were somehow related to, but distinct from, the Edomites.

Scripture records the long-lasting feud between the Amalekites and the Israelites and God's direction to wipe the Amalekites off the face of the earth (Exodus 17:8–13; 1 Samuel 15:2; Deuteronomy 25:17). Why God would call His people to exterminate an entire tribe is a puzzling, but history may give insight. Amalekites were nomadic. Numbers 13:29 has them native to the Negev, the desert between Egypt and Canaan. The Babylonians called them Sute, Egyptians the Sittiu, Amarna tablets refer to them as Khabbati, or "plunderers."

The Amalekites' unrelenting brutality toward the Israelites began with an attack at Rephidim (Exodus 17:8–13). This is recounted in Deuteronomy 25:17–19 with this admonition: "Remember what the Amalekites did to you along the way when you came out of Egypt. When you were weary and worn out, they met you on your journey and attacked all who were lagging behind [typically women and children]: they had no fear of God. When the LORD your God gives you rest from all the enemies around you in the land he is giving you to possess as an inheritance, you shall blot out the name of Amalek from under heaven. Do not forget!"

Shabbat Zakhor (shah-BAHT zah-KHAWR) The sabbath on which we read Parshat Zakhor, one of the Four Parshiyot, Torah readings added to the weekly cycle of readings during the month before Pesach (Passover). It contains the commandment regarding the tribe of Amalek.

Amorite, member of an ancient Semitic-speaking people who dominated the history of Mesopotamia, Syria, and Palestine from about 2000 to about 1600 BC. In the oldest cuneiform sources (*c.* 2400–*c.* 2000 BC), the Amorites were equated with the West, though their true place of origin was most likely Arabia, not Syria. They were troublesome nomads and were believed to be one of the causes of downfall of the 3rd dynasty of Ur (2112– 2004 BC).

During the 2nd millennium BC the Akkadian term Amurru referred not only to an ethnic group but also to a language and to a geographic and political unit in Syria and Palestine. At the beginning of the millennium, a large-scale migration of great tribal federations from Arabia resulted in the occupation of Babylonia proper, the mid-Euphrates region, and Syria-Palestine. They set up a mosaic of small kingdoms and rapidly assimilated the Sumero-Akkadian culture. It is possible that this group was connected with the Amorites mentioned in earlier sources; some scholars, prefer to call this second group Eastern Canaanites, or Canaanites.

Almost all of the local kings in Babylonia (such as Hammurabi of Babylon) belonged to this stock. One capital was at Mari (modern Tall al-Ḥarīrī, Syria). Farther west, the political centre was Ḥalab (Aleppo); in that area, as well as in Palestine, the newcomers were thoroughly mixed with the Hurrians. The region then called Amurru was northern Palestine, its centre at Hazor, and neighboring Syrian desert.

In the time between about 1600 to 1100 BC, language of the Amorites disappeared from Babylonia and the mid-Euphrates; in Syria and Palestine, becoming dominant. In Assyrian inscriptions from about 1100 BC, the term Amurru designated part of Syria and all of Phoenicia and Palestine but no longer referred to any specific kingdom, language, or population.

Girgashite, dwelling in clayey soil, the descendants of the fifth son of Canaan (Genesis 10:16), one of the original tribes inhabiting the land of Canaan before the time of the Israelites (Genesis 15:21 ; Deuteronomy 7:1).

Girgashites (Heb. גִּרְגָּשִׁי) are one of the tribes who invaded the land of Canaan as mentioned in Gen. 15:21; Deut. 7:1; Josh. 3:10; Neh.[1] 9:8. The Girgashites are also known as the fifth ethnic group that descended from Canaan (Gen. 10:16; i Chron. 1:14).[2] Although the Girgashites are not referred to in the narrative of the wars of conquests, and their locality is not stated, they are named by Joshua among the peoples the Israelites dispossessed (24:11).[3] This apparent inconsistency may be due to their emigrating to North Africa prior to Israelites entering the land.[4] This is supported by Procopius (Wars 4.10.13-22), stating Phoenician diaspora settled in the western end of the Mediterranean, in the vicinity of Carthage. [5]

They have been uncertainly identified with the Qaraqisha, allies of the Hittites in their wars with Ramses II.[6] If that identification is correct the Girgashites would have been part of the southward migrations from Anatolia of peoples displaced by the fall of the Hittite empire ca.1200 B.C.E. A personal name grgš appears in Ugaritic, but its connection with this people is unknown.[7] The sibilant termination of the biblical name suggests a Hurrian origin.

1. *Hastings, James; Selbie, John Alexander; Davidson, Andrew Bruce; Driver, Samuel Rolles; Swete, Henry Barclay (1899).* A Dictionary of the Bible: Dealing with Its Language, Literature, and Contents, Including the Biblical Theology. *T. & T. Clark.*
2. *Kitto, John (1864).* A Cyclopædia of Biblical Literature. *A. & C. Black.*
3. *Groot, N. G. De (1879).* History of the Israelites and Judæans: Philosophical and Critical. *Trübner & Co.*
4. "Jerusalem Talmud Sheviit 6:1:13". *www.sefaria.org.* Retrieved 2022-09-05.
5. "The Project Gutenberg eBook of History of the Wars, Books III and IV (of 8), by Procopius". *www.gutenberg.org.* Retrieved 2022-09-05.
6. *Allen, Clifton J. (1970).* The Broadman Bible Commentary: Acts. Romans. 1 Corinthians. *Broadman Press.* ISBN 978-0-8054-1125-6.
7. *Hastings, James; Selbie, John Alexander; Davidson, Andrew Bruce; Driver, Samuel Rolles; Swete, Henry Barclay (1899).* A Dictionary of the Bible: Dealing with Its Language, Literature, and Contents, Including the Biblical Theology. *T. & T. Clark.*

The Hittites (/ˈhɪtaɪts/) were an Anatolian Indo-European people who played an important role in establishing a kingdom in Kussara (before 1750 BC), then the Kanesh or Nesha kingdom (c. 1750–1650 BC), and next an empire centered on Hattusa in north-central Anatolia (around 1650 BC).[2][3] This empire reached its peak in mid-14th century BC, when it encompassed most of Anatolia and parts of the northern Levant and Upper Mesopotamia.

Between the 15th and 13th centuries BC, the Empire of Hattusa—in modern times conventionally called the Hittite Empire—came into conflict with the New Kingdom of Egypt, the Middle Assyrian Empire, and the empire of Mitanni for control of the Near East. The Middle Assyrian Empire eventually emerged as the dominant power and annexed much of the Hittite Empire, the remainder was sacked by Phrygian newcomers. From late 12th century BC, during Late Bronze Age collapse, Hittites splintered into independent Syro-Hittite states, some survived until the 8th century BC before succumbing to the Neo-Assyrian Empire.

The Hittite language was a distinct member of the Anatolian branch of the Indo-European language family. Along with the closely related Luwian language, Hittite is the oldest historically attested Indo-European language,[4] referred to by its speakers as *nešili*, "the language of Nesa". The Hittites called their kingdom *Hattusa* (*Hatti* in Akkadian), a name received from the Hattians, an earlier people who inhabited and ruled the central Anatolian region until beginning of the second millennium BC, and who spoke an unrelated language known as Hattic.[5] The modern conventional name "Hittites" is the initial identification of the people of Hattusa with Biblical Hittites by 19th-century archaeologists. Hittites would have called themselves "Neshites" or "Neshians" after the city of Nesha, which flourished two hundred years until king Labarna renamed himself Hattusili I (meaning "man of Hattusa") sometime around 1650 BC and established his capital city at Hattusa.[6]

History of the Hittite civilization is known mostly from cuneiform texts found in the area of their kingdom, and from diplomatic and commercial correspondence found in archives in Assyria, Babylonia, Egypt and the Middle East, the decipherment of which was a key event in the history of Indo-European studies.

Scholars once attributed the development of iron-smelting to the Hittites of Anatolia during the Late Bronze Age, with their success seen as largely based on the advantages of a monopoly on ironworking at the time. But the idea of a Hittite iron monopoly has come under scrutiny and no longer has scholarly consensus-support.[7] The Late Bronze Age collapse, leading into the Iron Age, saw the slow, comparatively continuous spread of ironworking technology in the region. While there are some iron objects from Bronze Age Anatolia, the number is comparable to that of iron objects found in Egypt; and only a small number of these objects are weapons.[8] X-ray spectrometry suggests "most or all irons from the Bronze Age are derived from" meteorites.[9] The Hittite military made successful use of chariots.[10]

In classical times, ethnic Hittite dynasties were in small kingdoms scattered around the present-day Syria, and into the Levant. Lacking a unifying continuity, their descendants scattered and ultimately merged into modern populations of the Levant, Türkiye, and Mesopotamia.[11]

The Hivites (Hebrew: חִוִּים Ḥīvvīm) were one group of descendants of Canaan, son of Ham, according to the Table of Nations in Genesis 10 (10:17). A variety of proposals have been made, but beyond the references in the Bible to Hivites in the land of Canaan, there is no consensus about their precise historical identity.[1]

1. Kloekhorst & Waal 2019.
2. Kloekhorst 2020.
3. "The peaks and troughs of Hittite". 7 July 2004. Archived from original on 3 Feb 2017.
4. Ardzinba, Vladislav. (1974): Notes on Typological Affinity Between Hattian and Northwest Caucasian (Abkhazo-Adygian) Languages. In: "Internationale Tagung der Keilschriftforscher der sozialistischen Länder", Budapest, 23–25. April 1974. Zusammenfassung der Vorträge (Assyriologica 1), pp. 10–15.
5. Cline, Eric H. (2021). "Of Arms and the Man". 1177 B.C.: The Year Civilization Collapsed. Princeton University Press. p. 32. ISBN 9780691208015.
6. Muhly, James D. (2003). "Metalworking/Mining in the Levant". In Richard, Suzanne (ed.). Near Eastern Archaeology. Eisenbrauns. pp. 174–183. ISBN 1-57506-083-3.
7. Waldbaum, Jane C. Bronze to Iron. Gothenburg: Paul Astöms Förlag (1978): 56–58.
8. Jambon, Albert (24 November 2017). "Bronze Age iron: Meteoritic or not? A chemical strategy". Journal of Archaeological Science. 88: 47–53. doi:10.1016/j.jas.2017.09.008. S2CID 55644155.
9. "Hittites". British Museum. London: Trustees of the British Museum. Arch 7 Nov 2014.
10. Ancient History Encyclopedia. "Sea Peoples." Sept 2009. Sea Peoples 18 June 2018 Wayback Machine

ANCIENT MAP EASTERN MEDITERRANEAN REGION

Etymology (origin of words)

E. C. Hostetter proposed that the name comes from "tent-dweller," as a cognate to the Hebrew word *hawwah* (חַוָּה), which means *tent-camp.*[1] No name resembling *Hivite* was found in Egyptian or Mesopotamian inscriptions, though *Hiyawa* in Luvian-Phoenician bilingual has been linked to the Biblical *Hiwwi.*[2]

Hivites, according to the Book of Joshua, lived in the hilly region of Lebanon from Lebo Hamath (Judges 3:3) to Mount Hermon (Joshua 11:3). Hivites are also mentioned further south in the Masoretic Text of the Hebrew Bible, which assigns to Hivites the towns of Gibeon, Kephirah, Beeroth, and Kiriath-Jearim (Joshua 9:17). However, the Septuagint reads these four towns as inhabited by Horites, suggesting that the name Hivite may have entered the Masoretic Text via a spelling error.[3]

The Masoretic Text of Joshua 11:3 described the Hivites as being "under Hermon in the land of Mizpeh." However, the Septuagint reads "Hittites" in place of "Hivites," suggesting that one text or the other has suffered an error.[3] Similarly in 2 Samuel 24:7 according to the Masoretic Text, Hivites are mentioned immediately after "the stronghold of Tyre," where the Septuagint once again reads "Hittites."[3]

Within the Hebrew Bible, Hivites are often listed among the inhabitants of Canaan, promised to the descendants of Abraham.[4] Genesis 36:2, in the Masoretic Text, mentions that one of Esau's wives was "Oholibamah the daughter of Anah, the daughter of Zibeon the Hivite" who is also described as "of the daughters of Canaan". However, textual evidence from the Septuagint and Genesis 36:20 suggest that Zibeon was originally referred to not as a Hivite, but a Horite.[3]

The Book of Joshua claims that Hivites were one of seven groups living in the land of Canaan when the Israelites under Joshua commenced their conquest of the land (Joshua 3:10). These seven nations were to be exterminated: Hittites, Girgashites, Amorites, Canaanites, Perizzites, Hivites and Jebusites.[5] In Joshua 9, Joshua enslaved the Hivites of Gibeon to be wood gatherers and water carriers for the Temple of YHWH (see Nethinim).

The Bible records David's census included Hivite cities.[6] During the reign of Solomon, they are described as slave labor for building projects.[7] It is not clear when they ceased to be separate.

Mizpah in Gilead (Joshua), where the Hivites were said to live.

Reference

1. Day, John (2007). "Gibeon and the Gibeonites in the Old Testament". In Robert Rezetko; Timothy Henry Lim; W. Brian Aucker (eds.). Reflection and Refraction: Studies in Biblical Historiography in Honour of A. Graeme Auld. *BRILL. p. 116.* ISBN 90-04-14512-5 – *Google Books.*

2. *Bryce, Trevor (2012). The World of the Neo-Hittite Kingdoms: A Political and Military History. Oxford University Press. p. 65.* ISBN 9780199218721.

3. North, Robert. "The Hivites." Biblica 54, no. 1 (1973): 56.

4. Genesis 10:15; Exodus 3:8, 3:17, 13:5, 23:23, 33:2, 34:11; Numbers 13:29; Deuteronomy 7:1, 20:17; Joshua 3:10, 9:1, 11:3, 12:8 24:11; Judges 3:5; 1 Kings 9:20; 1 Chronicles 1:13; 2 Chronicles 8:7; Ezra 9:1.

5. Exodus 34:11, 23:23, Deuteronomy 7:1–3 (Exodus 3:8

6. 2 Samuel 24:1–7

7. 1 Kings 9:20–21, 2 Chronicles 8:7–8

Jebusites (/ˈdʒɛbjəˌsaɪts/; Hebrew: יְבוּסִי, Modern: Yevūsī, Tiberian: Yəḇūsī ISO 259-3 Ybusi) were, according to the books of Joshua and Samuel from the Tanakh, a Canaanite tribe that inhabited Jerusalem, then called Jebus (Hebrew: יְבוּס Yəḇūs, "trampled place") prior to the conquest initiated by Joshua (Joshua 11:3, 12:10) and completed by King David (2 Samuel 5:6–10), although a majority of scholars agree that the Book of Joshua holds little historical value for early Israel and most likely reflects a much later period.[1] The Books of Kings as well as 1 Chronicles state that Jerusalem was known as Jebus prior to this event (1 Chronicles 11:4). Identification of Jebus with Jerusalem is sometimes disputed by scholars.[2] According to some biblical chronologies, the city was conquered by King David in 1003 BCE.[3]

The identification of Jebus with Jerusalem[4] has been disputed, principally by Niels Peter Lemche. Supporting his case, every non-biblical mention of Jerusalem found in the ancient Near East refers to the city as "Jerusalem". An example of these records are the Amarna letters, which were written by the chieftain of Jerusalem Abdi-Heba and call Jerusalem either Urusalim (URU ú-ru-sa-lim) or Urušalim (URU ú-ru-ša10-lim) (1330s BCE).[5] In Amarna, it is called Beth-Shalem, house of Shalem.[6]

The Sumero-Akkadian name for Jerusalem, uru-salim,[7] is variously etymologised to mean "foundation of [or: by] the god Shalim": from Hebrew/Semitic yry, "to found, to lay a cornerstone", and Shalim, the Canaanite god of the setting sun and the nether world, as well as of health and perfection.[8][9][10][11]

The Hebrew Bible describes the Jebusites as dwelling in the mountains besides Jerusalem.[21] In Exodus, the "good and large land, flowing with milk and honey" which was promised to Moses as the future home of the oppressed Hebrew people included land of the Jebusites.[22] According to Book of Joshua, Adonizedek led a confederation of Jebusites, and the tribes from the neighboring cities of Jarmut, Lachish, Eglon and Hebron against Joshua,[23] but was soundly defeated.

Identification of Jebus

Joshua 15:63 states that Judah could not dislodge the people. Judges 1:21 portrays the Jebusites as continuing to dwell at Jerusalem, within the territory occupied by the Tribe of Benjamin. According to the Second Book of Samuel, the Jebusites still had control of Jerusalem at the time of King David, but David wished to take control of the city. Understandably the Jebusites contested his attempt to do this, and since Jebus was the strongest fortress in Canaan they gloated that even the blind and lame could withstand David's siege.[26] According to the version of the story in the Masoretic Text, David managed to conquer the city by a surprise attack, led by Joab, through the water supply tunnels (Jerusalem has no natural water supply except for the Gihon Spring). Ever since its discovery in the 19th century, Warren's Shaft, part of a system which connects the spring to the city, has been cited as evidence for the plausibility of such a line of attack; however, the discovery, at the turn of the 21st century, of a set of heavy fortifications, including towers, around the base of the Warren's Shaft system and the spring, has made archaeologists now regard this line of attack as implausible, as it would be an attack against one of the most heavily fortified parts, and hardly a surprise.[27]

A Jebusite is mentioned also in The Acts of Barnabus as accompanying his martyrdom. "And having bound him to take him away to the governor, and a pious Jebusite, a kinsman of Nero, having come to Cyprus, the Jews, learning this, took Barnabas by night, and bound him with a rope by the neck; and having dragged him to the hippodrome from the synagogue, and having gone out of the city, standing round him, they burned him with fire, so that even his bones became dust. And straightway that night, having taken his dust, they cast it into a cloth; and having secured it with lead, they intended to throw it into the sea. But I, finding an opportunity in the night, and being able along with Timon and Rhodon to carry it. we came to a certain place, and having found a cave, put it down there, where the nation of the Jebusites formerly dwelt. And having found a secret place in it, we put it away, with the documents which he had received from Matthew. And it was the fourth hour of the night of the second of the week." [32]

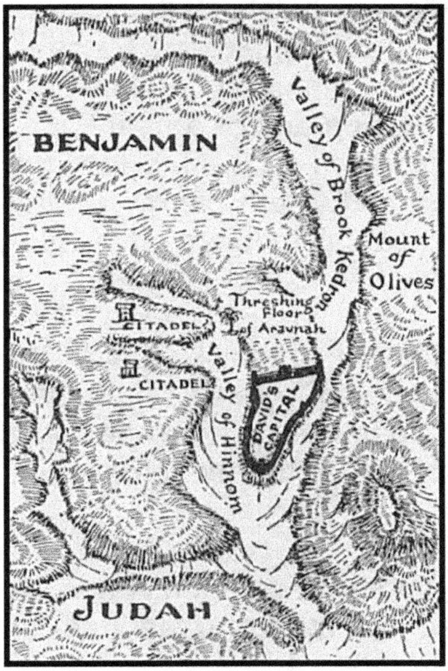

(Jebus becomes Jerusalem)

The account in 1 Chronicles mentions the advantage of a speedy attack but does not mention use of the water shafts [28] and according to many textual scholars the claim in the Masoretic Text could simply be a scribal error; the Septuagint version of the passage states that the Israelites had to attack the Jebusites with their dagger[s] rather than through the water shaft.

The Books of Kings state that once Jerusalem had become an Israelite city, the surviving Jebusites were forced by Solomon to become serfs;[29] though since some archaeologists believe that the Israelites were simply an emergent subculture in Canaanite society, it is possible this is an a etiological explanation for serfs rather than a historically accurate one.[24] It is unknown what became of these Jebusites.

According to the "Jebusite Hypothesis,"[30] Jebusites persisted as inhabitants of Jerusalem and comprised an important faction in the Kingdom of Judah, including such notables as Zadok the priest, Nathan the prophet, and Bathsheba, the queen and mother of the next monarch, Solomon. According to this hypothesis, after the disgrace of a rival Elide faction of priests in the struggle for succession to David,[31] the family of Zadok became the sole authorized Jerusalem clergy, so that a Jebusite family monopolized the Jerusalem clergy for many centuries before becoming sufficiently attenuated to be indistinguishable from other Judeans.

The First Book of Chronicles states that the inhabitants of Jebus forbade King David from coming to Jerusalem shortly after he was made king. Joab went up first and took the city and became chief and captain of David's armed forces.[32]

The earliest possible iteration or documentation of STATES is now represented in a map of Israel depicting the TRIBES and their geographic territory.

Map of Israel in the New Testament

1. Lemche 2010.
2. Gunn 2003, p. 262.
3. (Joshua 15:8 Archived 2016-03-04 at the Wayback Machine, 18:28 Arch 2016-11-06 at Wayback Machine; Judges 19:10 Archived 2016-11-12 at the Wayback Machine)
4. Urusalim e.g., in EA 289:014, Urušalim e.g., in EA 287:025. Transcription online at "The El Amarna Letters from Canaan". *Tau.ac.il.* Retrieved 11 Sept 2010.; translation by Knudtzon 1915 (English in Percy Stuart Peache Handcock, Selections from the Tell El-Amarna letters (1920).
5. See, e.g., Holman Bible Dictionary, op. cit. supra.
6. Victor P. Hamilton, Genesis, Chapters 1-17, p. 410 (1990). Hamilton asserts Sumerian uru is y^{e}rû,- "city."
7. Meir Ben-Dov, Historical Atlas of Jerusalem, Continuum Int'l Pub Group, 2002, p. 23.
8. *Binz, Stephen J. (2005).* Jerusalem, the Holy City. *Connecticut, USA.: Twenty-Third Publications. p.* 2. ISBN 9781585953653. Retr 17 December 2011. *Jerusalem, the Holy City By Stephen J. Binz.*
9. See the Anchor Bible Dictionary for an extensive discussion with citations. "SHALEM (DEITY) – the Anchor Bible Dictionary". *Archived from* the original *on 2014-02-21.*
10. See Holman Bible Dictionary, http://www.studylight.org/dic/hbd/print.cgi?n=3384 Archived 2014-02-23 at the http://education.nationalgeographic.com/media/file/Jerusalem_ED_Sheets.FasFacts.pdf Archived 2014-02-21 Wayback Machine ("Meaning of name, assumed compound of West Semitic "yrw" and "s[h]lm," interpreted "Foundation (the god) Shalem." Shalem, from Ugaritic mythology text as god of twilight.").
11. Lemche 2010, p. 161.
12. Pinches Archived 2015-11-19 at Wayback Machine, Theophilus G., The Old Testament: In the Light of the Historical Records and Legends of Assyria and Babylonia (London: SPCK, 1908), p. 324.
13. "Jebusites". Jewish Encyclopedia.
14. Lipinski 2004, p. 502.
15. Biblical Archaeology Review 32:02, March–April 2006, Who Were Jebusites?. "The letter refers to an Amorite ethnic group known as Yabusi'um. This, Lipinski says, implies existence of a tribe/clan of Yabusi, or Jebusites.(Semitic letter Y becomes J in Germanic languages English.) Clan of Jebusites in Mari letter may not be same as Jebusites living pre-Davidic Jerusalem. More than one clan/tribe have same name."
16. Detlev Groddek, Silvin Košak, and Marina Zorman, Tabularia Hethaeorum, p. 155 (20007).
17. 1 Chron. 21:15, "And the angel of the LORD stood by the threshing floor of Ornan the Jebusite."
18. Communication Jonathan D. Safren Arch 2016-03-11 Wayback Machine, Dept. of Biblical Studies, Beit Berl College, Israel (Aug 1, 2000.) Gwilym H. Jones, (Jan 1990) Https://books.google.com/books?id=73OtAwAAQBAJ&pg=PA122 Nathan Narratives (JSOT Supp) p. 122
19. Richard Hess, "Getting Personal: What Names in Bible Teach Us," Bible Review 13/6 (Dec 1997) 30, 34–36.
20. Numbers 13:29, Joshua 11:3
21. Exodus 3:8
22. Joshua 10:1–3
23. Finkelstein & Silberman 2002.
24. *Dever, William G. (2006-03-31).* Who Were the Early Israelites and Where Did They Come From?. *Wm. B. Eerdmans Publishing.* ISBN 978-0-8028-4416-3.

25. Peake's Commentary on the Bible
26. Reich & Shukron 1999.
27. 1 Chronicles 11:5
28. 1 Kings 9:20–21. This is inconsistent with other Biblical passages, however, that suggest that a Jebusite faction at King David's court (possibly including Bathsheba, Nathan, and Zadok) helped highjack the monarchic succession from David's older son, to the younger Solomon.
29. See:
    - Zadok and Nehushtan Rowley 1939, pp. 113–41
    - Melchizedek and Zadok Rowley 1950, pp. 461–72
    - Rowley 1939, pp. 113–41
    - Melchizedek and Zadok Rowley 1950, pp. 461–72
    - A History of Israelite Religion in the Old Testament Period Albertz 1994
    - The Nathan Narratives Jones 2009, pp. 20–25, 40–42, 131–35
    - See also Canaanite Myth and Hebrew Epic: Essays in History of Religion of Israel Cross 1997
30. 1 Kings i. 7, 19, 25; ii. 22, 26.
31. 1 Chronicles 11:3–8
32. "The Acts of Barnabas". *www.gnosis.org*. Retrieved 2023-09-17.

The Perizzites (Hebrew: פְּרִזִּי, romanized: *pərīṣṣī*) are a group of people mentioned many times in the Bible as having lived in the land of Canaan before the arrival of the Israelites. The name may be related to a Hebrew term meaning "rural person."[1]

Biblical mentions of Perizzites extend from the time of Abraham (Genesis 13:7) to the time of Ezra and Nehemiah (Ezra 9:1–2). According to Michael LeFebvre, Ezra's reference to the Perizzites does not imply that a group still known as Perizzites existed in the land in Ezra's time. It is instead to be a literary reference by Ezra to passages such as Exodus 34:11–16, Exodus 33:2 and Deuteronomy 7:1–5, which prohibited intermarriage with non-Israelite peoples, including Perizzites, among others.[2]

The time during which Perizzites were most in conflict with the Israelites is the time of Joshua to the early period of the Judges.

According to Joshua, Perizzites were in Judah and Ephraim (Joshua 11:3, 17:14–15). In 1 Kings 9:21, they were enslaved.

Jewish Encyclopedia Entry

Canaanitish tribe settled in the south of Canaan between Hor and Negeb, although it is not mentioned in the genealogy in Gen. x. According to the Biblical references, Abraham, when he entered Canaan, found the Perizzites dwelling near the Canaanites (ib. xiii. 7), and God promised to destroy both these peoples (ib. xv. 20). Jacob reproved his sons because of the crime of Shechem, inasmuch as he feared the Perizzites and the Canaanites (ib. xxxiv. 30). Moses promised the Israelites to bring them to the place of the Perizzites and Amorites (Ex. xxx. 8); and later, the tribes of Simeon and Judah conquered the Canaanites and Perizzites (Judges i. 4). Perizzites were tribes not subjected to tribute by Solomon (I Kings ix. 20–22), while the complaint was brought to Ezra that priests and Levites would not separate themselves from the Perizzites and other peoples of the land (Ezra ix. 1).

- Riehm, Handwörterb. 2nd ed., p. 1211
- Cheyne and Black, Encyclopedia Biblica, s.v.;
- Hastings' Dictionary of the Bible, s.v.
- Zondervan Pictorial Encyclopedia of Bible; Merrill Tenney, ed., Zondervan Publishing, ©1976;Vol.4, p. 704

1. For the etymology, see David Noel Freedman; Allen C. Myers (31 December 2000). Eerdmans Dictionary of the Bible. Amsterdam U Press. p. 1030. ISBN 978-9-05356-503-2.
2. Michael LeFebvre (1 October 2006). Collections, Codes, and Torah: The Re-characterization of Israel's Written Law. A&C Black. p. 114. ISBN 978-0-56702-882-2.

Chapter 14. LEGAL CODE IN BIBLICAL CHAPTER AND VERSE

Throughout this writing, the reader will be inundated with Biblical Chapter and Verse, along with US Constitution Articles and Sections. Chapter and Verse are essential so as to demonstrate the source of the 613 laws identified as laws by Maimonides. The purpose of this book is to establish a far greater linkage of our Holy Bible and modern day legal codes and the US Constitution. This is the very first discovery and rendering of the totality of which the US Constitution conforms to the Holy Bible. While Maimonides discoveries of the Mosaic Law represent the earliest legal code that continues to be applied today, our new discoveries will render the full extent to which the US Constitution is in strong conformity to the Holy Bible.

BIBLICAL CHAPTERS CONTAINING MOST LEGAL CODE

Leviticus 18 King James Version

18:1 And the LORD spake unto Moses, saying,
2 Speak unto the children of Israel, and say unto them, I am
the LORD your God.
3 After the doings of the land of Egypt, wherein ye dwelt, shall ye
not do: and after the doings of the land of Canaan, whither I bring
you, shall ye not do: neither shall ye walk in their ordinances.
4 Ye shall do my judgments, and keep mine ordinances, to walk
therein: I am the LORD your God.
5 Ye shall therefore keep my statutes, and my judgments: which if
a man do, he shall live in them: I am the LORD.
6 None of you shall approach to any that is near of kin to him, to
uncover their nakedness: I am the LORD.
7 The nakedness of thy father, or the nakedness of thy mother,
shalt thou not uncover: she is thy mother; thou shalt not uncover
her nakedness.
8 The nakedness of thy father's wife shalt thou not uncover: it’s
father's nakedness.

9 The nakedness of thy sister, daughter of thy father, or daughter
of thy mother, whether she be born at home, or abroad, their
nakedness thou shalt not uncover.
10 The nakedness of thy son's daughter, or of thy daughter's
daughter, even their nakedness thou shalt not uncover: for theirs
is thine own nakedness.
11 The nakedness of thy father's wife's daughter, begotten of thy
father, she is thy sister, thou shalt not uncover her nakedness.
12 Thou shalt not uncover nakedness of father's sister: she is thy
father's kin.
13 Thou shalt not uncover nakedness of mother's sister: for she is
thy mother's kin.
14 Thou shalt not uncover the nakedness of thy father's brother,
thou shalt not approach to his wife: she is thine aunt.
15 Thou shalt not uncover the nakedness of thy daughter in law:
she is thy son's wife; thou shalt not uncover her nakedness.
16 Thou shalt not uncover nakedness of brother's wife: it's thy
brother's nakedness.
17 Thou shalt not uncover the nakedness of a woman and her
daughter, neither shalt thou take her son's daughter, or her
daughter's daughter, to uncover her nakedness; for they are her
near kinswomen: it is wickedness.
18 Neither shalt thou take a wife to her sister, to vex her, to
uncover her nakedness, beside the other in her life time.
19 Also thou shalt not approach unto a woman to uncover her
nakedness, as long as she is put apart for her uncleanness.
20 Thou shalt not lie carnally with thy neighbour's wife, to defile
thyself with her.
21 Thou shalt not let thy seed pass through the fire to Molech,
neither shalt thou profane the name of thy God: I am the LORD.
22 Thou shalt not lie with mankind, as with womankind: it is
abomination.
23 Neither shalt thou lie with any beast to defile thyself therewith:
neither shall any woman stand before a beast to lie down thereto:
it is confusion.
24 Defile not ye yourselves in any of these things: for in all these
the nations are defiled which I cast out before you:

25 And the land is defiled: therefore I do visit the iniquity thereof
upon it, and the land itself vomit out her inhabitants.
26 Ye shall keep my statutes and judgments, shall not commit
abominations; neither of your own nation, nor a stranger that
sojourneth among you:
27 (For all these abominations have the men of the land done, the
land is defiled;)
28 The land spue not you out also, when ye defile it, spued out
nations before you
29 For whosoever shall commit any of these abominations, even
the souls that commit them shall be cut off from their people.
30 Therefore shall ye keep mine ordinance, that ye commit none of
these abominable customs, which were committed before you,
that ye defile not yourselves therein: I am the LORD your God.

Leviticus 19 King James Version

19:1 And the LORD spake unto Moses, saying,
2 Speak unto all the congregation of the children of Israel, and say
unto them, Ye shall be holy: for I, the LORD your God am holy.
3 Ye shall fear every man his mother, and his father, and keep my
sabbaths: I am the LORD your God.
4 Turn not unto idols, nor make to yourselves molten gods: I am
the LORD your God.
5 If ye offer a sacrifice of peace offerings to the LORD, ye shall
offer it at your will.
6 It shall be eaten the same day ye offer it, and on the morrow:
and if it ought remain until the third day, it shall be burnt in the
fire.
7 And if it be eaten at all on the third day, it is abominable; it shall
not be accepted.
8 Therefore every one that eateth it shall bear his iniquity,
because he profaned the hallowed thing of the LORD: and that
soul shall be cut off from among his people.
9 And when ye reap the harvest of your land, thou shalt not wholly
reap the corners of thy field, neither shalt thou gather the
gleanings of thy harvest.

10 Thou shalt not glean thy vineyard, shalt not gather every grape
of thy vineyard; thou shalt leave them for the poor and stranger: I
am the LORD your God.
11 Ye shall not steal, neither deal falsely, nor lie one to another.
12 And ye shall not swear by my name falsely, neither shalt thou
profane the name of thy God: I am the LORD.
13 Thou shalt not defraud thy neighbour, neither rob him: wages of
him that is hired shall not abide with thee all night until morning.
14 Thou shalt not curse the deaf, nor put a stumbling block before
the blind, but shalt fear thy God: I am the LORD.
15 Ye shall do no unrighteousness in judgment: thou shalt not
respect the person of the poor, nor honor the person of the
mighty: but in righteousness shalt thou judge thy neighbour.
16 Thou shalt not go up and down as a talebearer among thy
people: neither shalt thou stand against the blood of thy
neighbour; I am the LORD.
17 Thou shalt not hate thy brother in thine heart: thou shalt in any
wise rebuke thy neighbour, and not suffer sin upon him.
18 Thou shalt not avenge, nor bear grudge against children of thy
people, thou shalt love thy neighbour as thyself: I am the LORD.
19 Ye shall keep my statutes. Thou shalt not let thy cattle gender
with a diverse kind: thou shalt not sow thy field with mingled seed:
neither a garment mingled of linen and woolen come upon thee.
20 And whosoever lieth carnally with a woman, that is a bondmaid,
betrothed to an husband, and not at all redeemed, nor freedom
given her; she shall be scourged; they shall not be put to death,
because she was not free.
21 And he shall bring his trespass offering unto the LORD, unto the
door of the tabernacle of the congregation, even a ram for a
trespass offering.
22 And the priest shall make an atonement for him with the ram of
the trespass offering before the LORD for his sin which he hath
done: and the sin which he hath done shall be forgiven.
23 And when ye shall come into the land, and shall have planted
all manner of trees for food, then ye shall count the fruit thereof
as uncircumcised: three years shall it be as uncircumcised unto
you: it shall not be eaten of.

[24] But in the fourth year all the fruit thereof shall be holy to praise
the LORD withal.
[25] And in the fifth year shall ye eat of the fruit thereof, that it may
yield unto you the increase thereof: I am the LORD your God.
[26] Ye shall not eat any thing with the blood: neither shall use
enchantment, nor observe times.
[27] Ye shall not round corners of your heads, neither mar corners
of thy beard.
[28] Ye shall not make any cuttings in your flesh for the dead, nor
print any marks upon you: I am the LORD. (Other translations use
two words - - "NO TATTOO."
[29] Do not prostitute thy daughter, to cause her to be a whore; lest
the land fall to whoredom, and the land become full of
wickedness.
[30] Ye shall keep my sabbaths, and reverence my sanctuary: I am
the LORD.
[31] Regard not them that have familiar spirits, neither seek after
wizards, to be defiled by them: I am the LORD your God.
[32] Thou shalt rise up before the hoary head, and honour the face
of the old man, and fear thy God: I am the LORD.
[33] If a stranger sojourn with thee in your land, ye shall not vex
him.
[34] But the stranger that dwelleth with you shall be unto you as one
born among you, and thou shalt love him as thyself; for ye were
strangers in the land of Egypt: I am the LORD your God.
[35] Ye shall do no unrighteousness in judgment, in meteyard, in
weight, or measure.
[36] Just balances, just weights, a just ephah, and a just hin, shall
ye have: I am the LORD your God, which brought you out of the
land of Egypt.
[37] Therefore shall ye observe all my statutes, and all my
judgments, and do them: I am the LORD.

20 And the LORD spake unto Moses, saying,
2 Again, thou shalt say to children of Israel, Whosoever he be of
children of Israel, or of the strangers that sojourn in Israel, that
giveth any of his seed unto Molech; he shall surely be put to
death: people of the land shall stone him with stones.
3 And I will set my face against that man, and will cut him off from
among his people; because he hath given of his seed unto
Molech, to defile my sanctuary, and to profane my holy name.
4 And if the people of the land do any ways hide their eyes from
the man, when he giveth of his seed unto Molech, and kill him
not:
5 Then I will set my face against that man, and against his family,
and will cut him off, and all that go a whoring after him, to commit
whoredom with Molech, from among their people.
6 The soul that turneth after such as have familiar spirits, and after
wizards, to go a whoring, I will set my face against that soul, and
will cut him off from his people.
7 Sanctify yourselves therefore, and be ye holy: for I am
the LORD your God.
8 And ye shall keep my statutes, and do them: I am
the LORD which sanctify you.
9 For every one that curseth his father or his mother shall be
surely put to death: he hath cursed his father or his mother; his
blood shall be upon him.
10 The man that committeth adultery with another man's wife, he
that committeth adultery with neighbour's wife, adulterer and
adulteress shall be put to death.
11 The man that lieth with his father's wife hath uncovered his
father's nakedness: both of them shall surely be put to death;
their blood shall be upon them.
12 And if a man lie with his daughter in law, both of them shall
surely be put to death: they have wrought confusion; their blood
shall be upon them.
13 If a man also lie with man, as he lieth with a woman, both have
committed an abomination: they shall surely be put to death; their
blood shall be upon them.

14 And if a man take a wife and her mother, it is wickedness: they
shall be burnt with fire, both he and they; that there be no
wickedness among you.
15 And if a man lie with a beast, he shall surely be put to death:
and slay the beast.
16 And if a woman approach any beast, and lie down thereto, thou
shalt kill woman, and the beast: they shall surely be put to death;
their blood shall be upon them.
17 If a man take his sister, his father's daughter, or his mother's
daughter, see her nakedness, and she see his nakedness; it is
wicked; they shall be cut off in the sight of their people: he hath
uncovered sister's nakedness; he shall bear iniquity.
18 And if a man shall lie with a woman having her sickness, and
shall uncover her nakedness; he hath discovered her fountain,
and she hath uncovered the fountain of her blood: and both of
them shall be cut off from among their people.
19 And thou shalt not uncover the nakedness of thy mother's
sister, nor of thy father's sister: for he uncovereth his near kin:
they shall bear their iniquity.
20 And if a man lie with his uncle's wife, he hath uncovered his
uncle's nakedness: they shall bear their sin; shall die childless.
21 And if a man take his brother's wife, it is an unclean thing: he
hath uncovered his brother's nakedness; they shall be childless.
22 Ye shall therefore keep all my statutes, and all my judgments,
and do them: that the land, whither I bring you to dwell therein,
spue you not out.
23 And ye shall not walk in the manners of the nation, which I cast
out before you: for they committed all these things, and therefore
I abhorred them.
24 I have said unto you, Ye shall inherit their land, and I will give it
to you to possess it, a land that floweth with milk and honey: I am
the LORD your God, which have separated you from other people.
25 Ye shall put difference between clean beasts and unclean,
unclean fowls and clean: ye shall not make your souls
abominable by beast, by fowl, by any manner of living thing that
creepeth on ground, which I have separated as unclean.

26 And ye shall be holy unto me: for I the LORD am holy, and have severed you from other people, that ye should be mine.
27 A man also or woman that hath a familiar spirit, or that is a wizard, shall surely be put to death: they shall stone them with stones: their blood shall be upon them.

Deuteronomic Code

Deuteronomic Code is the name given by academics to the law code set out in chapters 12 to 26 of the Book of Deuteronomy in the Hebrew Bible.[1] The code outlines a special relationship between the Israelites and Yahweh[2] and provides instructions covering "a variety of topics including religious ceremonies and ritual purity, civil and criminal law, and the conduct of war".[1] They are similar to other collections of laws found in the Torah (the first five books of the Tanakh) such as the Covenant Code at Exodus 20–23,[1][3] except for the portion discussing the Ethical Decalogue, which is usually treated separately. This separate treatment stems not from any concern over authorship, but merely because the Ethical Decalogue is treated academically as a subject in its own right.

Almost the entirety of Deuteronomy is presented as the last few speeches of Moses, beginning with an historical introduction and a second introduction which expands on Ethical Decalogue, ending with speeches and final encouragement. Between these is found the law code, at Deuteronomy 12–26. In critical scholarship, this portion, and the remainder of Deuteronomy, was written by the Deuteronomist.

The following bullet points are an idea of how the Deuteronomic Code Laws of Religious Observance, prophesy tripartite government, and possibly Separation of Powers.

Laws of religious observance

- Do not worship other gods and commit human sacrifice, Deut. 12:29–31
- Prohibiting deliberate disfigurement as an act of mourning, Deut. 14:1–2
- Concerning clean and unclean animals, at Deut. 14:3–20
- Prohibiting consumption of animals not killed by man, Deut. 14:21
- Against Asherah groves and ritual pillars, at Deut. 16:21–22
- Against blemished sacrifices, at Deuteronomy 17:1

Laws concerning officials

- Ordering impartiality of judges, at Deuteronomy 16:19–20

Criminal law

- Concerning witnesses, at 19:15–21
- Concerning adultery and seduction, at Deut. 22:22–29
- Against kidnap, at Deuteronomy 24:7
- Ordering just weights and measures, at Deut. 25:13–16

Civil law

- Order restoration of lost property once found, Deut.22:1–4
- Prohibition of mixing kinds, at Deuteronomy 22:9–11
- Concerning tzitzit, at Deuteronomy 22:12
- Against marrying a step-mother, at Deuteronomy 22:30
- Against usury, at Deuteronomy 23:19–20
- Concerning vows, at Deuteronomy 23:21–23
- Concerning pledges, at Deuteronomy 24:6, and 24:10–13
- Concerning leprosy, at Deuteronomy 24:8–9
- Concerning wages of a hired servant, at Deut. 24:14–15
- Ordering justice towards strangers, widows, and orphans, Deut. 24:17–18
- Concerning scraps of crops, at Deuteronomy 24:19–22

Laws differing from the Torah

Laws of religious observance

- Prohibiting offerings and vows outside a central sanctuary, Deut. 12:1–28
- Concerning the tithe, at Deuteronomy 14:22–29
- Concerning relief of debt in the seventh year, at Deuteronomy 15:1–11
- Ordering the offering to Yahweh of the firstborn males, Deut. 15:19–23
- Concerning the three annual feasts, at Deut. 16:1–17

Criminal law

- Concerning manslaughter and murder, at Deut. 19:1–13

Civil laws

- Concerning slavery, at Deuteronomy 15:12–18
- Concerning cleanliness in the camp, at Deut. 23:9–14

Unique Laws within Torah

Laws of religious observance

- Against false prophets, at Deuteronomy 13
- Ordering idolaters to be stoned to death, at Deut. 17:2–7

Laws concerning officials

- Ordering judges to be appointed in every city, Deut. 16:18
- Ordering a supreme central tribunal, Deut. 17:8–13
- Restrictions on the king, at Deuteronomy 17:14–20
- Concerning rights, and revenue of Levites, Deut. 18:1–8
- Concerning future (unspecified) prophet, Deut. 18:9–22
- Restrictions on admittance to the priesthood, Deut. 23:1–8

Military law

- Concerning behavior during war, at Deut. 20, 21:10–14

Criminal law

- Ordering ritual atonement, untraced murder,Deut.21:1–9
- Concerning the corpse of a criminal, at Deut. 21:22–23

Civil laws

- Against the removal of boundary markers, at Deut. 19:14
- Concerning primogeniture, at Deuteronomy 21:15–17
- Ordering undutiful sons to be stoned to death, at Deuteronomy 21:18–21
- Against crossdressing, at Deuteronomy 22:5
- Prohibiting taking a mother bird at the same time as its nest, Deut. 22:6–7
- Order roofs constructed with parapets, at Deut. 22:8
- Prohibiting newly married women from being slandered, Deut. 22:13–21
- Concerning escaped slaves, at Deuteronomy 23:15–16
- Against religious prostitution, at Deuteronomy 23:17–18
- Concerning the crops of a neighbour, at Deut. 23:24–25
- Concerning divorce, at Deuteronomy 24:1–4
- Against punishing the family of a criminal, at Deut. 24:16
- Limiting the number of lashes, at Deuteronomy 25:1–3
- Against muzzling oxen during threshing, at Deut. 25:4
- Concerning levirate marriage, at Deuteronomy 25:5–10
- Ordering women to be modest, at Deuteronomy 25:11–12

Ritual

- Ritual of the firstfruits and of the tithe, including a prayer, Deut. 26:1–15
    1. Coogan 2009, p. 149
    2. Deuteronomy 26:16–19
    3. Kent 1901, 270-283.
    4. Finkelstein & Silberman 2002, p. 208.
    5. Coogan 2009, p. 150

Coogan, Michael D. (2009). A Brief Introduction to the Old Testament: The Hebrew

Chapter 15.

US CONSTITUTION BASIS, BIBLICAL CHAPTER AND VERSE
613 MITZVOT, BIBLICAL CHAPTER AND VERSE
BIBLICAL PROPHECY POINTS IN US CONSTITUTION

Within this document, we are introduced to 3 separate branches and functions of government. The foundational establishment for government is found in Exodus Chapter 18 beginning verse 20. The first Organization Chart in history is established and further Chapter and Verse establishes how the different government elements were ordered to function by the Word of God.

Separation of Powers

Within the body of this book, we will document and footnote heavy numbers of Biblical Chapter and Verse that correspond to the many issues discussed. Within this overview, we summarize the major findings that correlate the US Constitution to the Bible. You must read on to understand the totality by which these two precious documents are in agreement, along with several major points of government not mentioned in our US Constitution.

Three Branches of US Government

Executive Branch of Government (Biblical Beginnings)

1. Samuel chapter devoted to warning of dangers of Kings
2. Daniel is first in history to be named a President.

Legislative Branch (Biblical Beginnings)

God established the beginnings of all legal codes.

Sanhedrin is established as arbiters initially, today they engage in legislation.

Judicial Branch based on "rule of law" and "due process." (Biblical Beginnings)

1. Judges ordered to be empaneled
2. Legal code established
3. Penalties prescribed
4. Innocent until proven guilty
5. Witnesses required
6. Provision made for those falsely accused
7. Natural rights embedded
8. Contract law established by 613 and Nahum 1:12, "quiet and likewise many"

ADDITIONAL LINKS TO US CONSTITUTION

MAJOR ISSUES NOT IDENTIFIED BY MAIMONIDES, included in our book.

This is not a criticism of Maimonides. Governments were still in infancy; most were secondary to royalty. Many of these points and philosophies had not yet been aired, albeit traceable to chapter and verse. All the bullet points below will be elaborated as they impact the US Constitution in an upcoming chapter dedicated to tracing our actual US Constitution to enabling bible chapter and verse:

- Natural rights first indicated in Genesis 1:28.
- First Statesmanship demonstrated by Abraham in trek through enemy territory.
- Scalable organizations followed since that time, Ex 18:20-22.
- Military organization (although elements are in his 613).
- Legislative branch (judicial, executive, indicated) reference to Sanhedrin.
- Elections (Moses number of leaders required, and that IS evidence of first elections) Ex 18:20-22 - Moses had to find 111,000 leaders by one calculation.
- Voting, see above, how did Moses find 111,000 leaders.

- QUIET AND LIKEWISE MANY indication civil law of contracts and property sale and title - Nahum 1:12 - 500-700 BC.
- First President in history, Daniel - - many points of modern government grow out of Daniels presidency but not fully indicated in Bible. Daniel, 700BC.
- LETTERS OF PLINY 1st Century AD indicate government infrastructure possibly initiated by Rome such as municipal water, sewer systems, taxes.
- Jerusalem from earliest days was a site of huge and ever-present underground springs of pristine drinking water, original example of municipal water provision.
- Ben Franklin at Constitutional convention calls for temporary application of Mosaic Law as a shortcut to creating Constitution, then create legal code later.
- The Authors reviewed the Chapter and Verse for all 613 laws.
- Extensive and repetitive. Many serve several purposes.
- Much "Church Law" and tithes is so finitely detailed and worded that it is surely a point of prophecy of the detail created by IRS and our acceptance of overloaded and bloated government, although not intended by God.
- Food law in Bible is forerunner of modern health law and FDA
- Many food guidelines in Bible are health, medical, safety, law.

Legacy in politics and Law

In a metaphorical sense, a "Moses" has been referred to as the leader who delivers people from a terrible situation. Presidents using Moses symbolism were Harry S. Truman, Jimmy Carter, Ronald Reagan, Bill Clinton, George W. Bush, Barack Obama, who referred to his supporters as "the Moses generation."[3]

Theologians linked the Ten Commandments with the formation of early democracy. Scottish theologian William Barclay described them as "the universal foundation of all things ... the law without which nationhood is impossible. ...

---

[3] Ifil, Gwen (2009). The Breakthrough: Politics and Race in the Age of Obama. Random House. p. 58.

Our society is founded upon it."[4] Pope Francis addressed the United States Congress in 2015 stating that all people need to "keep alive their sense of unity by means of just legislation ... [and] the figure of Moses leads us directly to God and thus to the transcendent dignity of the human being". Allen, Jonathan (September 24, 2015). "Pope Francis addresses Congress".[5]

In United States History Pilgrims

References to Moses were used by the Puritans, who relied on the story of Moses to give meaning and hope to Pilgrims seeking religious and personal freedom in North America. John Carver was first governor of Plymouth colony and first signer of the Mayflower Compact, which he wrote in 1620 during the ship *Mayflower*'s three-month voyage. He inspired the Pilgrims with a "sense of earthly grandeur and divine purpose", notes historian Jon Meacham,[6] and was called "Moses of the Pilgrims".[7] Early American writer James Russell Lowell noted similarity of founding of America by the Pilgrims to that of ancient Israel by Moses:

> Next to the fugitives whom Moses led out of Egypt, the little shipload of outcasts who landed at Plymouth are destined to influence the future of the world. The spiritual thirst of mankind has for ages been quenched at Hebrew fountains; but the embodiment in human institutions of truths uttered by the Son of Man eighteen centuries ago was to be mainly the work of Puritan thought and Puritan self-devotion. ... If their municipal regulations smack somewhat of Judaism, yet there can be no nobler aim or more practical wisdom than theirs; for it was to make the law of man a living counterpart of the law of God, in their highest conception of it.[8]

---

[4] Barclay,William (1998)[1973].The Ten Commandments.Westminster JohnKnox Press.p. 4.
[5] Allen, Jonathan (September 24, 2015). "Pope Francis addresses Congress"
[6] Meacham 2006, p. 40.
[7] *Talbot, Archie Lee (1930),* A New Plymouth Colony at Kennebeck, *Library of Congress.*
[8] Lowell, James Russell (1913), The Round Table, Boston: Gorham Press, pp. 217–18

Following Carver's death, William Bradford became governor. He feared the Pilgrims would not survive the hardships of the new land, half their people having died within months of arriving. Bradford evoked Moses to the weakened Pilgrims to help calm them and give them hope: "Violence will break all. Where is the meek, humble spirit of Moses?"[9] William G. Dever explains the attitude of the Pilgrims: "We considered ourselves the 'New Israel', particularly we in America. We knew who we were, what we believed in and valued, and what our 'manifest destiny' was."[10],[11]

On July 4, 1776, immediately after the Declaration of Independence was passed, the Continental Congress asked John Adams, Thomas Jefferson, and Ben Franklin to design a seal that would clearly represent a symbol for the new United States. They chose the symbol of Moses leading the Israelites to freedom.[12]

Founding Fathers of the United States

After the death of George Washington in 1799, his eulogies referred to him as "America's Moses", one saying "Washington has been the same to us as Moses to the Children of Israel."[13]

Ben Franklin, in 1788, saw difficulties the newly independent states were having forming a government, and proposed that until new laws could be agreed, they should be governed by "the laws of Moses", in the Old Testament.[14] He justified his proposal by explaining the laws had worked in biblical times: "The Supreme Being ... having rescued them from bondage by many miracles, performed by his servant Moses, personally delivered to that chosen servant, in the presence of the whole nation, a constitution and code of laws for their observance."[15]

---

[9] Arber, Edward (1897). The Story of the Pilgrim Fathers. Houghton Mifflin. p. 345.

[10] Dever 2006, pp. ix, 234.

[11] Moses, Adolph (1903). Yahvism and Other Discourses. Louisville Council of Jewish Women. p. 93. [The pilgrims were clearly] animated by the spirit of the Hebrew prophets and law-givers. They walked by light of the Scriptures, and were resolved to form a Commonwealth in accordance with social laws and ideas of the Bible. ... they were true descendants of Israel.

[12] Feiler 2009, p. 35

[13] Feiler 2009, p. 102.

[14] Franklin 1834, p. 504.

[15] Franklin 1834, p. 211.

John Adams, 2nd President of the US, stated why he relied on the laws of Moses over Greek philosophy for establishing the United States Constitution:

> "As much as I love, esteem, and admire the Greeks, I believe the Hebrews have done more to enlighten and civilize the world. Moses did more than all their legislators and philosophers."[16] Swedish historian Hugo Valentin credited Moses as "first to proclaim the rights of man".[17]

In the 1960s, a leading civil rights figure was Martin Luther King Jr., who was called "a modern Moses", and often referred to Moses in his speeches: "The struggle of Moses, the struggle of his devoted followers as they sought to get out of Egypt. This is something of the story of every people struggling for freedom."[18]

BOOK OF NUMBERS=ORGANIZATION PLAN FOR MILITARY & GOVERNMENT

Several chapters of the book of NUMBERS could be referred to as the Chapters of Military Organization, Chapter of Municipal Organization, and Chapter of Government Organization, and Chapter of Human Care. Adding a highly important section of Exodus 18:20-26, we are gifted the world's very first form of Biblical Organization Chart that is perfectly scalable, as expected within the Professional Management Community in our modern day.

---

[16] Meacham 2006, p. 40.

[17] *Shuldiner, David Philip (1999). Of Moses and Marx. Greenwood. p. 35.*

[18] King, Martin Luther Jr. (2000) [1957, 1968]. *The Papers.* University of California Press. p. 155. I want to preach this morning from the subject, 'The Birth of a New Nation' And I would like to use as a basis for our thinking together, a story that has long since been stenciled on the mental sheets of succeeding generations. It is the story of the Exodus, the story of the flight of the Hebrew people from the bondage of Egypt, through the wilderness and finally, to the Promised Land. ... The struggle of Moses, struggle of his devoted followers as they sought to get out of Egypt.

Exodus 18:20-27
20 And thou shalt teach them ordinances and laws, and shalt
shew them the way wherein they must walk, and the work they
must do.
21Moreover thou shalt provide out of all the people able men,
such as fear God, men of truth, hating covetousness; and place
such over them, *to be* rulers of thousands, *and* rulers of
hundreds, rulers of fifties, and rulers of tens:
22And let them judge the people at all seasons: and it shall
be *that* every great matter they shall bring unto thee, but every
small matter they shall judge: so shall it be easier for thyself, and
they shall bear *the burden* with thee.
23If thou shalt do this thing, and God command thee *so*, then
thou shalt be able to endure, and all this people shall also go to
their place in peace.
24Moses hearkened to the voice of his father in law, and did all
that he had said.
25And Moses chose able men out of all Israel, and made them
heads over the people, rulers of thousands, rulers of hundreds,
rulers of fifties, and rulers of tens.
26They judged the people at all seasons: the hard causes they
brought unto Moses, every small matter they judged themselves.
27And Moses let his father in law depart; and he went his way
into his own land.

NUMBERS CHAPTER 1

And the LORD spake unto Moses in the wilderness of Sinai, in
the tabernacle of the congregation, on the first *day* of the second
month, in the second year after they were come out of the land of
Egypt, saying,
2Take ye the sum of all the congregation of children of Israel,
after their families, by the house of their fathers, with the number
of *their* names, every male by polls;
3From twenty years old and upward, all that are able to go forth
to war in Israel: thou and Aaron shall number them by their
armies.

4With you there shall be a man of every tribe; every head of
house of his fathers.
5Names of men that shall stand with you: *tribe of* Reuben; Elizur
son of Shedeur.
6Of Simeon; Shelumiel the son of Zurishaddai.
7Of Judah; Nahshon the son of Amminadab.
8Of Issachar; Nethaneel the son of Zuar.
9Of Zebulun; Eliab the son of Helon.
10Of the children of Joseph: of Ephraim; Elishama the son of
Ammihud: of Manasseh; Gamaliel the son of Pedahzur.
11Of Benjamin; Abidan the son of Gideoni.
12Of Dan; Ahiezer the son of Ammishaddai.
13Of Asher; Pagiel the son of Ocran.
14Of Gad; Eliasaph the son of Deuel.
15Of Naphtali; Ahira the son of Enan.
16These *were* the renowned of the congregation, princes of the
tribes of their fathers, heads of thousands in Israel.
17Moses and Aaron took these men which are expressed
by *their* names:
18They assembled the congregation together on first *day* of
second month, and declared their pedigrees after their families,
by house of their fathers, according to the number of the names,
from twenty years old and upward, by their polls.
19As the LORD commanded Moses, he numbered them in
wilderness of Sinai.
20And the children of Reuben, Israel's eldest son, by their
generations, after their families, by the house of their fathers,
according to number of the names, by their polls, every male
twenty years old and upward, all that were able to go to war;
21Those that were numbered of them, *even* of the tribe of
Reuben, *were* forty and six thousand and five hundred.
22Of the children of Simeon, by their generations, after their
families, by the house of their fathers, those that were numbered
of them, according to the number of the names, by their polls,
every male from twenty years old and upward, all that were able
to go forth to war;

23Those that were numbered of them, *even* of the tribe of
Simeon, *were* fifty and nine thousand and three hundred.
24Of the children of Gad, by their generations, after their families,
by the house of their fathers, according to the number of the
names, from twenty years old and upward, all that were able to
go forth to war;
25Those that were numbered of them, *even* of the tribe of
Gad, *were* forty and five thousand six hundred and fifty.
26Of the children of Judah, by their generations, after their
families, by the house of their fathers, according to the number of
the names, from twenty years old and upward, all that were able
to go forth to war;
27Those that were numbered of them, *even* of the tribe of
Judah, *were* threescore and fourteen thousand and six hundred.
28Of the children of Issachar, by their generations, after their
families, by the house of their fathers, according to the number of
the names, from twenty years old and upward, all that were able
to go forth to war;
29Those that were numbered of them, *even* of the tribe of
Issachar, *were* fifty and four thousand and four hundred.
30Of the children of Zebulun, by their generations, after their
families, by the house of their fathers, according to the number of
the names, from twenty years old and upward, all that were able
to go forth to war;
31Those that were numbered of them, *even* of the tribe of
Zebulun, *were* fifty and seven thousand and four hundred.
32Of the children of Joseph, *namely*, of children of Ephraim, by
their generations, after their families, by the house of their fathers,
according to the number of the names, from twenty years old and
upward, all that were able to go forth to war;
33Those numbered, *even* of tribe of Ephraim, *were* thousand
and five hundred.
34Of the children of Manasseh, by their generations, after their
families, by the house of their fathers, according to the number of
the names, from twenty years old and upward, all that were able
to go forth to war;

35Those that were numbered of them, *even* of the tribe of
Manasseh, *were* thirty and two thousand and two hundred.
36Of the children of Benjamin, by their generations, after their
families, by the house of their fathers, according to the number of
the names, from twenty years old and upward, all that were able
to go forth to war;
37Those that were numbered of them, *even* of the tribe of
Benjamin, *were* thirty and five thousand and four hundred.
38Of the children of Dan, by their generations, after their families,
by the house of their fathers, according to the number of the
names, from twenty years old and upward, all that were able to
go forth to war;
39Those that were numbered of them, *even* of the tribe of
Dan, *were* threescore and two thousand and seven hundred.
40Of the children of Asher, by their generations, after their
families, by the house of their fathers, according to the number of
the names, from twenty years old and upward, all that were able
to go forth to war;
41Those that were numbered of them, *even* of the tribe of
Asher, *were* forty and one thousand and five hundred.
42Of the children of Naphtali, throughout their generations, after
their families, by the house of their fathers, according to the
number of the names, from twenty years old and upward, all that
were able to go forth to war;
43Those that were numbered of them, *even* of the tribe of
Naphtali, *were* fifty and three thousand and four hundred.
44These *are* those that were numbered, which Moses and Aaron
numbered, and the princes of Israel, *being* twelve men: each one
was for the house of his fathers.
45So were all those numbered of the children of Israel, by house
of their fathers, from twenty years old and upward, all that were
able to go forth to war in Israel;
46All numbered were six hundred thousand three thousand five
hundred and fifty.
47But the Levites after the tribe of their fathers were not
numbered among them.
48For the LORD had spoken unto Moses, saying,

49Only thou shalt not number the tribe of Levi, neither take the
sum of them among the children of Israel:
50Thou shalt appoint Levites over the tabernacle of testimony,
over all the vessels thereof, over all things that *belong* to it: they
shall bear the tabernacle, and all vessels; they shall minister unto
it, and shall encamp round about the tabernacle.
51And when the tabernacle setteth forward, the Levites shall take
it down: and when the tabernacle is to be pitched, the Levites
shall set it up: and the stranger that cometh nigh shall be put to
death.
52And the children of Israel shall pitch their tents, every man by
his own camp, and every man by his own standard, throughout
their hosts.
53But the Levites shall pitch round about the tabernacle of
testimony, that there be no wrath upon the congregation of the
children of Israel: and the Levites shall keep the charge of the
tabernacle of testimony.
54And the children of Israel did according to all the LORD
commanded Moses.

NUMBERS CHAPTER 3

1These also *are* the generations of Aaron and Moses in the
day *that* the LORD spake with Moses in mount Sinai.
2These names of sons of Aaron; Nadab the firstborn, and Abihu,
Eleazar, Ithamar.
3These *are* the names of the sons of Aaron, the priests anointed,
whom he consecrated to minister in the priest's office.
4And Nadab and Abihu died before the LORD, when they offered
strange fire before the LORD, in the wilderness of Sinai, they had
no children: and Eleazar and Ithamar ministered in the priest's
office in the sight of Aaron their father.
5And the LORD spake unto Moses, saying,
6Bring tribe of Levi, present them before Aaron the priest, so they
minister to him.
7And they shall keep his charge, and the charge of the whole
congregation before the tabernacle of the congregation, to do the
service of the tabernacle.

8And they shall keep all the instruments of the tabernacle of the
congregation, and the charge of the children of Israel, to do the
service of the tabernacle.
9And thou shalt give the Levites unto Aaron and to his sons:
they *are* wholly given unto him out of the children of Israel.
10And thou shalt appoint Aaron and his sons, and they shall wait
on their priest's office: and the stranger that cometh nigh shall be
put to death.
11And the LORD spake unto Moses, saying,
12 I, have taken the Levites from among the children of Israel
instead of all firstborn that openeth the matrix among the children
of Israel: therefore Levites shall be mine;
13Because all the firstborn *are* mine; *for* on the day that I smote
all the firstborn in the land of Egypt I hallowed unto me all the
firstborn in Israel, both man and beast: mine shall they be:
I *am* the LORD.
14The LORD spake to Moses in the wilderness of Sinai, saying,
15Number the children of Levi after the house of their fathers, by
their families: every male from a month old and upward shalt thou
number them.
16Moses numbered them according to word of the LORD, as he
was commanded.
17These were the sons of Levi by their names; Gershon, and
Kohath, and Merari.
18These *are* the names of sons of Gershon by their families;
Libni, and Shimei.
19And the sons of Kohath by families; Amram, and Izehar,
Hebron, and Uzziel.
20And the sons of Merari by their families; Mahli, and Mushi.
These *are* the families of the Levites according to the house of
their fathers.
21Of Gershon *was* the family of the Libnites, and the family of the
Shimites: these *are* the families of the Gershonites.
22Those that were numbered, according to the number of all
males, from a month old upward, *even* those numbered of
them *were* seven thousand five hundred.
23The families of the Gershonites shall pitch behind the
tabernacle westward.

24Chief of the house of the father of Gershonites *shall*
be Eliasaph son of Lael.
25And the charge of the sons of Gershon in the tabernacle of the
congregation *shall be* the tabernacle, tent, covering thereof, the
hanging for door of the tabernacle of the congregation,
26Hangings of the court, and the curtain for the door of the court,
which *is* by the tabernacle, and by the altar round about, and
cords of it for all the service thereof.
27Of Kohath *was* family of Amramites, and family of Izeharites,
and family of the Hebronites, and family of the Uzzielites:
these *are* the families of the Kohathites.
28Number of all the males, from a month old upwards *were* eight
thousand six hundred, keeping charge of the sanctuary.
29Families of sons of Kohath shall pitch on the side of the
tabernacle southward.
30And the chief of the house of the father of the families of the
Kohathites *shall be* Elizaphan the son of Uzziel.
31Their charge *shall be* the ark, and the table, the candlestick,
the altars, and the vessels of the sanctuary wherewith they
minister, and the hanging, and all the service thereof.
32And Eleazar the son of Aaron the priest *shall be* chief over the
chief of the Levites, *and have* the oversight of them that keep the
charge of the sanctuary.
33Of Merari *was* the family of the Mahlites, and the family of the
Mushites: these *are* the families of Merari.
34And those that were numbered of them, according to the
number of all the males, from a month old and upward, *were* six
thousand and two hundred.
35And the chief of the house of the father of the families of
Merari *was* Zuriel the son of Abihail: *these* shall pitch on the side
of the tabernacle northward.
36And *under* the custody and charge of the sons of Merari *shall*
be the boards of the tabernacle, and the bars thereof, and the
pillars thereof, and the sockets thereof, and all the vessels
thereof, and all that serveth thereto,
37The pillars of the court round about, their sockets, their pins,
and their cords.

38But those that encamp before the tabernacle toward the
east, *even* before the tabernacle of the congregation
eastward, *shall be* Moses, and Aaron and his sons, keeping the
charge of the sanctuary for the charge of the children of Israel;
and the stranger that cometh nigh shall be put to death.
39All numbered of the Levites, Moses and Aaron numbered at
commandment of the LORD, throughout their families, all males a
month old and upward, *were* twenty two thousand.
40The LORD said unto Moses, Number all firstborn of the males
of the children of Israel from a month old and upward, and take
the number of their names.
41Tthou shalt take the Levites for me (I *am* the LORD) instead of
all the firstborn among the children of Israel; and cattle of Levites
instead of all firstlings among the cattle of the children of Israel.
42Moses numbered, as the LORD commanded, firstborn among
children of Israel.
43All firstborn males by number of names, from a month old
upward, numbered of them, were twenty two thousand two
hundred threescore and thirteen.
44And the LORD spake unto Moses, saying,
45Take the Levites instead of the firstborn among the children of
Israel, and cattle of the Levites instead of their cattle; and the
Levites shall be mine: I *am* the LORD.
46And for those that are to be redeemed of the two hundred and
threescore and thirteen of the firstborn of the children of Israel,
which are more than the Levites;
47Thou shalt take five shekels apiece by poll, after the shekel of
the sanctuary shalt thou take *them*: (the shekel *is* twenty gerahs:)
48And thou shalt give the money, wherewith the odd number of
them is to be redeemed, unto Aaron and to his sons.
49And Moses took the redemption money of them that were over
and above them that were redeemed by the Levites:
50Of the firstborn of the children of Israel took he the money; a
thousand three hundred and threescore and five *shekels*, after
the shekel of the sanctuary:
51Moses gave money of the redeemed unto Aaron and his sons,
according to word of the LORD, the LORD commanded Moses.

NUMBERS CHAPTER 4

1And the LORD spake unto Moses and unto Aaron, saying,
2Take the sum of the sons of Kohath from among the sons of
Levi, after their families, by the house of their fathers,
3From thirty years old and upward even until fifty years old, all
that enter into the host, to do the work in the tabernacle of the
congregation.
4This *shall be* the service of the sons of Kohath in the tabernacle
of the congregation, *about* the most holy things:
5And when the camp setteth forward, Aaron shall come, and his
sons, and they shall take down the covering vail, and cover the
ark of testimony with it:
6And shall put thereon the covering of badgers' skins, and shall
spread over *it* a cloth wholly of blue, and shall put in the staves.
7And upon the table of shewbread they shall spread a cloth of
blue, and put thereon the dishes, and the spoons, and the bowls,
and covers to cover withal: continual bread shall be thereon:
8They shall spread upon them a cloth of scarlet, cover the same
with a badgers' skins, and shall put in the staves thereof.
9They shall take a cloth of blue, and cover the candlestick of light,
and lamps, and tongs, and snuff dishes, and all the oil vessels,
wherewith they minister unto it:
10And they shall put it and all the vessels thereof within a
covering of badgers' skins, and shall put *it* upon a bar.
11And upon the golden altar they shall spread a cloth of blue, and
cover it with a covering of badgers' skins, and shall put to the
staves thereof:
12They shall take all the instruments of ministry, wherewith they
minister in the sanctuary, put *them* in a cloth of blue, and cover
them with badgers' skins, and shall put *them* on a bar:
13They shall take away ashes from the altar, and spread a purple
cloth thereon:
14They shall put upon it all the vessels thereof, wherewith they
minister about it, *even* the censers, fleshhooks, shovels, and
basons, all vessels of the altar; and they shall spread upon it a
covering of badgers' skins, and put to the staves of it.

15When Aaron and his sons have made an end of covering the
sanctuary, and all the vessels of the sanctuary, as the camp is to
set forward; after that, the sons of Kohath shall come to bear *it*:
but they shall not touch *any* holy thing, lest they die. These *things*
are burden of sons of Kohath in tabernacle of the congregation.
16The office of Eleazar the son of Aaron the priest *pertaineth* the
oil for the light, and the sweet incense, and the daily meat
offering, and the anointing oil, *and* the oversight of all the
tabernacle, and of all that therein *is*, in the sanctuary, and in the
vessels thereof.
17And the LORD spake unto Moses and unto Aaron, saying,
18Cut ye not off the tribe of the families of the Kohathites from
among the Levites:
19Thus do unto them, that they may live, and not die, when they
approach unto the most holy things: Aaron and his sons shall go
in, appoint them every one to his service and his burden:
20But they shall not go in to see when the holy things are
covered, lest they die.
21And the LORD spake unto Moses, saying,
22Take the sum of the sons of Gershon, throughout houses of
their fathers,
23From thirty years old upward until fifty years old shalt thou
number them; all that enter in to perform the service, to do the work
in tabernacle of the congregation.
24This *is* the service of the families of the Gershonites, to serve,
and for burdens:
25And they shall bear the curtains of the tabernacle, and the
tabernacle of the congregation, his covering, and the covering of
the badgers' skins that *is* above upon it, and the hanging for the
door of the tabernacle of the congregation,
26And hangings of the court, and the hanging for the door of the
gate of the court, which *is* by the tabernacle and by the altar round
about, and their cords, and all the instruments of their service, and
all that is made for them: so shall they serve.
27At the appointment of Aaron and his sons shall be all the service
of the sons of the Gershonites, in all their burdens, and in all their
service: and ye shall appoint unto them in charge all their burdens.

28This *is* service of families of sons of Gershon in tabernacle of the
congregation: and their charge *shall be* under the hand of Ithamar
the son of Aaron the priest.
29Sons of Merari, number them after their families, by the house
of their fathers;
30From thirty years and upward even unto fifty years old shalt thou
number them, every one that entereth service, to do work of the
tabernacle of the congregation.
31This *is* the charge of their burden, according to all their service
in the tabernacle of the congregation; the boards of the tabernacle,
and the bars thereof, and the pillars thereof, and sockets thereof,
32And the pillars of the court round about, and their sockets, and
their pins, and their cords, with all their instruments, and with all
their service: and by name ye shall reckon the instruments of the
charge of their burden.
33This *is* the service of families of sons of Merari, according to all
their service, in tabernacle of the congregation, under hand of
Ithamar the son of Aaron the priest.
34And Moses and Aaron and the chief of the congregation
numbered the sons of the Kohathites after their families, and after
the house of their fathers,
35Thirty years old upward unto fifty years old, every one that
entered the service, for work in the tabernacle of the
congregation:
36Those numbered of them by families were two thousand seven
hundred fifty.
37These *were* they that were numbered of the families of the
Kohathites, all that might do service in the tabernacle of the
congregation, which Moses and Aaron did number according to the
commandment of the LORD by the hand of Moses.
38And those that were numbered of the sons of Gershon,
throughout their families, and by the house of their fathers,
39Thirty years old and upward unto fifty years old, every one that
entereth into service, for work in the tabernacle of the
congregation,
40Even those that were numbered of them, throughout their
families, by the house of their fathers, were two thousand and six
hundred and thirty.

41These *are* they that were numbered of the families of the sons
of Gershon, of all that might do service in the tabernacle of the
congregation, whom Moses and Aaron did number according to
the commandment of the LORD.
42And those that were numbered of the families of the sons of
Merari, throughout their families, by the house of their fathers,
43From thirty years old and upward even unto fifty years old,
every one that entereth into the service, for the work in the
tabernacle of the congregation,
44Those numbered of their families, three thousand two
hundred.
45These *be* those that were numbered of the families of the sons
of Merari, whom Moses and Aaron numbered according to the
word of the LORD by Moses.
46All those that were numbered of the Levites, whom Moses and
Aaron and the chief of Israel numbered, after their families, and
after the house of their fathers,
47From thirty years old upward even unto fifty years old, every
one that came to do service of the ministry, and service of the
burden in tabernacle of congregation,
48Numbered of them were eight thousand five hundred
fourscore.
49According to the commandment of the LORD they were
numbered by the hand of Moses, every one according to his
service, and according to his burden: thus were they numbered of
him, as the LORD commanded Moses.

SAMUEL INTRODUCES THE COMING DANGER OF KINGS

The very first Biblical prophet to introduce separation of powers is Samuel who authored the Biblical books of 1st and 2nd Samuel, 1st and 2nd Kings, 1st, and 2nd Chronicles. It was Samuel whom God ordered to anoint David as King. (David who slew Goliath.)

Israel Demands a King 1 Samuel Chapter 8 King James Bible

1And it came to pass, when Samuel was old, that he made his sons judges over Israel. 2Now the name of his firstborn was Joel; and the name of his second, Abiah: *they were* judges in Beersheba. 3And his sons walked not in his ways, but turned aside after lucre, and took bribes, and perverted judgment.
4Then all the elders of Israel gathered themselves together, and came to Samuel unto Ramah, 5And said unto him, Behold, thou art old, and thy sons walk not in thy ways: now make us a king to judge us like all the nations. 6The thing displeased Samuel, when they said, Give us a king to judge us. And Samuel prayed unto the LORD. 7The LORD said unto Samuel, Hearken unto the voice of the people in all that they say unto thee: they have not rejected thee, but have rejected me, that I should not reign over them.
8According to all the works which they have done since the day that I brought them up out of Egypt even unto this day, wherewith they have forsaken me, and served other gods, so do they also unto thee. 9Now therefore hearken unto their voice: howbeit yet protest solemnly unto them, and shew them the manner of the king that shall reign over them.
10And Samuel told all the words of the LORD unto the people that asked of him a king. 11And he said, This will be the manner of the king that shall reign over you: He will take your sons, and appoint *them* for himself, for his chariots, and *to be* his horsemen; and *some* shall run before his chariots. 12And he will appoint him captains over thousands, and captains over fifties; and *will set them* to ear his ground, and to reap his harvest, and to make his instruments of war, and instruments of his chariots. 13And he will take your daughters *to be* confectionaries, and *to be* cooks, and *to be* bakers.

14And he will take your fields, and your vineyards, and your
oliveyards, *even* the best *of them*, and give *them* to his
servants. 15And he will take the tenth of your seed, and of your
vineyards, and give to his officers, and to his servants. 16And he
will take your menservants, and your maidservants, and your
goodliest young men, and your asses, and put *them* to his
work. 17He will take the tenth of your sheep: and ye shall be his
servants. 18Ye shall cry out in that day because of your king which
ye shall have chosen; the LORD will not hear you.

God Grants the Request

19Nevertheless the people refused to obey the voice of Samuel;
and they said, Nay; but we will have a king over us; 20That we also
may be like all the nations; and that our king may judge us, and go
out before us, and fight our battles. 21And Samuel heard all the
words of the people, and he rehearsed them in the ears of the
LORD. 22And the LORD said to Samuel, Hearken unto their voice,
and make them a king. And Samuel said unto the men of Israel,
Go ye every man unto his city.

Modern Commentary

Samuel was correct in his condemnations of Kings and dangers to society the Kings would create. The extensive record documented by History makes clear, Kings could not become the God fearing protector of society envisioned by ancient people. Kings would murder, slaughter, annihilate, ethnically cleanse, massacre and crucify hundreds of millions of innocent people. Modern demographers calculated the numbers who died at the hands of Kings and Wars between 300 million and 2 billion.

Socrates may have been first to widely discuss Democracy, Plato authored Plato's Republic, Aristotle writes three most insightful works on Democracy.

Athens, Greece form of democracy came first and survived 800 years, being replaced by Kings and Royalty. The Roman democratic Republic began after the Greek beginnings of democracy, and survived 500 years, to be replaced by the Roman Empire, by which Emperors ruled with more despotism than Kings. (American Democratic Republic, 1776 to 2026 will reach 250 years.)

Pliny (ancient Roman Parliamentarian/Philosopher)

Shortly after beginning of the Roman Empire, Pliny exchanges 200 letters with the Emperor, to discuss; municipal water, sewers, taxes, less punishment for Christians.

Born in 68 AD, Pliny became an important Roman and becomes Governor of Bithynia, not many years after Apostle Paul is preaching there. Pliny exchanged 200 letters with Emperor Trajan asking advice on many matters. The letters provide a grand view of daily life and advancements within the Roman Empire.

In the letters of Pliny, we can infer conditions that governed daily life, 2000 years ago. Those political conditions are not unlike what we deal with in 2020's. These letters prove how closely ancient Rome influenced development of our modern world. The same principles have been proven or indicated throughout history. In his letters Pliny provides detail on the following political and government issues traceable to Mosaic Law and Maimonides 613 Mitzvot.

- Taxation
- Religious practices in Rome
- Level of Persecution of Christians
- Public Health and Safety
- Sewer systems not seen in England before 1600AD
- Public provision of drinking water supplies
- Governance of military matters
- The Rule of Law
- Justiciable Rules of Evidence applied in that day
- Organization of levels of government
- Statutory clauses allowing “cheating” and “political trickery”

(Many sources on Pliny are summarized in DEMOKRATIA TO DEMOCRACY, THE REQUIEM, beginning Chapter 46.)

Commencing closely on the heels of the demise of Roman Republic, reaching fruition about 500 AD, world society is beset by the Dark Ages, during which time the great developments of history are lost and buried, many not yet rediscovered. All worldwide society was thrust into reverse. History suggests that only the Monasteries survived, many of which were ignored by the Goths and Pagans, and society quickly began to store texts, books, documents, and valuables in the Monasteries, many of which have never as yet been translated.

Charlemagne in France, begins to restore the march to modernity and organized government. He was a reluctant King, expecting his older brother to become King, then his brother dies and Charlamagne is “tricked” into showing up at a Cathedral where the Pope had prepared a lavish coronation for Charlamagne. Perhaps Charlamagne believed in the warnings of Samuel.

Democracy transitions were attempted across central and eastern Europe, the sub-continent and Asia, only to fail.

The great missing link defeating democracy, was realized by Machiavelli, then Montesquieu and John Locke - - called SEPARATION OF POWERS. The great philosophers realized the Kings were defeating the transition, yet they expected to be executed if they dared to call for removal of Royalty. Machiavelli was first to attempt to convince the Kings that they should be far more benevolent, if not to relinquish royal power to other levels of government. John Locke echo’s and adds power to removal of kings. Montesquieu writes widely of the required intricacies of government not in place and is first to establish a term that has taken modern democracy/republic forms of government to their present zenith - -

SEPARATION OF POWERS.

Chapter 16. CONSTITUTION CLAUSES DERIVED FROM BIBLE

Our United States Constitution establishes powers and forms of government never delineated beyond our Holy Bible. Many attempts throughout history intended to develop a democracy, yet with limited results and limited life. Athens, Greece built the longest surviving true democracy of some 800 years. Rome moved from Kingdom to democratic Republic to empire, with the democratic Republic surviving 500 years. Our Founding Fathers established democracy as the basic philosophy of government and then went one step further and declared America a Republic. In our Founders lengthy debate at Constitutional Convention, they determined that a true democracy could only work within a City/State setting. That is to say, if all people were to vote on all things, the physical geography of America would require months to notify the people on issues requiring a vote, and another period of months to return all the vote totals back in our nations capitol. The founder's solution was to establish our system of elected Senators and Representatives to do the voting and stand for re-election every 6 or 2 years.

While God dictated the Bible to Moses, he provided many elements of government we would require, even today, 3500 years later. However, elements of government appear different due to the dramatically smaller population of the day, which did not require the extensive or bloated government in place today, along with a much different language, transitioning from Bible to Constitution.

This long chapter provides the modern US Constitution, parallel to biblical chapter and verse provided by God and Moses.

In our original US Constitution, the Founders established a system of ARTICLE, then SECTION complete with many points of law. Today, those points have been numbered as CLAUSES. This writing remains with the original format.

The balance of this chapter will utilize a format by which the actual Articles and Sections/Clauses of the Constitution appear underlined. An appropriate discussion will then appear to demonstrate those Biblical Chapter and Verse writings that provide the basis for each and every clause of the US Constitution.

Article. I

Section 1.

Establishes all legislative powers that shall be vested in a Congress consisting of a Senate and House of Representatives.

Moses had his Tribal Elders (12 men, one for each tribe). He was then given the organization chart depicted in Exodus 18:20-26, scalable enough to provide all government bodies and leaders.

"More correctly Sanhedrin (Gr. synedrion), meaning "a sitting" "together," or a "council." This word (rendered "council,")" is frequently used in the New Testament (KJV Matt. 5:22; 26:59; Mark "15:1, etc.) to denote the supreme judicial and administrative" "council of the Jews, which, it is said, was first instituted by" "Moses, and was composed of seventy men (KJV Num. 11:16, 17). The name is first "employed by the Jewish historian Josephus. This "council" is" "referred to simply as the "chief priests and elders of the" "people" (KJV Matt. 26:3, 47, 57, 59; 27:1, 3, 12, 20, etc.), before" whom Christ was tried on the charge of claiming to be the Messiah. Peter and John were also brought before it for promulgating heresy (Acts. 4:1-23; 5:17-41); as was also Stephen "on a charge of blasphemy (Acts 6:12-15), and Paul for violating a" temple by-law (Acts 22:30; 23:1-10). "The Sanhedrin is said to have consisted of seventy-one members, the high priest being leader, (called president of the Sanhedrin in some modern Bibles). They were of three classes (1) "the chief priests, or heads of the twenty-four priestly courses" "(KJV 1 Chr. 24), (KJV 1 Chr. 24:5 refers to these people as governors of the house of God, (2) the scribes, and (3) the elders. As the highest" "court of judicature, "in all causes and over all persons," "ecclesiastical and civil, supreme," its decrees were binding," "not only on the Jews in Palestine, but on all Jews wherever" scattered abroad. Its jurisdiction was greatly curtailed by "Herod, and afterwards by the Romans. Its usual place of meeting" "was within the precincts of the temple, in the hall "Gazith," but it sometimes met also in the house of the high priest (Matt. "26:3)."

Article. I

Section 2

1.The House of Representatives shall be composed of Members chosen every second Year by the People of the several States, and the Electors in each State shall have the Qualifications requisite for Electors of the most numerous Branch of the State Legislature.

The Bible provided an organization according to the twelve tribes; thus the leadership would be established via the twelve tribes instead of states. The Bible will later establish specific geographic locations for those tribes. As for qualifications, the Bible established several points of training and experience required for those positions delineated by the Bible.

2.No Person shall be a Representative who shall not have attained to the Age of twenty five Years, and been seven Years a Citizen of the United States, and who shall not, when elected, be an Inhabitant of that State in which he shall be chosen.

These sections define rules and minimum age for Representative,25, Senator, 30.

The Bible provides an early indicator of the rightfulness of these minimum ages

– Joseph was 30 years old when he became second in command to Pharaoh, after being in prison, a slave in Egypt (Genesis 41:46).
–Priests officially entered service at age 30 (Numbers 4:3).
– Saul became King when he was 30 years old (1 Samuel 13:1).
– David became King when he was 30 years old (2 Samuel 5:4).
– Ezekiel was called by God as a prophet at age 30 (Ezekiel 1:1).
– Jesus officially started his ministry at age 30 (Luke 3:23).

Is there biblical significance to age 30? The second example (priestly ministry) offers most compelling evidence in favor of yes. After having a 5-year internship (Numbers 8:24), priests began a 20-year ministry, lasting from age 30 to 50 (Numbers 4:3). Jesus, our Great High Priest (Hebrews 4:14) followed this pattern to fulfill all righteousness (Matthew 3:13-15).

3.Representatives and direct Taxes shall be apportioned among the several States which may be included within this Union, according to their respective Numbers, which shall be determined by adding to the whole Number of free Persons, including those bound to Service for a Term of Years, and excluding Indians not taxed, three fifths of all other Persons. The actual Enumeration shall be made within three Years after the first Meeting of the Congress of the United States, and within every subsequent Term of ten Years, in such Manner as they shall by Law direct. The Number of Representatives shall not exceed one for every thirty Thousand, but each State shall have at Least one Representative; and until such enumeration shall be made, the State of New Hampshire shall be entitled to chuse three, Massachusetts eight, Rhode-Island and Providence Plantations one, Connecticut five, New-York six, New Jersey four, Pennsylvania eight, Delaware one, Maryland six, Virginia ten, North Carolina five, South Carolina five, and Georgia three.

This clause discusses number of representatives and taxation. The Moses organization chart identified at Exodus 18:20-26 identifies a number of leaders determined by a rule of "tens." This would determine the number of leaders throughout the entire organization chart, to include those involved with government.

All taxation issues may be determined in that day by the level of "Tithe" delineated in the Bible. The Church was Government in this day, thus the tithe was the level of taxation.

4.When vacancies happen in Representation from any State, the Executive Authority thereof shall issue Writs of Election to fill such Vacancies.

The Biblical replacement plan calls for selection or election from within those qualified within tribes, consistent with the great Mosaic Organization Chart. (p.131), Exodus Chapter 18:18-26

5.The House of Representatives shall chuse their Speaker and other Officers; and shall have the sole Power of Impeachment.

We refer to the Mosaic organization chart in Exodus and other chapter and verse. Moses was Biblically granted many levels of leadership to support him. This clause would have gone to the highest levels, culminating with the Twelve Tribal Elders and their immediate subordinate group of two per tribe. Easily true for the selection of officers and the Power of Impeachment.

Article. I

Section. 3.

1.The Senate of the United States shall be composed of two Senators from each State, chosen by the Legislature thereof, for six Years; and each Senator shall have one Vote.

The Bible provided just a few "terms of service, yet Senators in a Sanhedrin sense, would be chosen from within each tribe of Israel.

2.Immediately after they shall be assembled in Consequence of the first Election, they shall be divided as equally as may be into three Classes. The Seats of the Senators of the first Class shall be vacated at the Expiration of the second Year, of the second Class at the Expiration of the fourth Year, and of the third Class at the Expiration of the sixth Year, so that one third may be chosen every second Year; and if Vacancies happen by Resignation, or otherwise, during the Recess of the Legislature of any State, the Executive thereof may make temporary Appointments until the next Meeting of the Legislature, which shall then fill such Vacancies.

This clause is intended to ensure that no more than one third of the Senate shall be elected in a single election. This was a Tribal issue within Israel, thus the tribes appointed leaders as required, further deferring to Moses for permission to make changes.

3.No Person shall be a Senator who shall not have attained to Age of 30 Years, and been 9 Years a Citizen of the United States, and who shall not, when elected, be an Inhabitant of that State for which he shall be chosen.

See the discussion of Age requirements, page 137.

4.The Vice President of the United States shall be President of the Senate, but shall have no Vote, unless they be equally divided.

Biblically, the legislative group reporting directly to Moses would first determine that a matter requiring a high vote was in fact within the "Will of God." If not will of God, the issue was likely rejected.

5.The Senate shall chuse their other Officers, and also a President pro tempore, in the Absence of the Vice President, or when he shall exercise the Office of President of the United States.

Commenced first within Sanhedrin, along with Organization Chart of Moses in Exodus Chapter 18 - - different titles were utilized.

6.The Senate shall have the sole Power to try all Impeachments. When sitting for that Purpose, they shall be on Oath or Affirmation. When the President of the United States is tried, the Chief Justice shall preside: And no Person shall be convicted without the Concurrence of two thirds of the Members present.

Biblical leaders could be replaced at the will of higher levels of the Moses Organization Chart, yet they would only act in event of a terrible outcome or illegal act as defined by the Laws of God.

IMPEACHMENT is delineated within these sections. The Bible tells us the following on impeachment, which is defined with different words across many bibles today.

King James Version Romans 8:33-34
33 Who shall lay any thing to the charge of God's elect? It is God that Justifieth.
34 Who is he that condemneth? It is Christ that died, yea rather that is risen again.

WNT Bible, (Weymouth New Testament)
Romans 8:33-39
33 Who shall impeach those God has chosen? God declares them free from guilt.
34 Who is there to condemn them? Christ Jesus died, or rather has risen to life again. He is also at the right hand of God, and is interceding for us.
35 Who shall separate us from Christ's love? Shall affliction or distress, persecution or hunger, nakedness or danger or sword?
36 As it stands written in the Scripture, "For Thy sake they are, all day long, trying to kill us. We have been looked upon as sheep destined for slaughter."
37 Amid all these things we are more than conquerors through Him who loved us.
38 For I am convinced neither death nor life, neither the lower ranks of evil angels nor the higher, neither things present nor things future, nor forces of nature,
39 nor height nor depth, nor any other created thing, will be able to separate us from the love of God which rests upon us in Christ Jesus our Lord.

7.Judgment in Cases of Impeachment shall not extend further than to removal from Office, and disqualification to hold and enjoy any Office of honor, Trust, or Profit under the United States: but the Party convicted shall nevertheless be liable and subject to Indictment, Trial, Judgment and Punishment, according to Law.

Biblically strict rules govern discipline and retraining, leading to reordination for Church officials and members, throughout many Biblical chapter and verse. These points are consistent with IMPEACHMENT. If for example, a Preacher sins, it is expected that he be removed from his lay post pending a strictly enforced review and retraining of God's word. Remember, that in Biblical days, the Church and religious officials were government.

Here we define minimum age: Representative (25) Senator (30)

The Bible provides an indicator of rightfulness of minimum ages.

– Joseph was 30 years old when he became second in command to Pharaoh, after being imprisoned as a slave (Genesis 41:46).
–Priests officially entered service at age 30 (Numbers 4:3).
– Saul became King when he was 30 years old (1 Samuel 13:1).
– David became King when he was 30 years old (2 Samuel 5:4).
– Ezekiel was called by God as a prophet at age 30 (Ezekiel 1:1).
– Jesus officially started his ministry at age 30 (Luke 3:23).

So is there biblical significance to age 30? The second example (priestly ministry) offers the most compelling evidence in favor of yes. After having a 5-year internship (Numbers 8:24), the priests began a 20-year ministry, lasting from age 30 to 50 (Numbers 4:3). Jesus, our Great High Priest (Hebrews 4:14) followed this pattern to fulfill all righteousness (Matt 3:13-15).

On the other hand, as we read the Scriptures we see people of all ages being used of God. The fact is it doesn't matter your age. If you have a heart to serve God, He will put you to work. Ten years ago, I never could have dreamed all that God had in store for my life. And as I look ahead to the next decade of my life, I can only imagine what God will do. How old are you? It really doesn't matter – 20, 40, 60, 80? It all starts with faith in Jesus Christ and trusting Him for salvation – after that, possibilities are endless. God can and will use you for the glory of His great name.

"Now to him who is able to do far more abundantly than all we ask or think, according to the power at work within us, to him be glory in the church and in Christ Jesus throughout all generations, forever and ever. Amen." Ephesians 3:20-21

- Daniel Stegeman, June 13, 2013
- https://pastoral-theology.com/2013/06/13/is-there-a-biblical-significance-to-age-30/

Article. I

Section. 4.

1.The Times, Places and Manner of holding elections for Senators and Representatives, shall be prescribed in each State by the Legislature thereof; but the Congress may at any time by Law make or alter such Regulations, except as to the Places of chusing Senators.

2.The Congress shall assemble at least once in every Year, and such Meeting shall be on the first Monday in December, unless they shall by Law appoint a different Day.

Elections for representative and Senators are established.

This is one area that the Bible only provided a method of selecting but not always electing leaders.

Exodus 18:20-26 makes clear that Moses had to empanel over 100,000 leaders, as the organization chart discussed is a rule of 10's. Therefore, given the 1.5 million Hebrews following Moses in Exodus, he had to find and select/empanel/elect 100,000+. It is a human impossibility to have enough knowledge of 100,000 people to make high quality leadership selection. Some form of election was essential, although not discussed biblically in that sense.

King James Version of the Bible speaks on the ELECT

Isaiah 42:1 Behold my servant, whom I uphold; mine elect, in whom my soul delighteth; I have put my spirit upon him: he shall bring judgment to the Gentiles.
Isaiah 45:4 For Jacob my servant's sake, and Israel mine elect, I have even called thee by thy name: I have surnamed thee, though thou hast not known me.
Isaiah 65:9 And I will bring forth a seed out of Jacob, and out of Judah an inheritor of my mountains: mine elect shall inherit it, my servants shall dwell there.
Isaiah 65:22 They shall not build, and another inhabit; they shall not plant, and another eat: for as the days of a tree are the days of my people, and mine elect shall long enjoy the work of their hands.
Matthew 24:22 And except those days should be shortened, there should no flesh be saved: but for the elect's sake those days shall be shortened.
Matthew 24:24 For there shall arise false Christs, and false prophets, and shall shew great signs and wonders; insomuch that, if it were possible, they shall deceive the very elect.
Matthew 24:31 He shall send his angels with a great sound of a trumpet, they shall gather together his elect from the four winds, one end of heaven to the other.
Mark 13:20 Except that the Lord had shortened those days, no flesh should be saved: but for the elect's sake, whom he hath chosen, he hath shortened the days.
Mark 13:22 For false Christs and false prophets shall rise, and shew signs and wonders, to seduce, if possible, even the elect.
Mark 13:27 Then shall he send his angels, and gather together his elect from the four winds, from the uttermost part of the earth to uttermost part of heaven.
Luke 18:7 And shall not God avenge his own elect, which cry day and night unto him, though he bear long with them?
Romans 8:33 Who shall lay any thing to God's elect? It is God that justifieth.

Colossians 3:12 Put on therefore, as the elect of God, holy and beloved, bowels of mercies, kindness, humbleness of mind, meekness, longsuffering;
1 Timothy 5:21 I charge thee before God, and the Lord Jesus Christ, and the elect angels, that thou observe these things without preferring one before another, doing nothing by partiality.
2 Timothy 2:10 Therefore I endure all things for the elect's sakes, so they may obtain salvation in Christ Jesus eternal glory.
Titus 1:1 Paul, a servant of God, and an apostle of Jesus Christ, according to the faith of God's elect, and the acknowledging of the truth which is after godliness;
1 Peter 1:2 Elect according to foreknowledge of God the Father, through sanctification of the Spirit, unto obedience and sprinkling the blood of Jesus Christ: Grace unto you, peace, be multiplied.
1 Peter 2:6 Wherefore also it is contained in scripture, Behold, I lay in Sion a chief corner stone, elect, precious: he that believeth on him shall not be confounded.

Bible verses on ELECTION

Romans 11:5 Even so then at this present time also there is a remnant according to the election of grace.
Romans 11:7 What then? Israel hath not obtained what he seeks; but the election hath obtained it, and the rest were blinded
Romans 11:28 Concerning the gospel, they are enemies for your sakes: touching the election, are beloved for the fathers' sakes.
1 Thess 1:4 Knowing, brethren beloved your election of God.
2 Peter 1:10 Wherefore brethren, give diligence to make your calling and election sure: if ye do these things, ye shall never fall:

Bible verses on ELECTED

1 Peter 5:13 The church that is at Babylon, elected together with you, saluteth you; and so doth Marcus my son.

We do not have evidence of an actual elections system in the Bible, except to infer some form of election HAD TO BE in place due to the need to place over 100,000 leaders during the day of Moses.

Article. I

Section. 5.

1.Each House shall be the Judge of the Elections, Returns and Qualifications of its own Members, and a Majority of each shall constitute a Quorum to do Business; but a smaller Number may adjourn from day to day, and may be authorized to compel the Attendance of absent Members, in such Manner, and under such Penalties as each House may provide.

Age and qualifications for members is discussed in many sections of this book. Biblically speaking, the members of each level would inspect any result of elections or qualifications, yet the final outcome would be confirmed by higher levels of the organization, consistent with Exodus 18:20-26.

2.Each House may determine the Rules of its Proceedings, punish its Members for disorderly Behaviour, and, with the Concurrence of two thirds, expel a Member.

Exodus Chapter 18 verse 20, provides the governing issue:
20 And thou shalt teach them ordinances and laws, and shalt shew them the way wherein they must walk, and the work they must do.
21 Moreover thou shalt provide out of all the people able men, such as fear God, men of truth, hating covetousness; and place such over them, to be rulers of thousands, and rulers of hundreds, rulers of fifties, and rulers of tens:
22 And let them judge the people at all seasons: and it shall be, that every great matter they shall bring unto thee, but every small matter they shall judge: so shall it be easier for thyself, and they shall bear the burden with thee.
23 If thou shalt do this thing, and God command thee so, then thou shalt be able to endure, and all this people shall also go to their place in peace.

3.Each House shall keep a Journal of its Proceedings, and from time to time publish the same, excepting such Parts as may in their Judgment require Secrecy; and the Yeas and Nays of the Members of either House on any question shall, at the Desire of one fifth of those Present, be entered on the Journal.

4.Neither House, during the Session of Congress, shall, without the Consent of the other, adjourn for more than three days, nor to any other Place than that in which the two Houses shall be sitting.

This section establishes Congress responsibility:

- Be Judge of elections
- Attendance of members
- Rules for Proceedings
- Journals of Proceedings
- Adjournment.

In the day of Moses, God provided all the rules and laws that would be required of government, Moses compiled those rules and laws into the first five books of our Bible. Elected people simply had to be sure the laws were communicated, followed, and enforced. It would not be until the day of the Roman Republic, 510BC to 28BC, that written forms of proceedings would commence.

Article. I

Section. 6.

1.The Senators and Representatives shall receive a Compensation for their Services, to be ascertained by Law, and paid out of the Treasury of the United States. They shall in all Cases, except Treason, Felony and Breach of the Peace, be privileged from Arrest during their Attendance at the Session of their respective Houses, and in going to and returning from the same; and for any Speech or Debate in either House, they shall not be questioned in any other Place.

Many forms of Compensation are identified in the Bible, to be drawn from tithes. While these compensations, titles, and positions may not line up equally with our present requirements, the system was in place deep in the heart of the Bible.

2.No Senator or Representative shall, during the Time for which he was elected, be appointed to any civil Office under the Authority of the United States, which shall have been created, or the Emoluments whereof shall have been encreased during such time; and no Person holding any Office under the United States, shall be a Member of either House during his Continuance in Office.

- Compensation -The Church provided all elements of government. Taxes took the form of tithes, (p.70)which became heavy for the rich during Church mandated festivals. Levites and other Churchmen received a form of compensation that was distributed from tithes. (See Chapter dealing with Tithes/Taxes.
- Can only be arrested or questioned by quorum of house members, unless Felony, Treason, or Breach of the Peace. God again, takes precedence and ordered heavy punishment for those involved in most crimes.
- No appointments or other government jobs while elected.

Article. I

Section. 7.

Clauses 1 through 3 will be detailed together in the adjacent discussion.

1.All Bills for raising Revenue shall originate in the House of Representatives; but the Senate may propose or concur with Amendments as on other Bills.

2.Every Bill which shall have passed the House of Representatives and Senate, shall, before it become a Law, be presented to the President of the United States; If he approve he shall sign it, but if not he shall return it, with his Objections to that House in which it shall have originated, who shall enter Objections at large on their Journal, and proceed to reconsider it. If after Reconsideration two thirds of that House shall agree to pass the Bill, it shall be sent, together with the Objections, to the other House, by which it shall likewise be reconsidered, and if approved by two thirds of that House, it shall become a Law. But in all Cases the Votes of both Houses shall be determined by yeas and Nays, and the Names of the Persons voting for and against the Bill shall be entered on the Journal of each House, respectively. If any Bill shall not be returned by the President within ten Days (Sundays excepted) after it shall have been presented to him, the Same shall be a Law, in like Manner as if he had signed it, unless the Congress by their Adjournment prevent its Return, in which Case it shall not be a Law.

3.Every Order, Resolution, or Vote to which the Concurrence of the Senate and House of Representatives may be necessary (except on a question of Adjournment) shall be presented to the President of the United States; and before the Same shall take Effect, shall be approved by him, or being disapproved by him, shall be repassed by two thirds of the Senate and House of Representatives, according to Rules and Limitations prescribed in the Case of a Bill.

Bills for Revenue, Presidential review and concurrence

Again, please refer to the chapter on Tithes/Taxes. God approved all the tithes/taxation required, and that process worked for 500 years, until Solomon began to build his huge wealth. Solomon expanded all areas and functions of Jerusalem and the Temple and Military infrastructure. Appearance indicates Solomon paid those costs out of the Temple treasures, which he doubled via international commerce during the Reign of Solomon.

We can see from scriptures that Solomon doubled his wealth from 3000 "talents" up to 6000 "talents" by dispatching the Hebrew trading fleet once every three years, loaded with the finest goods produced in Israel. Ship Captains were ordered not to return until the entire cargo was converted to Gold or precious objects.

The Bible contains many strange terms for weights and measures. Modern conversion tables exist for all those strange terms. Talent was a standard for the amount of weight a man could be expected to carry on his back all day at the time. The Standard Talent was 75 pounds. The Royal Talent was 150 pounds. The reader is urged to translate these numbers and learn that with 2026 gold valuation, the gold Wealth of Solomon would reach over $75 Billion. The Bible tells us he had 10 times as much Silver.

As for review and concurrence by the President - - no scripture outlines this requirement, yet we can be sure the lead Priests at the top of the Organization Chart of Moses would fulfill that need by means of close review of the word of God memorialized in the Pentateuch, the first five books of the Bible. It would not be until the Day of Daniel that the concept of President was first used, 1000 years beyond Moses. Daniel was first to be named President, a position he retained during two World Empires.

God and his instructions within the Bible fully expected higher levels of government/church to ensure any changes were reviewed for compliance with the WILL OF GOD.

Article. I

Section. 8.

Correlation between the US Constitution and Bible for is extensive. An overview will be provided next to each statement, with an extensive description at the end of constitutional provisions.

1.The Congress shall have Power To lay and collect Taxes, Duties, Imposts and Excises, to pay the Debts and provide for the common Defence and general Welfare of the United States; but all Duties, Imposts and Excises shall be uniform throughout the United States;

In the Old Testament, all taxation was ordered and paid via church tithes, as the church was essentially the government in those days. In a very few instances, the word "tribute" is used when nations or armies demanded payment. Then in the New Testament, Nations and Governments or Emperors took charge and began the process of Taxation. Render therefore unto Caesar the things which are Caesar's; and unto God the things that are God's.

In this next lengthy section, note the various rules for tithe's, taxes, tribute, or valuation. (page 70)

<u>2.To borrow Money on the credit of the United States;</u>

Obviously, the Bible made no reference to the United States, however, there are a number of rules for credit or contracts enumerated within this book. See the section that discusses JOINT AND SEVERAL RESPONSIBILITY as a result of Nahum 1:12 - - "though they be quiet and likewise many."

<u>3.To regulate Commerce with foreign Nations, and among the several States, and with the Indian Tribes;</u>

There were no rules for commerce among foreign nations. Often, the word "Tribute" is used to describe a process akin to taxation or imposts on foreign trade, as you will see in the section on TITHES AND TAXATION. (page 70)

<u>4.To establish an uniform Rule of Naturalization, and uniform Laws on the subject of Bankruptcies throughout the United States;</u>

Following this overview, you will see the rules for Third Generation and Tenth Generation as a means of Naturalization or granting Citizenship, also, laws or custom on Contracts (Bankruptcy)

<u>5.To coin Money, regulate the Value thereof, and of foreign Coin, and fix the Standard of Weights and Measures;</u>

“Barter” was the primary medium of exchange until our modern day, however, you may download many pages of Standards of Weights and Measures, from Gold to lengths and measures.

6.To provide for the Punishment of counterfeiting the Securities and current Coin of the United States;

God provided guidance for Fair Weights, Measures, Balances

7.To establish Post Offices and post Roads; see below

8.To promote the Progress of Science and useful Arts, by securing for limited Times to Authors and Inventors the exclusive Right to their respective Writings and Discoveries;

Patents were not law (future discovery notwithstanding) until:
The Venetian Patent Statute -- 1474

- The English Statute of Monopolies – 1624
- U.S. Patent Law: The Patent Act –1790
- Patent Law in Revolutionary France – 1791

Patent and Copyright were so new that Benjamin Franklin argued against patents, stating that such inventions should benefit all society, not just the inventor.

9.To constitute Tribunals inferior to the supreme Court;

10.To define and punish Piracies and Felonies committed on the high Seas, and Offences against the Law of Nations;

11.To declare War, grant Letters of Marque and Reprisal, and make Rules concerning Captures on Land and Water;

12.To raise and support Armies, but no Appropriation of Money to that Use shall be for a longer Term than two Years; - -

Moses numbered all the fighting age men and established what resembled a militia military force numbering over 600,000.

13.To provide and maintain a Navy; (see below)

14.To make Rules for Government and Regulation of land and naval Forces;

15.To provide for calling forth the Militia to execute the Laws of the Union, suppress Insurrections and repel Invasions;

16.To provide for organizing, arming, and disciplining, the Militia, and for governing such Part of them as may be employed in the Service of the United States, reserving to the States respectively, the Appointment of the Officers, and the Authority of training Militia according to the discipline prescribed by Congress;

17.To exercise exclusive Legislation in all Cases whatsoever, over such District (not exceeding ten Miles square) as may, by Cession of particular States, and the Acceptance of Congress, become the Seat of the Government of the United States, and to exercise like Authority over all Places purchased by the Consent of the Legislature of the State in which the Same shall be, for the Erection of Forts, Magazines, Arsenals, dock-Yards, and other needful Buildings;—And

18.To make all Laws which shall be necessary and proper for carrying into Execution the foregoing Powers, and all other Powers vested by this Constitution in the Government of the United States, or in any Department or Officer thereof.

This section details many varied points for senate and congress.

1.Power to lay and collect taxes and pay government debts.

Over and above the concept of Tithe's, the greatest single Bible verse related to the concept of taxation comes from the words of Jesus in Matthew 22:17-21

[17] Tell us, What thinkest thou? Is it lawful to give tribute to Caesar?
[18] But Jesus perceived their wickedness, and said, Why tempt ye me, *ye* hypocrites?
[19] Shew me the tribute money. And they brought unto him a penny.
[20] And he saith unto them, Whose *is* this image and superscription?
[21] They say unto him, Caesar's. Then saith he unto them, Render therefore unto Caesar the things which are Caesar's; and unto God the things that are God's.

God provided all the law needed for taxation in the day of Moses. Remember that the only government in that day was the Church. All tithes were intended to support the church which was government. The same instruction and laws from God may easily apply today if our modern congress can learn to control itself.

The verse about tithing one-tenth of your income is found in Leviticus 27:30: "'A tithe of everything from the land, whether grain from the soil or fruit from the trees, belongs to the Lord; it is holy to the Lord." The 10% requirement specifically comes from the Hebrew translation of tithe, "עשר" or "ten".

2 Kings 23:35 And Jehoiakim gave the silver and the gold to Pharaoh; but he taxed the land to give the money according to the commandment of Pharaoh: he exacted the silver and the gold of the people of the land, of every one according to his taxation, to give it unto Pharaoh Nechoh.

Luke 2:2 (And this taxing was first made when Cyrenius was governor of Syria.)

What Does Bible Say About Tithing One Tenth? (Balance of this section is guided by https://get.tithe.ly/blog/tithing-in-the-new-testament-what-does-it-say

The verse about tithing one-tenth of your income is found in Leviticus 27:30: "'A tithe of everything from the land, whether grain from the soil or fruit from the trees, belongs to the Lord; it is holy to the Lord." The 10% requirement specifically comes from the Hebrew translation of tithe, "עשר" or "ten".

Other passages also talked about tithing, such as the following:

- Numbers 18:26: "Speak to the Levites and say: 'When you receive from the Israelites the tithe I give you as inheritance, you must present a tenth of that as the Lord's offering."
- Deuteronomy 14:22: "Be sure to set aside a tenth of all that your fields produce each year."
- 2 Chronicles 31:5: "As soon as the order went out, Israelites generously gave the first fruits of their grain, new wine, olive oil and honey and all the fields produced. They brought a great amount, tithe of everything."

So, does the Bible actually say to give 10%? Yes. Even before tithes were required by Mosaic law, Abraham tithed once (Genesis 14:20) and Jacob pledged to tithe all that he had (Genesis 28:22).

Later, the Old Testament Law required *multiple* tithes for the Levites, temple operations and feasts, and the poor and unfortunate. In total, tithes came out to 20-30% of incoming money, plus any additional voluntary giving of first-fruit and freewill offerings, which we will detail in the next section.

Law of Tithes and Offerings

In the Old Testament books of Exodus, Leviticus, Numbers, and Deuteronomy, God gave Moses the Law that included instructions on how to generously give to God and His people.

Here are some of the required tithings and offerings that the Israelites had to give:

- The First Tithe: All Israelite families were asked to give one-tenth of their produce, flocks, and herds. That amount was set aside and given to the Lord annually to support the Levites in their priestly service, as they had no other source of income or land ownership (Leviticus 27:30-33 - Numbers 18:21-24).

- The Festival Tithe: Israelites, mainly in Jerusalem, had to give another tenth of their resources to sponsor religious feasts and festivals throughout the year. These events were grand religious celebrations, so the Israelites spared nothing to bring thanks and praise to God (Deuteronomy 14:22-27).
- The Poor Tithe: Israelites had to give a tithe to the poor and needy every third year. It is unclear whether this is a third full tithe or the second Festival Tithe was being donated to the poor that year (Deuteronomy 14:28-29), but there was certainly a tithe set aside for the unfortunate.

The point of tithing is to support the ongoing work of God's people. This is different from the purpose of offerings, which acted as a personal thanksgiving and repentance of sins:

- Propitiatory Offerings: These offerings were meant as a material sacrifice to atone for one's sins, both known and unknown. There are two types in this category: the Sin Offering mentioned in Exodus 29:14, 36, and Leviticus 4, and the Guilt Offering mentioned in Leviticus 5:14 to 6:7.
- Dedicatory Offerings: These offerings reminded the Israelites of the goodness of God. There were three types in this category: the Burnt Offering of Levi 1:3-17, the Cereal Offering in Levi 2:1-16, and Drink Offering in Num 28:14 and 29:6.
- Communal Offerings: These offerings include the Peace Offering in Leviticus 3 and 7:11-26 and the Votive Offering in Leviticus 7:16-17 and Numbers 6:21.

What Does New Testament Say About Tithing?

We've established that the Old Testament had a lot of tithing and offering rules, but what does the New Testament say about tithing? After Jesus saved humanity from eternal death, He introduced a new perspective on tithing and offerings (John 3:16). Jesus endorses tithing but expects His followers to *excee*d righteousness of the Scribes and Pharisees whom He encouraged to continue tithing (Matt 23:23).

Here are the key ideas of the principle of giving:

- God owns everything, and His people are "money managers." God continues to give everything they need, including money (1 Corinthians 10:26). In turn, they are to manage the money so His blessings and generosity are not wasted. Moreover, gaining money is only possible through Him, so Christians may show their gratitude by returning a portion to Him.
- Giving to God, best antidote for materialism. Money cannot buy happiness. Instead, happiness is gained by *who* a person has (God) rather than by *what* the person has gained (things). "Command those who are rich in this present world not to be arrogant nor to put their hope in wealth… But put their hope in God, who provides us with everything." (1Tim 6:17)
- Christians are to give to the church in proportion to God's provision. Instead of asking, "How much is required?" Christians are to ask, "How much can I give?" Old Testament tithing established rules for proportionate giving. Today, anyone dedicated to Christ should offer an appropriate portion of their wealth voluntarily to support ongoing operations of their church.

A note on Hebrews 7, a passage that parallels Melchizedek to whom Abraham gave one-tenth of what he had.

This Melchizedek was king of Salem and priest of God Most High. He met Abraham returning from the defeat of the kings and blessed him, and Abraham gave him a tenth of everything. First, the name Melchizedek means "king of righteousness;" then also, "king of Salem" means "king of peace." Without father or mother, without genealogy, without beginning of days or end of life, resembling the Son of God, remains a priest forever. (Heb 7:1-3)

The Old Covenant of keeping Laws to gain forgiveness is fulfilled in the New Covenant of faith in Jesus. The writer of Hebrews says, Jesus is a High Priest forever in the order of Melchizedek. The first tithe was given to Melchizedek by Abraham. Christians are children from the seed of Abraham.

Jesus receives tithes from believers who deem Him their High Priest, as Melchizedek did from Abraham.

Is Tithing 10%

A tithe is a tenth, but it doesn't have intrinsic spiritual value. A tenth of the spoils Abraham gave could be interpreted as "top of the heap." It was the first best Abraham had, and he gave it.

Paul makes it clear that generosity should be cheerful and voluntary (2 Corinthians 9:6-7). We should not allow the Old Covenant law of tithing to become an obstacle to embracing the New Covenant's behavior of generosity. Some people may start at 1% and work their way from there. The point is breaking the curse of "love of money" through rearranging our priorities on building the Kingdom of God.

We will close this point by quoting perfectly prophetic verse from DANIEL that continues to resound across the previous three millennia. Daniel Chapter 11 foretells the Greco-Persian Wars and the rise and fall of the final Kings of the Second World Empire, partly as a negative prophecy of the dangers of taxation.

Daniel Chapter 11

1I in first year of Darius the Mede, *even* I, stood to confirm and to strengthen him.
2 And now will I shew thee the truth. Behold, there shall stand up yet three kings in Persia; and the fourth shall be far richer than *they* all: and by his strength through his riches he shall stir up all against the realm of Grecia.
3 And a mighty king shall stand up, that shall rule with great dominion, and do according to his will.
4 And when he shall stand up, his kingdom shall be broken, and shall be divided to the four winds of heaven; and not to his posterity, nor according to his dominion which he ruled: for his kingdom shall be plucked up, for others beside those.
17 He shall also set his face to enter with the strength of his whole kingdom, and upright ones with him; thus shall he do: and he shall give him the daughter of women, corrupting her: but she shall not stand *on his side*, neither be for him.

18 After this shall he turn his face unto the isles, and shall take
many: but a prince for his own behalf shall cause the reproach
offered by him to cease; without his own reproach he shall cause
it to turn upon him.
19 Then he shall turn his face toward the fort of his own land: but
he shall stumble and fall, and not be found.
20 Then shall stand up in his estate A RAISER OF TAXES *in* the
glory of the kingdom: but within few days he shall be destroyed,
neither in anger, nor in battle.
21 And in his estate shall stand up a vile person, to whom they
shall not give honour of the kingdom: but shall come peaceably,
and obtain the kingdom by flatteries.
22 And with the arms of a flood shall they be overflown from before
him, and shall be broken; yea, also the prince of the covenant.
23 And after the league *made* with him he shall work deceitfully:
for he shall come up, and shall become strong with a small people.
24 He shall enter peaceably even upon the fattest places of the
province; and he shall do *that* which his fathers have not done, nor
his fathers' fathers; he shall scatter among them the prey, and
spoil, and riches: *yea*, and he shall forecast his devices against the
strong holds, even for a time.
25 And he shall stir up his power and his courage against the king
of the south with a great army; and the king of the south shall be
stirred up to battle with a very great and mighty army; but he shall
not stand: for they shall forecast devices against him.
26 Yea, they that feed of the portion of his meat shall destroy him,
and his army shall overflow: and many shall fall down slain.

"TRIBUTE" BIBLICAL DISCUSSION

Genesis 14:20 And blessed be God Most High, Who has delivered your enemies into your hand." He gave him a tenth of all.

Romans 13:6-7 - For this cause pay ye tribute also: for they are God's ministers, attending continually upon this very thing.

Matthew 22:17-21 - Tell us therefore, What thinkest thou? Is it lawful to give tribute unto Caesar, or not?

Romans13: 6 For this cause pay ye tribute also: for they are God's ministers, attending continually upon this very thing.
Romans 13:7 Render therefore to all their dues: tribute to whom tribute *is due*; custom to whom custom; fear to whom fear; honour to whom honour.

Luke 3: 12 Then came also publicans to be baptized, and said unto him, Master, what shall we do?
Luke 3:13 And he said unto them, Exact no more than that which is appointed you.

BIBLICAL DISCUSSION OF TAXATION

Genesis 14:20 And blessed be God Most High, Who has delivered your enemies into your hand." He gave him a tenth of all.

Exodus 30:11-16 The Lord also spoke to Moses, saying, "When you take a census of the sons of Israel to number them, then each one of them shall give a ransom for himself to the Lord, when you number them, so that there will be no plague among them when you number them. This is what everyone who is numbered shall give: half a shekel according to the shekel of the sanctuary (the shekel is twenty gerahs), half a shekel as a contribution to the Lord.

Leviticus 27:30-33 'Thus all the tithe of the land, of the seed of the land or of the fruit of the tree, is the Lord's; it is holy to the Lord. If, therefore, a man wishes to redeem part of his tithe, he shall add to it one-fifth of it. For every tenth part of herd or flock, whatever passes under the rod, the tenth one shall be holy to the Lord.
Numbers 18:21 "To the sons of Levi, behold, I have given all the tithe in Israel for an inheritance, in return for their service they perform, the service of the tent of meeting.

Deuteronomy 14:28-29 “At the end of every third year you shall bring out all the tithe of your produce in that year, and shall deposit it in your town. The Levite, because he has no portion or inheritance among you, and the alien, the orphan and the widow who are in your town, shall come and eat and be satisfied, in order that the Lord your God may bless you in all the work of your hand which you do.

Judges 3:15 But when the sons of Israel cried to the Lord, the Lord raised up a deliverer for them, Ehud the son of Gera, the Benjamite, a left-handed man. And the sons of Israel sent tribute by him to Eglon the king of Moab.

1 Kings 4:21 Now Solomon ruled over all the kingdoms from the River to the land of the Philistines and to the border of Egypt; they brought tribute and served Solomon all the days of his life.

2 Kings 17:4 But the king of Assyria found conspiracy in Hoshea, who had sent messengers to So king of Egypt and had offered no tribute to the king of Assyria, as he had done year by year; so the king of Assyria shut him up bound in prison.

2 Kings 23:35 So Jehoiakim gave the silver and gold to Pharaoh, but he taxed the land in order to give the money at the command of Pharaoh. He exacted the silver and gold from the people of the land, each according to his valuation, to give it to Pharaoh Neco.

2 Kings 17:3 Shalmaneser king of Assyria came up against him, and Hoshea became his servant and paid him tribute.

1 Chronicles 18:2 He defeated Moab, and the Moabites became servants to David, bringing tribute.

1 Chronicles 18:6 Then David put garrisons among the Arameans of Damascus; and the Arameans became servants to David, bringing tribute. And the Lord helped David wherever he went.

2 Chronicles 17:11 Some of the Philistines brought gifts and silver as tribute to Jehoshaphat; Arabians also brought him flocks, 7,700 rams and 7,700 male goats.

2 Chronicles 24:4-12 Now it came about after this that Joash decided to restore the house of the Lord. He gathered the priests and Levites and said to them, "Go out to the cities of Judah and collect money from all Israel to repair the house of your God annually, and you shall do the matter quickly." But the Levites did not act quickly. So the king summoned Jehoiada the chief priest and said to him, "Why have you not required the Levites to bring in from Judah and Jerusalem the levy fixed by Moses the servant of the Lord on the congregation of Israel for the tent of the testimony?"

Ezra 4:13 Now let it be known to the king, if that city is rebuilt and walls are finished, they will not pay tribute, custom or toll, and it will damage the revenue of the kings.

Nehemiah 5:4 Also there were those who said, "We have borrowed money for the king's tax on our fields and our vineyards.

Isaiah 16:1 Send the tribute lamb to the ruler of the land, From Sela by way of the wilderness to mountain of the daughter of Zion.
Hosea 10:6 The thing itself will be carried to Assyria As tribute to King Jareb; Ephraim will be seized with shame And Israel will be ashamed of its own counsel.

Malachi 3:8-10 "Will a man rob God? Yet you are robbing Me! But you say, 'How have we robbed You?' In tithes and offerings. You are cursed with a curse, for you are robbing Me, the whole nation of you! Bring the whole tithe into storehouse, so there may be food in My house, test Me now in this," says the Lord of hosts, "if I will not open for you the windows of heaven and pour out for you a blessing until it overflows.

Matthew 17:24-26 When they came to Capernaum, those who collected the two-drachma tax came to Peter and said, "Does your teacher not pay the two-drachma tax?" He *said, "Yes."

And when he came into the house, Jesus spoke to him first, saying, "What do you think, Simon? From whom do the kings of the earth collect customs or poll-tax, from their sons or from strangers?" When Peter said, "From strangers," Jesus said to him, "Then sons are exempt.

Luke 23:1-2 Then the whole body of them got up and brought Him before Pilate. And they began to accuse Him, saying, "We found this man misleading our nation and forbidding to pay taxes to Caesar, and saying that He Himself is Christ, a King."

Romans 13:7 Render to all what is due: tax to whom tax is due; custom to whom custom; fear to whom fear; honor to whom honor. Source: https://bible.knowing-jesus.com/topics/Taxation

Rules for Naturalization and Bankruptcy (continued from above)

(It should appear strange to the reader, just why our Founding Fathers chose to couple naturalization and bankruptcy in the same constitutional statement. You are reminded that Benjamin Franklin opened debate one morning at Constitutional Convention with a recommendation that they could save much time and debate by declaring the Mosaic Law to be the law of the land, until they could take the time to go further. This point seems to prove they followed this Franklin recommendation.)

God chose to prohibit certain people from becoming naturalized into citizenship. Many others were allowed to become citizens in the third generation beyond their parents' migration into the country.

God provided laws for loaning, Deuteronomy Chapter 23

1He that is wounded in the stones, or hath his privy member cut off, shall not enter into the congregation of the LORD.
2 A bastard shall not enter into congregation of the LORD; even to his tenth generation shall he not enter congregation of the LORD.

3 An Ammonite or Moabite shall not enter into the congregation of
the LORD; even to their tenth generation shall they not enter the
congregation of the LORD for ever:
4 Because they met you not with bread and with water, when ye
came forth out of Egypt; and because they hired against thee
Balaam the son of Beor of Pethor of Mesopotamia, to curse thee.
5 Nevertheless the LORD thy God would not hearken unto Balaam;
but the LORD thy God turned the curse into a blessing, because
the LORD thy God loved thee.
6 Thou shalt not seek their peace nor prosperity for ever.
7 Thou shalt not abhor an Edomite; for he *is* thy brother: thou shalt
not abhor an Egyptian; because thou wast a stranger in his land.
8 The children that are begotten of them shall enter into the
congregation of the LORD in their third generation.

BANKRUPTCY

Originally based upon money or goods. These laws were based upon the concept of "usury" which is today called "interest rate loans." The Bible doe does not apply the word BANKRUPTCY, although the rules applied today, were in a formative stage, via the verses indicated herein requiring bonding or a form of contract such as the passage from Nahum 1:12 "Quiet and Likewise Many, or joint and several responsibility for the contract and its terms.

Deuteronomy Chapter 23

19 Thou shalt not lend upon usury to thy brother; usury of money,
usury of victuals, usury of any thing that is lent upon usury:
20 Unto a stranger thou mayest lend upon usury; but unto thy
brother thou shalt not lend upon usury: that the LORD thy God may
bless thee in all that thou settest thine hand to in the land whither
thou goest to possess it.
21 When thou shalt vow a vow unto the LORD thy God, thou shalt
not slack to pay it: for the LORD, thy God will surely require it of
thee; and it would be sin in thee.

Later in the book of NAHUM, we are given a phrase that was only learned in the past 100 years to have been a contract term for loans that seems to be utilized across many countries of the middle east. The Book of Nahum is an extension and point of finality from the Book of Jonah.

God orders Jonah to become the world's first traveling Evangelist and orders Jonah to travel to Nineveh (2-hour drive north of Baghdad) and evangelize that evil and sinful city. Nineveh is the world's largest city of the day, with a population between 120,000 and 140,000. Jonah runs away at first, boards a ship bound for Spain, is thrown overboard, the whale gobbles-up Jonah, three days later spits Jonah out on a beach of Israel. Jonah begs God's forgiveness and then travels to Nineveh.

God has already given Nineveh its order to cease their untold sin on penalty of being destroyed. Now the people of Nineveh see a strange man, Jonah, having come a long distance to preach. Josephus tells us the complexion of Jonah had been changed a strange color by the acid in the belly of the whale. IT WORKED. In just a single day, Jonah brought the world's largest city back to the worship of God and a cessation of sin. Then about 100 years later, they backslid heavily, and God destroyed the city. (612 BC) Just 25 years later, God ordered Nebuchadnezzar to take Jerusalem into captivity due to their sins.

As for bankruptcy, we learn from modern Archaeologists that huge libraries of clay tablets were unearthed from Nineveh that were first learned to contain the statement from Nahum 1:12; "Though they be Quiet and Likewise many." Decades of Archaeology were required to understand the statement. Later findings revealed this was a legal phrase contained in contracts and deeds. Quiet and Likewise Many is considered to be the old world equivalent of our modern legal phrase, JOINT AND SEVERAL RESPONSIBILITY for contracts or deeds or land title.

This is a huge indication that a court centered Rule of Law was in process for a lengthy period. Such contracts continue today to be a standard for determining the personal assets of individuals and corporations facing bankruptcy.

5.To coin money, regulate the value thereof, and of foreign coin, and fix the standard of weights and measures;

Money was not coined or standardized until the era of Jesus Christ. Barter was the primary means of trade in the Old Testament. They utilized far different weights and measures than our present day. The reader can find many conversion tables on the Internet that allow you to compare the weight and measure methods of the old testament to our modern day. Understand that weights and measures did in-fact exist in these earliest days.

6.To provide for the punishment of counterfeiting the securities and current coin of the United States.

- Not to commit fraud in measuring (Lev. 19:35)
- To ensure that scales and weights are correct (Lev. 19:36)
- Not to possess inaccurate measures and weights (Deut. 25:13-14

Exodus Chapter 22 provides rules for restitution

1If a man shall steal an ox, or a sheep, and kill it, or sell it; he shall restore five oxen for an ox, and four sheep for a sheep.
2 If a thief be found breaking up, and be smitten that he die, *there shall* no blood *be shed* for him.
3 If the sun be risen upon him, *there shall be* blood *shed* for him; *for* he should make full restitution; if he have nothing, then he shall be sold for his theft.
4 If the theft be certainly found in his hand alive, whether it be ox, or ass, or sheep; he shall restore double.

7. To Provide Post Roads.

The Bible begins to talk of roads in the book of Genesis. The following appear as Gods instruction for building of Roads.

- Isaiah 43:16 This is the word of the Lord, who makes a way in the sea, and a road through the deep waters;
- Jeremiah 6:16 This is what the Lord said: Take your place looking out on the ways; make search for the old roads, saying, where is the good way? And go in it that you may have rest for your should. But they said, We will not go in in.
- Jeremiah 31:21 Put up guiding pillars, make road signs for yourself: give attention to the highway, even the way in which you went: be turned again, O virgin of Israel, be turned to these your towns.
- Acts 8:26 But an angel of the Lord said to Philip, Get up, and go to the south, to the road which goes from Jerusalem to Gaza, through the waste land.
- Acts 26:13 In the middle of the day, on the road I saw a light from heaven, brighter than the sun, shining round me and those who were journeying with me.
- Hebrews 12:13 Make straight roads for your feet, so the feeble may not be turned out of the way, but may be made strong.

8. To promote the Progress of Science and useful Arts, by securing for limited Times to Authors and Inventors the exclusive Right to their respective Writings and Discoveries;

There were discoveries and inventions in the old testament, although lack of communication mediums prevented knowledge of discoveries beyond knowledge of the inventor. Such Patents would not appear for the next thousand years.

Contract law seeming to be established in Book of Nahum suggests legal remedies existed to deal with inventions and patents.

We find repetition of issues in the US Constitution. We often repeat sections of chapter and verse that apply to many issues.

The book of NAHUM contains a phrase that was only learned in the past 100 years to have been a contract term for loans that seems to be utilized across many countries of the middle east. The Book of Nahum is an extension and point of finality from the Book of Jonah.

God orders Jonah to become the first traveling Evangelist and orders Jonah to Nineveh (2 hour drive north of Baghdad) and evangelize that evil sinful city. Nineveh is the world's largest city of the day, with a population between 120,000 and 140,000. Jonah runs, boards a ship to Spain, is thrown overboard, the whale gobbles-up Jonah, three days later spits Jonah out on a beach of Israel. Jonah begs God's forgiveness and travels to Nineveh.

God has already given Nineveh its order to cease their untold sin on penalty of being destroyed. Now the people of Nineveh see a strange man, Jonah, having come a long distance to preach. Josephus tells us the complexion of Jonah had been changed a strange color by the acid in the belly of the whale. IT WORKED. In just a single day, Jonah brought the world's largest city back to the worship of God and a cessation of sin. Then about 100 years later, they backslid heavily and God destroyed the city. (612 BC) Just 25 years later, God ordered Nebuchadnezzar to take Jerusalem into captivity due to their sins.

As for inventions and patents or science, we learn from modern Archaeologists that huge libraries of clay tablets were unearthed from Nineveh that were first learned to contain the statement from Nahum 1:12 Though they be Quiet and Likewise many. Decades of Archaeology were required to understand the statement. Later findings revealed this was a legal phrase contained in contracts and deeds. Quiet and Likewise Many is considered to be the old world equivalent of our modern legal phrase JOINT AND SEVERAL RESPONSIBILITY for contracts or deeds or land title. The same applied to inventors patents.

Bible verses about science are:

- 1 Timothy 6:20, warns against false science and knowledge.
- Luke 11:52, which criticizes the lawyers for taking away the key of knowledge.
- Romans 2:20, mock Jews as being instructors of foolish, teachers of babes.
- Genesis 2:4-25, creation of heavens, earth, first humans.
- Revelation 11:15-18, which prophesies the coming of God's kingdom and the destruction of those who destroy the earth.

9. To constitute tribunals inferior to the Supreme Court

Our Constitution only established one Supreme Court, yet gave Congress the power to establish a lesser level of court as Congress believed were needed. Congress established District Courts and Court of Appeal subordinate to the US Supreme Court. The States were allowed to establish Courts for state purposes.

The Bible provided several means of establishing courts. The original court structure appears in the Moses Organization Chart beginning at Exodus 18:20. In Moses system, the people were to bring complaints or issues to the lower level leader, if the matter was not be resolved at lower level, then elevated.

- To appoint judges and officers in every community of Israel (Deut. 16:18).
- Not to appoint as a judge, a person who is not well versed in the laws of the Torah, even if he is expert in other branches of knowledge (Deut. 1:17).
- To accept rulings of every Supreme Court in Israel (Deut. 17:11).
- Not to rebel against the orders of the Court (Deut. 17:11).

1 Samuel Chapter 7
15 And Samuel judged Israel all the days of his life.
16 And he went from year to year in circuit to Bethel, and Gilgal, and Mizpeh, and judged Israel in all those places.

10.To define and punish piracies and felonies committed on the high seas, and offences against the law of Nations;

High Seas and Piracy would not become an issue for 2000 years. The major nations had not yet established Naval forces. There was not yet a LAW OF NATIONS. However, Mosaic Law provides a few provisions that move in that direction:

1. Not to make covenant with seven idolatrous nations (Ex. 23:20-32; Deut. 7:2). (Amorites, Hittites, Perizzites, the Canaanites, Hivites, Jebusites, or Philistines)
2. Not to keep alive any individual of the seven Canaanite nations (Deut. 20:16).
3. To exterminate the seven Canaanite nations from the land of Israel (Deut. 20:17).
4. Not to offer peace to Ammonites and Moabites before waging war on them, as should be done to other nations (Deut. 23:7).

11.To declare War, Grant Letters of Marque and Reprisal, and make rules concerning captures on Land and Water.

The Bible applies the word WAR over 250 times. Declaration of War is never indicated, while peace is a constant theme of the Bible. Instead of Declaration of War, God ordered the Hebrew people following Exodus, to engage in several wars so that they could retake the Holy Land following their absence of 430 years. Understand that the Hebrews abandoned the Holy Land during an extended period of famine that nearly starved them to death. They remained in Egypt 430 years, until God ordered Moses to "get my people out."

Chapter and Verse regarding Warfare.

- 1 Chronicles 12:33 Of Zebulun, such as went forth to battle, expert in war, with all instruments of war, fifty thousand, they were not of double heart.

- Joel 3:9 Proclaim ye this among the Gentiles; Prepare war, wake up the mighty men, let all the men of war draw near; let them come up:
- Numbers 31:6 And Moses sent them to the war, a thousand of every tribe, them, and Phinehas the son of Eleazar the priest, to the war, with the holy instruments, and the trumpets to blow.
- 1 Chronicles 5:18 The sons of Reuben, and the Gadites, and half the tribe of Manasseh, of valiant men, able to bear buckler and sword, to shoot with bow, skillful in war, were four and forty thousand seven hundred and threescore.
- 1 Kings 2:5 Moreover thou knowest also what Joab the son of Zeruiah did to me, and what he did to the two captains of the hosts of Israel, unto Abner the son of Ner, and unto Amasa the son of Jether, whom he slew, and shed the blood of war in peace, and put the blood of war upon his girdle that was about his loins, and in his shoes that were on his feet.
- 2 Samuel 22:35 He teacheth my hands to war; so that a bow of steel is broken by mine arms.
- Psalms 18:34 He teacheth my hands to war, so that a bow of steel is broken by mine arms.

The 613 Laws have delineated many chapter and verse statements regarding the rules of war.

<u>12.To raise and support armies, but no appropriation of money to that use shall be for a longer term than two years.</u>

God had Moses to number the fighting age men of each of the twelve tribes and to be prepared to make war when and if needed.

NUMBERS CHAPTER 1

19As the LORD commanded Moses, he numbered them in the wilderness of Sinai.
20The children of Reuben, Israel's eldest son, by their generations, after their families, by the house of their fathers, according to the number of the names, by their polls, every male from twenty years old upward, all that were able to go to war;

21Those that were numbered of them, *even* of the tribe of
Reuben, *were* forty and six thousand and five hundred.
23Those that were numbered of them, *even* of the tribe of
Simeon, *were* fifty and nine thousand and three hundred.
24Of the children of Gad, by their generations, after their families,
by the house of their fathers, according to the number of names,
twenty years old and upward, all that were able to go forth to war;
25Those that were numbered of them, *even* of the tribe of
Gad, *were* forty and five thousand six hundred and fifty.
26Of the children of Judah, by their generations, after their families,
by the house of their fathers, according to the number of names,
twenty years old and upward, all that were able to go forth to war;
27Those that were numbered of them, *even* of the tribe of
Judah, *were* threescore and fourteen thousand and six hundred.
28Of the children of Issachar, by their generations, after their
families, by the house of their fathers, according to the number of
the names, from twenty years old and upward, all that were able to
go forth to war;
29Those that were numbered of them, *even* of the tribe of
Issachar, *were* fifty and four thousand and four hundred.
30Of the children of Zebulun, by their generations, after their
families, by the house of their fathers, according to the number of
the names, from twenty years old and upward, all that were able to
go forth to war;
31Those that were numbered of them, *even* of the tribe of
Zebulun, *were* fifty and seven thousand and four hundred.
32Of the children of Joseph, *namely*, of the children of Ephraim, by
their generations, after their families, by the house of their fathers,
according to the number of the names, from twenty years old and
upward, all that were able to go forth to war;
33Those that were numbered of them, *even* of the tribe of
Ephraim, *were* forty thousand and five hundred.
34Of the children of Manasseh, by their generations, after their
families, by the house of their fathers, according to the number of
the names, from twenty years old and upward, all that were able to
go forth to war;

35Those that were numbered of them, *even* of the tribe of
Manasseh, *were* thirty and two thousand and two hundred.
36Of the children of Benjamin, by their generations, after their
families, by the house of their fathers, according to the number of
the names, from twenty years old and upward, all that were able to
go forth to war;
37Those that were numbered of them, *even* of the tribe of
Benjamin, *were* thirty and five thousand and four hundred.
38Of the children of Dan, by their generations, after their families,
by the house of their fathers, according to the number of names,
twenty years old and upward, all that were able to go forth to war;
39Those that were numbered of them, *even* of the tribe of
Dan, *were* threescore and two thousand and seven hundred.
40Of the children of Asher, by their generations, after their families,
by the house of their fathers, according to the number of names,
twenty years old and upward, all that were able to go forth to war;
41Those that were numbered of them, *even* of the tribe of
Asher, *were* forty and one thousand and five hundred.
42Of the children of Naphtali, throughout their generations, after
their families, by the house of their fathers, according to the number
of the names, from twenty years old and upward, all that were able
to go forth to war;
43Those that were numbered of them, *even* of the tribe of
Naphtali, *were* fifty and three thousand and four hundred.
44These *are* those that were numbered, which Moses and Aaron
numbered, and the princes of Israel, *being* twelve men: each one
was for the house of his fathers.
45So all those that were numbered of the children of Israel, by the
house of their fathers, twenty years old and upward, all that were
able to go forth to war in Israel;
46Even all they that were numbered were six hundred thousand
and three thousand and five hundred and fifty.
47But the Levites after the tribe of their fathers were not numbered.
48For the LORD had spoken unto Moses, saying,
49Only thou shalt not number the tribe of Levi, neither take the sum
of them among the children of Israel:

50But thou shalt appoint the Levites over the tabernacle of testimony, and over all the vessels thereof, and over all things that *belong* to it: they shall bear the tabernacle, and all the vessels thereof; and they shall minister unto it and shall encamp round about the tabernacle.

Bible Chapter and Verse on Warfare supports many Clauses

- 1 Chronicles 12:33 Of Zebulun, such as went forth to battle, expert in war, with all instruments of war, fifty thousand, which could keep rank: they were not of double heart.
- Joel 3:9 Proclaim ye this among the Gentiles; Prepare war, wake up the mighty men, let all the men of war draw near; let them come up:
- Numbers 31:6 And Moses sent them to the war, a thousand of every tribe, them and Phinehas the son of Eleazar the priest, to the war, with holy instruments, and trumpets to blow in his hand.
- 1 Chronicles 5:18 The sons of Reuben, and the Gadites, and half the tribe of Manasseh, of valiant men, men able to bear buckler and sword, and to shoot with bow, and skillful in war, were four and forty thousand seven hundred and threescore, that went out to the war.
- 1 Kings 2:5 Moreover thou knowest also what Joab the son of Zeruiah did to me, and what he did to the two captains of the hosts of Israel, unto Abner the son of Ner, and unto Amasa the son of Jether, whom he slew, and shed the blood of war in peace, and put the blood of war upon his girdle that was about his loins, and in his shoes that were on his feet.
- 2 Samuel 22:35 He teacheth my hands to war; so that a bow of steel is broken by mine arms.
- Psalms 18:34 He teacheth my hands to war, so that a bow of steel is broken by mine arms.

As you can see, God and Moses provided 603,550 men for war from among the twelve tribes of the Hebrews.

13.To provide and maintain a Navy;

There were merchant cargo ships at work around the Mediterranean in the old Testament. The first Navy ships for warfare were not documented prior to the Greco-Persian Wars , 499 – 449 BC. Navy was never a factor in Biblical days.

The very first sea-faring ship was The Ark of Noah, Genesis 6. Some 5000 years would pass until the buildup of military requirements would call for other ships greater than the Ark. God provided many advancing rules, increasing in requirement for improvements and technology. There are no military ships until about 600 BC.

14.To make rules for the Government and regulation of the land and Naval forces;

You are urged to review, once again, the 613 laws contained in the Mitzvot. You will see simple rules for government and military. During Biblical days, world population was so low that there was no need for the more difficult and demanding rules we follow today for government.

God did not provide regulations for armies. He did provide battle plans and some humanistic guidelines. The Hebrew won every battle when following the battle plan provided by God, best exemplified in the Book of Joshua.

God also tells us in Old and New Testament to care for the Widows and Orphans. This seems to appear once warfare destroyed so many men.

Now these points begin the transition from Old Testament Church Law to modern day legal code for health law, safety law, family law, and health law. Consider ramification of the following:

All Waiting Children Have a Father

God is the loving Father of all children who have been orphaned. Psalm 68:5 tells us, "Father of the fatherless and protector of widows is God in his holy habitation." His aim is to show orphans mercy, care, and protection, because waiting children are essential to him, they should be essential to us as his Church.

Children Who Have Been Orphaned Is an Injustice of This World

Justice is a fundamental part of God's character, as we are shown in the Bible. That even one child does not know the love of a family is a great injustice, and there are millions of children living in this reality.

Deuteronomy 10:18 says, "He executes justice for the fatherless and the widow, and loves the sojourner, giving him food and clothing."

Psalm 10:14 says, "But you do see, for you note mischief and vexation, that you may take it into your hands; to you the helpless commits himself; you have been the helper of the fatherless."

God promises protection and help for those who cannot protect themselves, and he redeems injustice through his unfailing love. He also asks us to do something about it. God invites everyone to play his or her part in working toward justice.

The People of God Will Care for Orphans

James 1:27 says, "Religion that is pure and undefiled before God, the Father, is: to visit orphans and widows in their affliction, to keep oneself unstained from the world."

The words of the Bible call God's people to actively pursue meeting the needs of children who have been orphaned, and a great place to start is through prayer. Your actions matter and there are many ways you can help make a difference, whether you are a prayer partner, a fundraiser, a Show Hope sponsor, or a prospective adoptive parent.

The People of God Share Their Resources With Orphans

The following verse comes from Deuteronomy where God is instructing his people about tithing. Deuteronomy 14:29 says, "And the Levite, because he has no portion or inheritance with you, and the sojourner, the fatherless, and the widow, who are within your towns, shall come and eat and be filled, that the LORD your God may bless you in all the work of your hands that you do."

People are called by God to care well for children who have been orphaned in their giving. Show Hope provides creative ways to get involved and make a difference. As you consider how God may be calling you to care for waiting children, take heart.

"He who calls you is faithful; he will surely do it" (1 Thessalonians 5:24).

15.To provide for calling forth the Militia to execute the Laws of the Union, suppress Insurrections and repel Invasions;

The US Constitution calls for regular Army and Navy, both full-time and reserves, as well as the concept of militia. In centuries prior to the Common Era, the Bible established levels of troop strength and the minimum ages of troops, along with allowances for men to be excused from military service. The Bible also chronicles how troops were to be armed. All able-bodied men were expected to be prepared to go into warfare when and if the situation called for battle.

In a previous section, we documented troop numbers established by the Bible. In this section, we will provide additional requirements established by the Bible. Bible verses related to Military Service from the King James Version (KJV) by Relevance

THE WHOLE ARMOUR OF GOD

Ephesians Chapter 6 10 Finally, my brethren, be strong in the Lord,
and in the power of his might.
11 Put on the whole armour of God, that ye may be able to stand
against the wiles of the devil.
12 For we wrestle not against flesh and blood, but against
principalities, against powers, against the rulers of darkness of this
world, against spiritual wickedness in high *places*.
13 Wherefore take unto you the whole armour of God, that ye may
be able to withstand in the evil day, and having done all, to stand.
14 Stand therefore, having your loins girt about with truth, and
having on the breastplate of righteousness;
15 And your feet shod with the preparation of the gospel of peace;
16 Above all, taking the shield of faith, wherewith ye shall be able
to quench all the fiery darts of the wicked.
17 Take the helmet of salvation, and the sword of the Spirit, which
is the word of God:
18 Praying always with all prayer and supplication in the Spirit, and
watching thereunto with all perseverance and supplication for all
saints;
Psalms 23:4 - Yea, though I walk through the valley of the shadow of death, I will fear no evil: for thou art with me; thy rod and thy staff they comfort me.

Deuteronomy 20:1 When thou goest out to battle against thine
enemies, and seest horses, and chariots, *and* a people more than
thou, be not afraid of them: for the LORD thy God *is* with thee,
which brought thee up out of the land of Egypt.
2 And it shall be, when ye are come nigh unto the battle, that the
priest shall approach and speak unto the people,
3 And shall say unto them, Hear, O Israel, ye approach this day
unto battle against your enemies: let not your hearts faint, fear not,
and do not tremble, neither be ye terrified because of them;
4 For the LORD your God *is* he that goeth with you, to fight for you
against your enemies, to save you.

16.To provide for organizing, arming, and disciplining, the Militia, and for governing such Part of them as may be employed in the Service of the United States, reserving to the States respectively, the Appointment of the Officers, and the Authority of training the Militia according to the discipline prescribed by Congress;

The bible provides signaling devices called Trumpets, along with weapons, training, and leadership.

The biblical plan for an Army is more in keeping with our modern concept of Militia instead of a standing army.

Deuteronomy 1:15 So I took the chief of your tribes, wise men, and known, and made them heads over you, captains over thousands, and captains over hundreds, and captains over fifties, and captains over tens, and officers among your tribes.

2 Samuel 18:1 And David numbered the people that were with him, and set captains of thousands and captains of hundreds over them.

Numbers 31:48 And the officers which were over thousands of the host, the captains of thousands, and captains of hundreds, came near unto Moses:

In addition to his God-ordered Militia, Solomon applied wealth to a military unit and produced a "gold-accented" horse-cavalry.

Antiquities of the Jews, 8.176—8.211
Flavius Josephus, translated by William Whiston
(Numbers in this paragraph correspond to Josephus page #)

Accordingly there went a great fame all around the neighboring countries, which proclaimed the virtue and wisdom of Solomon, insomuch that all the kings every where were desirous to see him, as not giving credit to what was reported, on account of its being almost incredible: they also demonstrated the regard they had for him by the presents they made him;

183for they sent him vessels of gold, and silver, and purple garments, and many sorts of spices, and horses, and chariots, and as many mules for his carriages as they could find proper to please the king's eyes, by their strength and beauty. This addition that he made to those chariots and horses which he had before from those that were sent him, augmented the number of his chariots by above four hundred, for he had a thousand before, and augmented the number of his horses by two thousand, for he had twenty thousand before. 184These horses also were so much exercised, in order to their making a fine appearance, and running swiftly, that no others could, upon comparison, appear either finer or swifter; but they were at once the most beautiful of all others, and their swiftness was incomparable also.

185Their riders also were a further ornament to them, being, in the first place, young men in the most delightful flower of their age, and being eminent for their largeness, and far taller than other men. They had also very long heads of hair hanging down, and were clothed in garments of Tyrian purple. They had also dust of gold every day sprinkled on their hair, so that their heads sparkled with the reflection of the sun-beams from the gold. 186The king himself rode upon a chariot in the midst of these men, who were still in armor, and had their bows fitted to them. He had on a white garment, and used to take his progress out of the city in the morning. There was a place fifty furlongs from Jerusalem, called Etham, pleasant it is in fine gardens, abounding in rivulets of water; thither did he go out in the morning, sitting high [in his chariot.

There were also the skilled slingers mentioned in the Bible.

"Among all this people *there were* seven hundred chosen men lefthanded; every one could sling stones at an hair *breadth*, and not miss" (Judges 20:16).

"And they beat down the cities, and on every good piece of land cast every man his stone, and filled it; and they stopped all the wells of water, and felled all the good trees: only in Kirharaseth left they the stones thereof; howbeit the slingers went about it, and smote it" (2 Kings 3:25).

"They were armed with bows, and could use both the right hand and the left in hurling stones and shooting arrows out of a bow, even of Saul's brethren of Benjamin" (1 Chronicles 12:2)

"Uzziah prepared for them throughout all the host shields, spears, helmets, and habergeons, and bows, and slings" (2 Chronicles 26:14).

"In Old Testament times, "slingers" were regular components of an army and were often used together with archers; during siege warfare their role was to pick off the enemy from the besieged city's ramparts. Such slingers could hurl a projectile at over one hundred miles an hour and their effective range was in excess of one hundred yards" (Alfred Hoerth, *Archaeology, and Old Testament*).

The most famous slinger in history is David.

SIGNAL INSTRUMENTS   Numbers Chapter 10

1And the LORD spake unto Moses, saying, **2Make thee two
trumpets of silver; of a whole piece shalt thou make them: that
thou mayest use them for the calling of the assembly, and for
the journeying of the camps.** 3And when they shall blow with
them, all the assembly shall assemble themselves to thee at the
door of the tabernacle of the congregation. 4And if they blow *but*
with one *trumpet*, then the princes, *which are* heads of the
thousands of Israel, shall gather themselves unto thee. 5When ye
blow an alarm, then the camps that lie on the east parts shall go
forward.

These trumpets of silver were the first metal musical instruments ever produced. A loud blast of a Trumpet may have been the very first technology advance for military purposes. Two Trumpets led the march of Hebrews, going before the Ark of The Covenant.

Judges 7:22 And the three hundred blew the trumpets, and the LORD set every man's sword against his fellow, even throughout all the host: and the host fled to Bethshittah in Zererath, and to the border of Abelmeholah, unto Tabbath.

17.To exercise exclusive Legislation in all Cases whatsoever, over such District (not exceeding ten Miles square) as may, by Cession of particular States, and Acceptance of Congress, become the Seat of the Government of the United States, and to exercise like Authority over all Places purchased by Consent of the Legislature of the State in which the Same shall be, for the Erection of Forts, Magazines, Arsenals, dock-Yards, and other needful Buildings;

US Constitution provides rules for the establishment of the Capital City of The United States. God established Jerusalem as the Seat of Power for the Hebrew people.

God established the headquarters and capital city of the Hebrews at Jerusalem. The original name was Shalem, or Shalom, or Salem, meaning Peace while Melchisedec was leader. The name changed to Jerusalem, meaning New Peace once David takes over. Jerusalem in the day of David was not as large as a big city shopping Mall, much smaller than 10 square miles. Jerusalem has remained the ceremonial center of the Hebrew world along with all Christian denominations and shall forever remain that center. Clearly very consistent with the National Capitol of these United States being established at Washington, DC.

18.To make all Laws which shall be necessary and proper for carrying into Execution the foregoing Powers, and all other Powers vested by this Constitution in the Government of the United States, or in any Department or Officer thereof.

God did not make provision for changes to the powers of the laws He provided, instead, God established a procedure for the National leader, along with the Twelve Tribal leaders and the elders to review a situation, to ensure any changes were consistent with the will of God, and to seek approval of the people. (Sounds much like a democratic republic situation). There was no intent to make an allowance to change the Word of God. However, God allowed his people to work together and craft other rules or regulations as necessary to strongly functioning society.

Article. I

Section. 9.

1.The Migration or Importation of such Persons as any of the States now existing shall think proper to admit, shall not be prohibited by the Congress prior to the Year one thousand eight hundred and eight, but a Tax or duty may be imposed on such Importation, not exceeding ten dollars for each Person

KJV Deuteronomy Chapter 23

1He that is wounded in the stones, or hath his privy member cut
off, shall not enter into the congregation of the LORD.
2 A bastard shall not enter into the congregation of the LORD; even
to his tenth generation shall he not enter into the congregation of
the LORD.
3 An Ammonite or Moabite shall not enter into the congregation of
the LORD; even to their tenth generation shall they not enter into
the congregation of the LORD for ever:
4 Because they met you not with bread and with water, when ye
came forth out of Egypt; and because they hired against thee
Balaam the son of Beor of Pethor of Mesopotamia, to curse thee.
5 Nevertheless the LORD thy God would not hearken unto Balaam;
but the LORD thy God turned the curse into a blessing, because
the LORD thy God loved thee.
6 Thou shalt not seek their peace nor their prosperity all thy days.
7 Thou shalt not abhor an Edomite; for he *is* thy brother: thou shalt
not abhor an Egyptian; because thou wast a stranger in his land.
8 The children that are begotten of them shall enter into the
congregation of the LORD in their third generation.

2.The Privilege of Writ of Habeas Corpus shall not be suspended, unless when in Cases of Rebellion or Invasion the public Safety may require it.

Habeus Corpus is a time-honored legal requirement whereby, a writ requiring a person under arrest to be brought before a judge or into court, especially to secure the person's release unless lawful grounds are shown for their detention, as in "his application for habeas corpus."

Biblical chapter and verse were written far before the day in which the process of Habeus corpus was established. However, chapter and verse make it clear that we must be granted a lawful decision based upon testimony, witnesses, evidence, with Judges who are men of courage, hating covetousness. Appeals are in order early in the second book of the Bible.

The following verses come close to Habeas Corpus.

Leviticus 5:1-19
"If anyone sins in that he hears a public adjuration to testify, and though he is a witness, whether he has seen or come to know the matter, yet does not speak, he shall bear his iniquity; or if anyone touches an unclean thing, whether a carcass of an unclean wild animal or a carcass of unclean livestock or a carcass of unclean swarming things, and it is hidden from him and he has become unclean, and he realizes his guilt; or if he touches human uncleanness, of whatever sort the uncleanness may be with which one becomes unclean, and it is hidden from him, when he comes to know it, and realizes his guilt; or if anyone utters with his lips a rash oath to do evil or to do good, any sort of rash oath that people swear, and it is hidden from him, when he comes to know it, and he realizes his guilt in any of these; when he realizes his guilt in any of these and confesses the sin he has committed,

Zephaniah 2:1-15
Gather together, yes, gather, O shameless nation, before the decree takes effect —before the day passes away like chaff— before there comes upon you the burning anger of the LORD, before there comes upon you the day of the anger of the LORD. Seek the LORD, all you humble of the land, who do his just commands; seek righteousness; seek humility; perhaps you may be hidden on the day of the anger of the LORD.

For Gaza shall be deserted, and Ashkelon shall become a desolation; Ashdod's people shall be driven out at noon, and Ekron shall be uprooted. Woe to you inhabitants of the seacoast, you nation of the Cherethites! The word of the LORD is against you, O Canaan, land of the Philistines; and I will destroy you until no inhabitant is left. ...

Matthew 7:1-29
"Judge not, that you be not judged. For with the judgment, you pronounce you will be judged, and with the measure you use it will be measured to you. Why do you see the speck that is in your brother's eye, but do not notice the log that is in your own eye? Or how can you say to your brother, 'Let me take the speck out of your eye,' when there is the log in your own eye? You hypocrite, first take the log out of your own eye, and then you will see clearly to take the speck out of your brother's eye. ...

John 3:16-21
"For God so loved the world, that he gave his only Son, that whoever believes in him should not perish but have eternal life. For God did not send his Son into the world to condemn the world, but in order that the world might be saved through him. Whoever believes in him is not condemned, but whoever does not believe is condemned already, because he has not believed in the name of the only Son of God. And this is the judgment: the light has come into the world, and people loved the darkness rather than the light because their works were evil. For everyone who does wicked things hates the light and does not come to the light, lest his works should be exposed. ...

In the investigation leading to the crucifixion of Jesus Christ, we see the principle of Habeas Corpus almost work. Jesus was taken before the high Judge/governor and questioned. The Roman governor Pontius Pilate, three times attempted to free Jesus as he found no fault. Then the misguided Sanhedrin caused habeas corpus principle to fail, leading to Jesus crucifixion.

Matthew 27

1.When the morning was come, all the chief priests and elders of the people took counsel against Jesus to put him to death:
2And when they had bound him, they led *him* away, and delivered him to Pontius Pilate the governor.
3Then Judas, which betrayed him, when he saw that he was condemned, repented himself, and brought again the thirty pieces of silver to the chief priests and elders,
4Saying, I have sinned in that I have betrayed the innocent blood. And they said, What *is that* to us? see thou *to that.*
5And he cast down the pieces of silver in the temple, and departed, and went and hanged himself.
6And the chief priests took the silver pieces, and said, It is not lawful for to put them into the treasury, it is the price of blood.
7They took counsel, and bought with them the potter's field, to bury strangers in.
8Wherefore that field was called, The field of blood, unto this day.
9Then was fulfilled that which was spoken by Jeremy the prophet, saying, And they took the thirty pieces of silver, the price of him that was valued, whom they of the children of Israel did value;
10And gave them for the potter's field, as the Lord appointed me.
11And Jesus stood before the governor: and the governor asked him, saying, Art thou the King of the Jews? And Jesus said unto him, Thou sayest.
12And when he was accused of the chief priests and elders, he answered nothing.
13Pilate said to him, Hearest thou not how many things they witness against thee?
14And he answered him to never say a word; and the governor marveled greatly.
15Now at *that* feast the governor was wont to release unto the people a prisoner, whom they would.
16And they had then a notable prisoner, called Barabbas.
17Therefore when they were gathered together, Pilate said unto them, Whom will ye that I release unto you? Barabbas, or Jesus which is called Christ?

18For he knew that for envy they had delivered him.
19When he was set down on the judgment seat, his wife sent unto
him, saying, Have thou nothing to do with that just man: for I have
suffered many things this day in a dream because of him.
20But the chief priests and elders persuaded the multitude that
they should ask Barabbas, and destroy Jesus.
21The governor answered and said unto them, Whether of the
twain will ye that I release unto you? They said, Barabbas.
22Pilate saith unto them, What shall I do then with Jesus which is
called Christ? *They* all say unto him, Let him be crucified.
23And the governor said, Why, what evil hath he done? But they
cried out the more, saying, Let him be crucified.
24When Pilate saw that he could prevail nothing, but *that* rather a
tumult was made, he took water, and washed *his* hands before the
multitude, saying, I am innocent of the blood of this just person:
see ye *to it*.
25Then answered all the people, and said, His blood *be* on us, and
on our children.
26Then released he Barabbas unto them: and when he had
scourged Jesus, he delivered *him* to be crucified.
27Then the soldiers of the governor took Jesus into the common
hall, and gathered unto him the whole band *of soldiers*.
28And they stripped him, and put on him a scarlet robe.
29And when they had platted a crown of thorns, they put *it* upon
his head, and a reed in his right hand: and they bowed the knee
before him, and mocked him, saying, Hail, King of the Jews!
30And they spit upon him, took the reed, smote him on the head.
31And after that they had mocked him, they took the robe off from
him, and put his own raiment on him, and led him away to
crucify *him*.
32And as they came out, they found a man of Cyrene, Simon by
name: him they compelled to bear his cross.
33When they were come unto a place called Golgotha, a place of
a skull,
34They gave him vinegar to drink mingled with gall: and when he
had tasted *thereof*, he would not drink.

35And they crucified him, and parted his garments, casting lots:
that it might be fulfilled which was spoken by the prophet, They
parted my garments among them, and upon my vesture did they
cast lots.
36And sitting down they watched him there;
37And set up over his head his accusation written,

THIS IS JESUS THE KING OF THE JEWS.

38There two thieves crucified with him, one on the right hand,
another on the left.
39And they that passed by reviled him, wagging their heads,
40And saying, Thou that destroyest the temple, and buildest *it* in
three days, save thyself. If thou be the Son of God, come down
from the cross.
41Likewise the chief priests mocking *him*, scribes and elders, said,
42He saved others; himself he cannot save. If he be the King of
Israel, let him come down from the cross, and we will believe him.
43He trusted in God; let him deliver him now, if he will have him:
for he said, I am the Son of God.
44The thieves also, which were crucified with him, cast the same
in his teeth.
45Now from the sixth hour there was darkness over all the land
unto the ninth hour.
46And about the ninth hour Jesus cried with a loud voice,
saying, Eli, Eli, lama sabachthani? that is to say, My God, my God,
why hast thou forsaken me?
47Some that stood there when they heard *that*, said,
This *man* calleth for Elias.
48And straightway one of them ran, and took a spunge, and
filled *it* with vinegar, and put *it* on a reed, and gave him to drink.
49The rest said, Let be, let us see whether Elias will save him.
50Jesus, when he had cried with a loud voice, yielded up the ghost.
51And, behold, the veil of the temple was rent in twain from the top
to the bottom; and the earth did quake, and the rocks rent;
52And the graves were opened; and many bodies of the saints
which slept arose,

53And came out of the graves after his resurrection, and went into
the holy city, and appeared unto many.
54Now when the centurion, and they that were with him, watching
Jesus, saw the earthquake, and those things that were done, they
feared greatly, saying, Truly this was the Son of God.

We have demonstrated that God ordered levels of courts and levels of Judges to deal with all possible legal scenarios. Please refer to the chapter of 613 laws.

3.No Bill of Attainder or ex post facto Law shall be passed.

Ex Post Facto means that laws may not be established that penalize any that came before, or cannot apply retroactively. In the Exodus, Moses remains on the mountain with God some 40 days (Exodus 32). One of the laws God gave Moses ordered no other gods be worshipped, yet while Moses is receiving the law, the Hebrews built the Golden Calf as a false god, thus when Moses returned and found the Hebrews worshipping the golden calf, he found a condition in which the new laws of God might not apply. We suggest God intended the principle of ex post facto, due to Moses throwing the tablets of the 10 commandments to destroy the golden calf and returning up the mountain to receive the laws once again, followed by God's refusal to allow those who worshipped the Golden Calf to return to the Promised Land.

In the Bible, we learn that God took offense to a Census, therefore taxation should not be applied on a census basis, as proven by the following Biblical verses.

Clause 4.
No Capitation or Direct Tax unless per Census

1 Chronicles 21

Satan stood up against Israel, provoked David to number Israel.
2 And David said to Joab and to the rulers of the people, Go,
number Israel from Beersheba even to Dan; and bring the
number of them to me, that I may know it.

3 And Joab answered, The LORD make his people an hundred
times so many more as they be: but my lord the king, are they not
all my lord's servants? why then doth my lord require this thing?
why will he be a cause of trespass to Israel?
4 The king's word prevailed against Joab. Wherefore Joab
departed, and went throughout all Israel, and came to Jerusalem.
5 And Joab gave the sum of the number of the people unto David.
And all they of Israel were a thousand thousand and an hundred
thousand men that drew sword: and Judah was four hundred
threescore and ten thousand men that drew sword.
6 Levi and Benjamin counted he not among them: for the king's
word was abominable to Joab.
7 God was displeased with this thing; therefore he smote Israel.
8 David said unto God, I have sinned greatly, because I have
done this thing: I beseech thee, do away the iniquity of thy
servant; for I have done very foolishly.
9 And the LORD spake unto Gad, David's seer, saying,
10 Go and tell David, saying, Thus saith the LORD, I offer thee
three things: choose thee one of them, that I may do it unto thee.
11 Gad came to David, and said unto him, Thus saith the LORD,
12 Either three years' famine; or three months to be destroyed
before thy foes, while sword of thine enemies overtaketh; or else
three days the sword of the LORD, even pestilence, in the land,
angel of the LORD destroying throughout all coasts of Israel.
13 And David said unto Gad, I am in a great strait: let me fall now
into the hand of the LORD; for very great are his mercies: but let
me not fall into the hand of man.
14 The LORD sent pestilence on Israel: there fell of Israel seventy
thousand men.
15 God sent an angel to destroy Jerusalem: as he was destroying,
the LORD beheld, he repented him of evil, and said to the angel
that destroyed, It is enough, stay thine hand. And the angel of the
LORD stood by the threshing floor of Ornan the Jebusite.
16 And David lifted up his eyes, and saw the angel of the LORD stand
between the earth and the heaven, having a drawn sword in his
hand stretched out over Jerusalem. Then David and the elders of
Israel, who were clothed in sackcloth, fell upon their faces.

[17] And David said unto God, Is it not I that commanded the people
to be numbered? even I it is that have sinned and done evil
indeed; but as for these sheep, what have they done? let thine
hand, I pray thee, O LORD my God, be on me, and on my father's
house; but not on thy people, that they should be plagued.
[18] The angel of the LORD commanded Gad to say to David, that
David should go up, and set up an altar unto the LORD in the
threshing floor of Ornan the Jebusite.
[19] David went up at the saying of Gad, which he spake in the
name of the LORD.
[20] And Ornan turned back, and saw the angel; and his four sons
with him hid themselves. Now Ornan was threshing wheat.
[21] And as David came to Ornan, Ornan looked and saw David,
and went out of the threshing floor, and bowed himself to David
with his face to the ground.
[22] Then David said to Ornan, Grant me the place of this threshing
floor, that I may build an altar to the LORD: thou shalt grant it me
for the full price: that the plague may be stayed from the people.
[23] And Ornan said unto David, Take it to thee, and let my lord the
king do that which is good in his eyes: lo, I give thee the oxen
also for burnt offerings, and the threshing instruments for wood,
and the wheat for the meat offering; I give it all.
[24] And king David said to Ornan, Nay; but I will verily buy it for the
full price: for I will not take that which is thine for the LORD, nor
offer burnt offerings without cost.
[25] So David gave to Ornan six hundred shekels of gold by weight.
[26] David built an altar unto the LORD, offered burnt offerings and
peace offerings, and called upon the LORD; he answered from
heaven by fire upon altar of offering.
[27] And the LORD commanded the angel; and he put up his sword.
[28] At that time, David saw that the LORD had answered him in the
threshing floor of Ornan the Jebusite, then he sacrificed there.
[29] For the tabernacle of the LORD, which Moses made in the
wilderness, and the altar of the burnt offering, were at that season
in the high place at Gibeon.
[30] But David could not go before it to enquire of God: for he was
afraid because of the sword of the angel of the LORD.

5.No Tax or Duty shall be laid on Articles exported from any State.

See explanation for Clause 6.

6.No Preference shall be given by any Regulation of Commerce or Revenue to the Ports of one State over those of another: nor shall Vessels bound to, or from, one State, be obliged to enter, clear, or pay Duties in another.

An argument can be made that the Twelve Tribes of Israel had been allotted State sized regions for their tribes habitation and therefore might be considered States.

The concept of States as subunits of nations had not come into utilization at this time in history. Concept of States may not have commenced until the Roman Empire spread around the Mediterranean Sea. The Bible does not discuss this issue. Beginning in the day of Nebuchadnezzar, outlying Provinces were recognized and by the time of Xerxes, we learn that the Second World Kingdom of Cyrus had gained control of 129 provinces, as documented beginning in the Books of Daniel and Esther. The concept of duties upon Ports had not yet commenced.

7.No Money shall be drawn from Treasury, but in Consequence of Appropriations made by Law; and a regular Statement and Account of the Receipts and Expenditures of all public Money shall be published from time to time.

The modern US Congress makes budgets for all expenditures and attempts to balance taxes collected with expenditures. In the Bible, we are told to pay tithes of differing amounts into the temple. These tithes were nearly the equivalent of taxes, as the church was the only government of the day, prior to the midpoint of the Roman Republic, at about 200BC. The ancient Church was to collect only those additional tithes that were sometimes required to ensure "plenty" at the religious festivals ordered by God.

The large sections above dealing with Biblical tithes will show you the orders of God that were implemented beginning in the day of Moses. Some of those tithes/taxes could be considered heavier, yet all were designed to provide enough to sustain the church, which was the government in that day. There were indeed many categories established for purposes of tithes to support.

The section above on Tithes/Taxes provides strong biblical intent.

<u>8.No Title of Nobility shall be granted by the United States: And no Person holding any Office of Profit or Trust under them, shall, without the Consent of Congress, accept of any present, Emolument, Office, or Title, of any kind whatever, from any King, Prince, or foreign State.</u>

When Moses establishes his organization chart, levels of leadership are referred to as Leaders, Judges, Captains. Other titles are Elders and Priests and Levites. No title of nobility enters the Biblical narrative until God allows Samuel to anoint Saul and David as King. The title of King was in use by non Hebrew nations.

Samuel actually provides an entire chapter outlining the dangers presented by the concept of Kings and/or Royalty.

1 Samuel 8 King James Version

1 And it came to pass, when Samuel was old, he made his sons judges over Israel.
2 Now the name of his firstborn was Joel; and the name of his second, Abiah: they were judges in Beersheba.
3 And his sons walked not in his ways, but turned aside after lucre, and took bribes, and perverted judgment.
4 Then all the elders of Israel gathered themselves together, and came to Samuel,
5 And said unto him, Behold, thou art old, and thy sons walk not in thy ways: now make us a king to judge us like all the nations.
6 But the thing displeased Samuel, when they said, Give us a king to judge us. And Samuel prayed unto the LORD.

7 The LORD said unto Samuel, Hearken unto the voice of the
people in all they say: they have not rejected thee, but have
rejected me, that I should not reign over them.
8 According to all the works which they have done since the day
that I brought them up out of Egypt even unto this day, wherewith
they have forsaken me, and served other gods, so do they also
unto thee.
9 Now therefore hearken unto their voice: howbeit yet protest
solemnly unto them, and shew them the manner of the king that
shall reign over them.
10 Samuel told all the words of the LORD unto the people that asked
of him a king.
11 This is the manner of the king reigning over you: He will take your
sons, appoint them for himself, his chariots, his horsemen; some
shall run before his chariots.
12 He will appoint captains of thousands, captains over fifties; set
them to his ground, to reap his harvest, make instruments of war,
and instruments of chariots.
13 And he will take your daughters to be confectionaries, to be
cooks, to be bakers.
14 And he will take your fields, and your vineyards, and your
oliveyards, even the best of them, and give them to his servants.
15 And he will take the tenth of your seed, and of your vineyards,
and give to his officers, and to his servants.
16 And he will take your menservants, and your maidservants, and
your goodliest young men, and your asses, put them to his work.
17 He will take the tenth of your sheep: and ye shall be his servants.
18 And ye shall cry out in that day because of your king which ye
shall have chosen you; and the LORD will not hear you in that day.
19 Nevertheless the people refused to obey the voice of Samuel;
and they said, Nay; but we will have a king over us;
20 That we be like all the nations; that our king may judge us, and
fight our battles.

1 Samuel 9 King James Version

9:1 There was a man of Benjamin, named Kish, the son of Abiel,
the son of Zeror, the son of Bechorath, the son of Aphiah, a
Benjamite, a mighty man of power.

2 And he had a son, whose name was Saul, a choice young man,
and a goodly: and there was not among the children of Israel a
goodlier person than he: from his shoulders and upward he was
higher than any of the people.
15 The LORD had told Samuel a day before Saul came, saying,
16 Tomorrow about this time I will send a man out of land of
Benjamin, thou shalt anoint him a captain over my people Israel,
that he may save my people from the Philistines: for I have
looked upon my people, because their cry is come unto me.
17 And when Samuel saw Saul, the LORD said unto him, Behold
the man whom I spake of! this same shall reign over my people.
18 Saul drew near Samuel, and said, Tell, where seer's house is.

1 Samuel 10:24 Samuel said to all the people, See ye him whom
the LORD hath chosen, that there is none like him among all the
people? And the people shouted, and said, God save the king.
25 Samuel told the people the manner of the kingdom, wrote it in a
book, and laid it before the LORD. Samuel sent the people away.
26 And Saul also went home to Gibeah; and there went with him a
band of men, whose hearts God had touched.

1 Samuel 16 GOD orders Samuel to anoint David as King.
And the LORD said unto Samuel, How long wilt thou mourn for
Saul, seeing I have rejected him from reigning over Israel? fill thine
horn with oil, and go, I will send thee to Jesse the Bethlehemite: for
I have provided me a king among his sons.
2And Samuel said, How can I go? if Saul hear *it*, he will kill me.
And the LORD said, Take an heifer with thee, and say, I am come
to sacrifice to the LORD.
12 He sent, and brought him in. Now he was rudy, and of a beautiful
countenance, and goodly to look at. And the LORD said, Arise,
anoint him: for this is he
13 Samuel took the horn of oil, anointed him in midst of his brethren:
and Spirit of the LORD came upon David from that day forward.
Samuel rose and went to Ramah.
14 Spirit of the LORD departed from Saul, an evil spirit from the
LORD troubled him.
15 And Saul's servants said unto him, Behold, an evil spirit from God
troubleth thee.

Article. I

Section. 10.

1.No State shall enter into any Treaty, Alliance, or Confederation; grant Letters of Marque and Reprisal; coin Money; emit Bills of Credit; make any Thing but gold and silver Coin a Tender in Payment of Debts; pass any Bill of Attainder, ex post facto Law, or Law impairing the Obligation of Contracts, or grant any Title of Nobility.

Solomon appears to be the first King in history, 900 BC, to establish EXPORT as a means to increase National Wealth. Solomon would order the Hebrew fleet, one year out of three, to load with the very finest produce of Israel and to travel and trade the produce until the entire cargo had been converted to Gold or Silver or other precious commodity. Solomon doubled the national wealth of Israel, often called the Wealth of Solomon, within 30 years.

1 Kings 10
14Now the weight of gold that came to Solomon in one year was six hundred threescore and six talents of gold,
15Beside *that he had* the merchantmen, and the traffic the spice merchants, and of all kings of Arabia, and of governors.
16Solomon made two hundred targets *of* beaten gold: six hundred *shekels* of gold went to one target.
17And *he made* three hundred shields *of* beaten gold; three pound of gold went to one shield: and the king put them in the house of the forest of Lebanon.
18Moreover the king made a throne of ivory, overlaid with gold.
19The throne had six steps, and the top of the throne *was* round: *there were* stays on either side on the place of the seat, and two lions stood beside the stays.
20And twelve lions stood there on the one side and on the other upon the six steps: there was not the like made in any kingdom.

21All king Solomon's drinking vessels *were of* gold, all the vessels of the house of the forest of Lebanon *were of* gold; none *were of* silver: it was nothing accounted of in the days of Solomon.
22For the king had at sea a navy of Tharshish with the navy of Hiram: once in three years came the navy of Tharshish, bringing gold, silver, ivory, apes, and peacocks.

2.Duties and Imposts, laid by any State on Imports or Exports, shall be for the Use of the Treasury of the United States; and all such Laws shall be subject to the Revision and Controul of the Congress.

We documented in many passages above that no tax, impost, or duty existed on imports or exports. Instead, Solomon utilized import/export as a means of building national wealth. About 500 years beyond Moses, Solomon attained massive wealth by export, and Solomon is first in history to profit so heavily on export.

3.No State shall, without the Consent of Congress, lay any Duty of Tonnage, keep Troops, or Ships of War in time of Peace, enter into any Agreement or Compact with another State, or with a foreign Power, or engage in War, unless actually invaded, or in such imminent Danger as will not admit of delay.

We have established above in many chapters that no taxes, duties, or imposts, non tonnage duties were utilized. Whereas the Hebrew leaders of each of the twelve tribes were assigned a large number of men to be prepared for war, there were no standing armies or navies. In our modern language, we can say that a "militia" force was always at the ready to defend if needed.

All the ship strength in that day was dedicated to mercantile shipping activity, albeit the ships could be called together for combat activity if needed. We established earlier that treaties were executed among sovereign Kings, who sealed the agreement by providing each other a wife from among his own family, creating a treaty on brotherhood.

We documented in many passages above that no tax, impost, or duty existed on imports or exports. Instead, Solomon utilized import/export as a means of building national wealth. About 500 years beyond Moses, Solomon attained massive wealth by export, Solomon seems first in history to profit so heavily on export.

Article. 2.

Section.1.

THIS SECTION ESTABLISHES THE OFFICE AND STATUS OF PRESIDENT AND VICE PRESIDENT OF THE UNITED STATES, PLUS ELECTION RULES AND CITIZENSHIP ISSUES!!

The original US Constitution contained scant lexicon on the citizenship issue. That is because more than half our population in 1776 were recent immigrants. Constitutional Convention delegates chose to leave the citizenship issue for a future time, following establishment of a working constitution, and then they would satisfy this clear issue called citizenship and establish the necessary laws to create citizenship.

Now in 2026, we are faced with an even greater plethora of actions that continue to skew legal immigration and citizenship. While Congress has not yet fully satisfied clear means to establish legal immigration and means to transcend to full citizenship, we are beset with another related issue being called "Birthright Citizenship" which has no clear passage of associated laws pro or con.

We have a need to write an account of where we stand today in 2026 so that future readers will understand why our book is less than clear on the birthright issue. That is because there is no clear prevailing law on these issues. The only clear citizenship rule is that you have been born in America to individuals who have been in country indefinitely, for some period of time. Then you become a natural born citizen at birth.

The Map of Israel below can be considered the equivalent of States in ancient days. Each of the twelve Tribes could be considered a State in our modern language and form of government.

THE TWELVE TRIBES OF ISRAEL
Around 1200-1050 B.C.
(according to the Book of Joshua)
Mediterranean Sea
ARAMEANS
ASHER
NAPHTALI
ZEBULUN
ISSACHAR
MANASSEH
BASAN
EPHRAIM
DAN
BENJAMIN
GAD
AMMON
REUBEN
JUDAH
PHILISTIA
SIMEON
MOAB
EDOM
AMALEK
Wilderness of Zin
Dead Sea
Sidon
Tyre
Ijon
Dan
Kedesh
Hazor
Chinnereth
Ashteroth
Achshaph
Hamath
Helkath
Mount Tabor
Jokneam
Dor
Edrei
Camon
Japhia
Megiddo
Jezreel
Taanach
Bethshean
Ramoth-Gilead
Tirzah
Shamir
Zaphon
Shechem
Mahanaim
Pirathon
Gathrimmon
Aphek
Shiloh
Joppa
Bethel
Bethoron
Ai
Gilgal
Jazer
Rabbath Ammon
Eltekeh
Gezer
Gibeon
Jericho
Gibbethon
Ekron
Jerusalem
Heshbon
Mephaath
Ashdod
Bezer
Mount Nebo
Ashkelon
Gath
Jarmuth
Bethlehem
Lachish
Hebron
Jahaza
Gaza
Debir
Eshtemoa
Gerar
Arad
Beersheba
Kirhareseth
Zoar
Tamar
Zalmona
Bozrah
Kadesh
Punon

America has established a number of procedures whereby immigrants may apply for citizenship. We will begin with the concepts of 1) birthright citizenship, 2) naturalized citizenship, 3) immigration rules, 4) refugee status if endangered in home country.

Birthright Citizenship has never been declared a valid form of citizenship. A modern court opinion has declared that the Civil War era Dred Scot case which sought clear citizenship for slaves provided precedent for Birthright Citizenship, wherein, if you are born in America, then you are a citizen. Now in the past decades, we have become overrun with foreign citizens coming to America to give birth, and expect then to return to the home country, expecting their children that are born in America are to be citizens. There is zero indication of birthright citizenship to be found in our Holy Bible. If it exists, then it is for Hebrews that have become scattered around the world. The Bible declares that those Hebrews remain citizens of Israel if they have continued to worship via all the ceremonies and beliefs declared by the bible.

Then we have naturalized citizenship procedures that have been legally established, albeit never in the Founding Fathers Constitution. The great philosopher Socrates once spoke that governments were free to establish rules for citizenship, and he concluded those remarks by saying "but the immigrant needs to have been in country for some length of time first. In modern legal terms, we apply the term assimilation, meaning they must assimilate to our language, customs, and laws and religion.

Immigration legalities are broad and varied. The bible applies the term "sojourners" or travelers. The bible says we should welcome the sojourners and they should be free to remain with us for a time, for as long as they obey our customs, laws, and religious rituals. Then this lays the groundwork for a rather stiff biblical rule for actual citizenship.

Refugee status laws have been crafted so that we in the freedom of America may assist those foreigners who are in great danger within their home countries. Refugee status may be brief and limited, or be allowed to continue for longer times.

Biblical Citizenship Rules ordered by God, dictated to Moses

There are three sets of rather simple but tough citizenship rules.

-Those from Friendly Nations (Third Generation in Country).
-Those from Unfriendly Nations (Tenth Generation in Country).
-Those hailing from our greatest enemy Nations (Never).

Third Generation, as stated in the bible indicates immigrants from friendly nations shall be allowed to apply for citizenship once they have resided in country for Three Generations beyond the original immigrant. (Deuteronomy 23:1-8)

Tenth Generation, as stated in the bible indicates that immigrants from unfriendly nations shall not be granted citizenship or allowed to apply for citizenship until they have resided in country for Ten Generations beyond the original immigrant. (Deuteronomy 23:1-8)

Those hailing from our greatest enemies shall never be allowed to become citizens. The endangered refugee issue may allow those truly endangered, an option after all. (Deut 23:1-8)

Bible chapter and verse spans broad sections of the bible, and often no clearly stated. However, the procedures stated above are consistent with US Constitution lexicon, presented by our Bible.

1.The executive Power shall be vested in a President of the United States of America. He shall hold his Office during the Term of four Years, and, together with the Vice President, chosen for the same Term, be elected, as follows.

The Bible documents the very first person in world history to be declared a President. It is important the reader understand the world setting of the day, along with the conditions in the palace before and after Daniel is named President. Nebuchadnezzar of Babylon will establish the first World Kingdom, with Daniel as his leading advisor. Nebuchadnezzar dies and a brief succession of leaders culminates with Darius becoming next King.

The World Kingdom established by Nebuchadnezzar was becoming a difficult governance task as 129 kingdoms had been conquered by Nebuchadnezzar, thus becoming the first World Empire (first indicated in Book of Daniel, verified by Book of Esther). Darius decides to seat a different plan of management featuring Daniel. Three Presidents were established with Daniel as the leading President. Daniel was retained as President through the next three successions of Kings, becoming the very first President of the First and Second World Empires.

Situations that led to Daniel becoming First President

Daniel Chapter 5
Belshazzar the king made a great feast to a thousand of his lords, and drank wine before the thousand.
2 Belshazzar, whiles he tasted the wine, commanded to bring the golden and silver vessels his father Nebuchadnezzar had taken out of the temple in Jerusalem; that the king, and his princes, his wives, and his concubines, might drink therein.
3 Then they brought the golden vessels that were taken out of the temple of the house of God which *was* at Jerusalem; and the king, and his princes, his wives, and his concubines, drank in them.
4 They drank wine, praised the gods of gold, silver, brass, iron, wood, and stone.
5 In the same hour came forth fingers of a man's hand, and wrote over against the candlestick upon the plaister of the wall of the king's palace: and the king saw the part of the hand that wrote.
6 Then the king's countenance was changed, and his thoughts troubled him, so that the joints of his loins were loosed, and his knees smote one against another.
7 The king cried aloud to bring in the astrologers, the Chaldeans, and the soothsayers. *And* the king spake, and said to the wise *men* of Babylon, Whosoever shall read this writing, and shew me the interpretation, shall be clothed with scarlet, and *have* a chain of gold about his neck, and shall be the third ruler in the kingdom.
8 Then came in all the king's wise *men*: but they could not read the writing, nor make known to the king the interpretation thereof.
9 Then was king Belshazzar greatly troubled, his countenance changed in him, and his lords were astonied.

10 *Now* the queen, by reason of the words of the king and his lords,
came into the banquet house: *and* the queen spake and said, O
king, live for ever: let not thy thoughts trouble thee, nor let thy
countenance be changed:
11 There is a man in thy kingdom, in whom *is* the spirit of the holy
gods; and in the days of thy father light and understanding and
wisdom, like the wisdom of the gods, was found in him; whom the
king Nebuchadnezzar thy father, the king, *I say*, thy father, made
master of the magicians, astrologers, Chaldeans, *and* soothsayers;
12 Forasmuch as an excellent spirit, knowledge, and
understanding, interpreting of dreams, shewing of hard sentences,
and dissolving of doubts, were found in Daniel, whom the king
named Belteshazzar: now let Daniel shew the interpretation.
13 Then was Daniel brought in before the king. *The* king spake and
said unto Daniel, *Art* thou Daniel, which *art* of the children of the
captivity of Judah, whom the king my father brought out of Jewry?
14 I have heard of thee, that the spirit of the gods *is* in thee, and
that light and understanding and excellent wisdom is found in thee.
15 And now the wise *men*, the astrologers, have been brought in
before me, that they should read this writing, and make known unto
me the interpretation thereof: but they could not shew the
interpretation of the thing:
16 And I have heard of thee, that thou canst make interpretations,
and dissolve doubts: now if thou canst read the writing, and make
known to me the interpretation thereof, thou shalt be clothed with
scarlet, and *have* a chain of gold about thy neck, and shalt be the
third ruler in the kingdom.
17 Then Daniel answered and said before the king, Let thy gifts be
to thyself, and give thy rewards to another; yet I will read the writing
unto the king, and make known to him the interpretation.
18 O thou king, the most high God gave Nebuchadnezzar thy
father a kingdom, and majesty, and glory, and honour:
19 And for the majesty that he gave him, all people, nations, and
languages, trembled and feared before him: whom he would he
slew; and whom he would he kept alive; and whom he would he
set up; and whom he would he put down.

20 But when his heart lifted up, and his mind hardened in pride, he
was deposed from his throne, and they took his glory from him:
21 And he was driven from the sons of men; and his heart was
made like the beasts, and his dwelling *was* with the wild asses:
they fed him with grass like oxen, and his body was wet with the
dew of heaven; till he knew that the most high God ruled in the
kingdom of men, and *that* he appointeth over it whomsoever he
will.
22 And thou his son, Belshazzar, hast not humbled thine heart,
though knewest this;
23 But hast lifted up thyself against the Lord of heaven; and they
have brought vessels of his house before thee, thou, and thy lords,
wives, and thy concubines, have drunk wine in them; and thou hast
praised the gods of silver, and gold, of brass, iron, wood, and
stone, which see not, nor hear, nor know: and the God in whose
hand thy breath *is*, and whose *are* all thy ways, hast thou not
glorified:
24 Then was the part of the hand sent from him; and this writing
was written.
25 And this *is* the writing that was written, MENE, MENE, TEKEL,
UPHARSIN.
26 This *is* interpretation: MENE; God hath numbered thy kingdom,
and finished it.
27 TEKEL; Thou art weighed in the balances, and art found
wanting.
28 PERES; Thy kingdom is divided, and given to the Medes and
Persians.
29 Then commanded Belshazzar, and they clothed Daniel with
scarlet, and *put* a chain of gold about his neck, and made a
proclamation that he should be the third ruler in the kingdom.
30 In that night was Belshazzar the king of the Chaldeans slain.
31 Darius the Median took the kingdom, *being* about threescore
and two years old.

Daniel Chapter 6

It pleased Darius to set over the kingdom an hundred and twenty
princes, which should be over the whole kingdom;
2 And over these three presidents; of whom Daniel *was* first: that
the princes might give accounts unto them, and the king should
have no damage.
3 Then this Daniel was preferred above the presidents and princes,
because an excellent spirit *was* in him; and the king thought to set
him over the whole realm.
4 Then the presidents and princes sought to find occasion against
Daniel concerning the kingdom; but they could find none occasion
nor fault; forasmuch as he *was* faithful, neither was there any error
or fault found in him.
5 Then said these men, We shall not find any occasion against this
Daniel, except we find *it* against him concerning the law of his God.
6 Then these presidents and princes assembled together to the
king, and said thus unto him, King Darius, live for ever.
7 All the presidents of the kingdom, the governors, and the princes,
the counsellors, and the captains, have consulted together to
establish a royal statute, and to make a firm decree, that
whosoever shall ask a petition of any God or man for thirty days,
save of thee, O king, he shall be cast into the den of lions.
8 Now, O king, establish the decree, and sign the writing, that it be
not changed, according to the law of the Medes and Persians,
which altereth not.
9 Wherefore king Darius signed the writing and the decree.
10 When Daniel knew that the writing was signed, he went into his
house; and his windows being open in his chamber toward
Jerusalem, he kneeled upon his knees three times a day, and
prayed, and gave thanks to his God, as he did aforetime.
11 Then these men assembled, and found Daniel praying and
making supplication before his God.

And now we see Daniel not so figuratively thrown in "The Lion's Den," and not so figuratively manifesting the continual situations facing a modern President of the United States.

Our Bible does not establish a Vice President, yet instead, that enduring organization chart first documented by Moses comes into full force and effect. Our constitution and form of government establishes many offices and titles, fully consistent with Exodus 18:16-26.

Exodus 18 When they have a matter, they come unto me; and I
judge between one and another, and I do make *them* know the
statutes of God, and his laws.
17 And Moses' father in law said unto him, The thing that thou
doest *is* not good.
18 Thou wilt surely wear away, both thou, and this people that *is*
with thee: for this thing *is* too heavy for thee; thou art not able to
perform it thyself alone.
19 Hearken now unto my voice, I will give thee counsel, and God
shall be with thee: Be thou for the people to God-ward, that thou
mayest bring the causes unto God:
20 And thou shalt teach them ordinances and laws, and shalt shew
them the way wherein they must walk, and work that they must do.
21 Moreover thou shalt provide out of all the people able men, such
as fear God, men of truth, hating covetousness; and place *such*
over them, *to be* rulers of thousands, *and* rulers of hundreds, rulers
of fifties, and rulers of tens:
22 And let them judge the people at all seasons: and it shall be,
that every great matter they shall bring unto thee, but every small
matter they shall judge: so shall it be easier for thyself, and they
shall bear *the burden* with thee.
23 If thou shalt do this thing, and God command thee, then thou
shalt endure, and all this people shall go to their place in peace.
24 So Moses hearkened to the voice of his father in law, and did
all he had said.
25 And Moses chose able men out of all Israel, and made them
heads over the people, rulers of thousands, rulers of hundreds,
rulers of fifties, and rulers of tens.
26 They judged the people at all seasons: the hard causes they
brought to Moses, but every small matter they judged themselves.

The organization chart indicated above may be found to govern the process of elections elaborated in the next constitutional sections. As we have documented above, the Bible applies the words “elect, and election.” Further, given the sheer numbers of leaders Moses had to appoint or elect being over 100,000, a system of election was strongly indicated, as no human can possibly know over 100,000 people closely enough to determine their fitness to become leaders, thus the Bible chapter and verse included herein serves as biblical “predetermination” of the many offices established by the US
Constitution and later actions of Congress to establish other offices and seat those leaders.

Different versions/translations of the Bible apply the words “predetermination, predestination, predestined” to indicate the intent of God.

Ephesians Chapter 1

4 According as he hath chosen us in him before the foundation of the world, that we should be holy and without blame before him in love:
5 Having predestinated us unto the adoption of children by Jesus Christ to himself, according to the good pleasure of his will,
Ephesians 1:11-12 - In whom also we obtained inheritance, being predestinated according to the purpose of him who worketh all things after counsel of his own will:

Romans Chapter 8
28 And we know that all things work together for good to them that love God, to them who are the called according to *his* purpose.
29 For whom he did foreknow, he also did predestinate *to be* conformed to the image of his Son, that he might be the firstborn among many brethren.
30 Whom he did predestinate, the also called: and whom he called, them he also justified: and whom he justified, them he also glorified.

2.Each State shall appoint, in such Manner as the Legislature thereof may direct, a Number of Electors, equal to the whole Number of Senators and Representatives to which the State may be entitled in the Congress: but no Senator or Representative, or Person holding an Office of Trust or Profit under the United States, shall be appointed an Elector.

3.The Electors shall meet in their respective States, and vote by Ballot for two Persons, of whom one at least shall not be an Inhabitant of the same State with themselves. And they shall make a List of all the Persons voted for, and of the Number of Votes for each; which List they shall sign and certify, and transmit sealed to the Seat of the Government of the United States, directed to the President of the Senate. The President of the Senate shall, in the Presence of the Senate and House of Representatives, open all the Certificates, and the Votes shall then be counted. The Person having the greatest Number of Votes shall be the President, if such Number be a Majority of the whole Number of Electors appointed; and if there be more than one who have such Majority, and have an equal Number of Votes, then the House of Representatives shall immediately chuse by Ballot one of them for President; and if no Person have a Majority, then from the five highest on the List the said House shall in like Manner chuse the President. But in chusing the President, the Votes shall be taken by States, the Representation from each State having one Vote; A quorum for this Purpose shall consist of a Member or Members from two thirds of the States, and a Majority of all the States shall be necessary to a Choice. In every Case, after the Choice of the President, the Person having the greatest Number of Votes of the Electors shall be the Vice President. But if there should remain two or more who have equal Votes, the Senate shall chuse from them by Ballot the Vice President.

4.The Congress may determine the Time of chusing the Electors, and the Day on which they shall give their Votes; which Day shall be the same throughout the United States.

Those paragraphs of US Constitution immediately above are designed to establish the acceptable rules by which the ELECTORAL COLLEGE shall function and audit and determine the ultimate outcome of national elections. Given the much smaller population in the day of the Bible, these rules were not necessary to insure a proper outcome of placing leaders in office. The Bible indicates many rules for qualification to hold office, and the number of those offices as identified by the Moses Organization Chart.

However, the Bible establishes that the legislative leadership element of Moses Organization Chart shall jointly review to ensure any changes are consistent with the Will of God. The many rules requiring review and approval of the twelve tribal elders and their associated highest ranking religious officials served a purpose very similar to our ELECTORAL COLLEGE.

<u>5.No Person except a natural born Citizen, or a Citizen of the United States, at the time of Adoption of this Constitution, shall be eligible to the Office of President; neither shall any Person be eligible to that Office who shall not have attained to Age of thirty five Years, and been fourteen Years a Resident within United States.</u>

The Bible gives us several indications that citizenship could be granted to all, yet was not automatic, and was to be controlled by the Third Generation or Tenth Generation from original migrant.

The rights and privileges of a citizen in distinction from a foreigner (Luke 15:15; 19:14; Acts 21:39). Under the Mosaic law "non-Israelites, with the exception of the Moabites and the" "Ammonites and others mentioned in Deut. 23:1-3, were admitted to" the general privileges of citizenship among the Jews (Ex. 12:19; "Lev. 24:22; Num. 15:15; 35:15; Deut. 10:18; 14:29; 16:10, 14)." "The right of citizenship under the Roman government was granted "by the emperor to individuals, and sometimes to provinces, as a" "favour or as a recompense for services rendered to the state, or" "for a sum of money (Acts 22:28). This "freedom" secured" privileges equal to those enjoyed by natives of Rome. Among the most notable of these was the provision that a man could not be "bound or imprisoned without formal trial (Acts 22:25, 26), or" scourged (16:37). All Roman citizens had right of appeal to Caesar (25:11).

Alien person indicated in the Bible:

Exodus 18:3 And her two sons; of which the name of the one was Gershom; for he said, I have been an alien in a strange land:

Isaiah 61:5 Strangers shall stand and feed your flocks, and the sons of the alien shall be your plowmen and your vinedressers.

Foreigner identified in the Bible:

Exodus 12:45 A foreigner and a hired servant shall not eat thereof.
Deuteronomy 15:3 Of a foreigner thou mayest exact it again: but that which is thine with thy brother thine hand shall release;

6.In Case of Removal of the President from Office, or of his Death, Resignation, or Inability to discharge Powers and Duties of said Office, the Same shall devolve on the Vice President, and Congress may by Law provide for the Case of Removal, Death, Resignation or Inability, both of the President and Vice President, declaring what Officer shall act as President, and such Officer shall act accordingly, until the Disability be removed, or a President shall be elected.

Subsection statement above is the Plan of Succession, unless another specific plan has been determined, (such as line of succession of the President prior to a succeeding election). This would give way to a Constitutional Amendment ordering a specific "line of succession," The 25th Amendment to the US Constitution.

The Biblical story of Judas gives a view of the biblical plan for replacement of ranking officials. Please recall that Judas Iscariot was a disciple of Jesus Christ. As a result of Judas betrayal of Jesus, Judas commits suicide and must be replaced as one of the twelve. The Bible indicated how Judas was replaced.

When the Apostles departed Jerusalem to commence their mission to spread the word to all the world, they appointed Stephen to be the leader of Jesus Christs preaching in Jerusalem. Stephen was killed and another was appointed in his place - - James the brother of Jesus.

These and other Bible stories provide the beginnings for the process of selecting leaders and for planned succession as well as non planned succession.

Acts Chapter 1

16 Men *and* brethren, this scripture must needs have been fulfilled, which the Holy Ghost by the mouth of David spake before concerning Judas, which was guide to them that took Jesus.
17 For he was numbered with us, and had obtained part of this ministry.
18 Now this man purchased a field with the reward of iniquity; and falling headlong, he burst asunder in the midst, and all his bowels gushed out.
19 And it was known unto all the dwellers at Jerusalem; insomuch as that field is called in their proper tongue, Aceldama, that is to say, The field of blood.
20 It is written in the book of Psalms, Let his habitation be desolate, let no man dwell therein: and his bishoprick let another take.
21 Wherefore of these men which have companied with us all the time that the Lord Jesus went in and out among us,
, 22 Beginning from the baptism of John, unto that same day that he was taken up from us, must one be ordained to be a witness with us of his resurrection.
23 And they appointed two, Joseph called Barsabas, who was surnamed Justus, and Matthias.

Acts Chapter 6 Stephen is appointed and replaced upon his death by James the half brother of Jesus.

And in those days, when the number of the disciples was multiplied, there arose a murmuring of the Grecians against the Hebrews, their widows were neglected in daily ministration.

2Then the twelve called the multitude of the disciples *unto them*,
and said, It is not reason that we should leave the word of God,
and serve tables.
3Wherefore, brethren, look ye out among you seven men of honest
report, full of the Holy Ghost and wisdom, whom we may appoint
over this business.
4We will give ourselves continually to prayer, ministry of the word.
5And the saying pleased the whole multitude: and they chose
Stephen, a man full of faith and of the Holy Ghost, and Philip, and
Prochorus, and Nicanor, and Timon, and Parmenas, and Nicolas
a proselyte of Antioch:
6Whom they set before the apostles: when they had prayed,
laid hands on them.
7And the word of God increased; and the number of the disciples
multiplied in Jerusalem greatly; and a great company of the priests
were obedient to the faith.
8Stephen, full of faith and power, did great wonders and miracles.
9Then there arose certain of the synagogue, which is called *the
synagogue* of the Libertines, and Cyrenians, and Alexandrians,
and of them of Cilicia and of Asia, disputing with Stephen.
10And they were not able to resist the wisdom and the spirit by
which he spake.
11Then they suborned men, which said, We have heard him speak
blasphemous words against Moses, and *against* God.
12And they stirred up the people, and the elders, and the scribes,
and came upon *him*, and caught him, brought *him* to the council,
13And set up false witnesses, which said, This man ceaseth not to
speak blasphemous words against this holy place, and the law:
14For we have heard him say, that this Jesus of Nazareth shall
destroy this place, and change the customs Moses delivered us.
15And all that sat in the council, looking stedfastly on him, saw his
face as it had been the face of an angel.

Acts Chapter 7 Execution of Stephen

54 When they heard these things, they were cut to the heart, and
they gnashed on him with *their* teeth.
55 He, being full of the Holy Ghost, looked up stedfastly into
heaven, saw the glory of God, Jesus standing on right hand of God,
56 And said, Behold, I see the heavens opened, and the Son of man
standing on the right hand of God.
57 They cried with a loud voice, stopped their ears, ran upon him
with one accord,
58 And cast *him* out of the city, and stoned *him*: and witnesses laid
down their clothes at a young man's feet, whose name was Saul.
59 They stoned Stephen, who called upon *God*, . . . Lord Jesus,
receive my spirit.
60 And he kneeled down, and cried with a loud voice, Lord, lay not
this sin to their charge. And when he had said this, he fell asleep.

Acts Chapter 8 Saul/Paul enters the story

And Saul was consenting unto his death. And at that time there
was a great persecution against the church which was at
Jerusalem; and they were all scattered abroad throughout the
regions of Judaea and Samaria, except the apostles.
2Devout men carried Stephen *to his burial*, and made great
lamentation over him.
3As for Saul, he made havock of the church, entering into every
house, and haling men and women committed *them* to prison.

Galatians 1

17Neither went I up to Jerusalem to them which were apostles; but
I went into Arabia, and returned again unto Damascus.
18after three years I went to Jerusalem to see Peter, abode with
him fifteen days.
19But other apostles saw I none, save James the Lord's brother.

Galatians 2 on James

And when James, Cephas, and John, who seemed to be pillars, perceived the grace that was given unto me, they gave to me and Barnabas the right hands of fellowship; that we *should go* unto the heathen, and they unto the circumcision. In recognition of these verses, the reader can realize succession planning or appointment to occur in the Bible, thus forerunner of our US Constitution succession.

7.The President shall, at stated Times, receive for his Services, a Compensation, which shall neither be encreased nor diminished during the Period for which he shall have been elected, and he shall not receive within that Period any other Emolument from the United States, or any of them.

In days of the Bible, Priests, and church officials along with those being appointed, elected, or anointed for church or government service were originally compensated from tithes, as we have indicated within the 613 laws.

8.Before he enter on the Execution of his Office, he shall take the following Oath or Affirmation:—"I do solemnly swear (or affirm) that I will faithfully execute the Office of President of the United States, and will to the best of my Ability, preserve, protect and defend the Constitution of the United States."

The Bible cautions us not to swear of affirm falsely:

1. To affirm a solemn declaration, with appeal to God for the truth of what is affirmed.
    a) Ye shall not *swear* by my name falsely. Leviticus 19:12.
    b) But I say unto you, *swear* not at all. Matthew 5:34.
2. To promise upon oath.
    a) Jacob said, *swear* to me this day; and he swore to him. Genesis 25:33.

Article. 2.

Section. 2.

1.The President shall be Commander in Chief of the Army and Navy of the United States, and of the Militia of the several States, when called into the actual Service of the United States; he may require the Opinion, in writing, of the principal Officer in each of the executive Departments, upon any Subject relating to the Duties of their respective Offices, and he shall have Power to grant Reprieves and Pardons for Offences against the United States, except in Cases of Impeachment.

We refer the reader once again to Exodus 18 organization chart. Our President is the leader of all elements of government of the United States. In the Exodus organization, the person atop the organization chart was the leader of more than just government. In sections above, we have delineated the biblical plan for establishment of military within and among twelve tribes of Israel.

Exodus 18:21 Moreover thou shalt provide out of all the people
able men, such as fear God, men of truth, hating covetousness;
and place such over them, to be rulers of thousands, and rulers of
hundreds, rulers of fifties, and rulers of tens:
22 And let them judge the people at all seasons: that every great
matter they shall bring unto thee, but every small matter they
shall judge: so shall it be easier for thyself, and they shall bear
the burden with thee.

In several subsections of chapters above, we have elaborated the Moses Organization Chart and plan of government. Again, the number one leader sat atop Moses Organization chart of Exodus 18:20-26. The Bible also indicates that many times, a plan of succession was in place, beginning with Joshua, replacement of Moses upon the death of Moses, along with a continuous succession of Hebrew leaders Chronicled by Samuel, through the Day of David and Solomon, albeit the succession was not always friendly, it remained in Hebrew hands.

As for requiring the opinion of the other principal officers, this is also established via the Organization Chart by which all matters are to matriculate up the lines of the organization. As for Reprieves and Pardons or Impeachment, these points are to be determined following the twelve elders and their 24 assistants' determination of the issue in question falling within or beyond the Will of God.

2.He shall have Power, by and with the Advice and Consent of the Senate, to make Treaties, provided two thirds of the Senators present concur; and he shall nominate, and by and with the Advice and Consent of the Senate, shall appoint Ambassadors, other public Ministers and Consuls, Judges of the supreme Court, and all other Officers of the United States, whose Appointments are not herein otherwise provided for, and which shall be established by Law: but the Congress may by Law vest the Appointment of such inferior Officers, as they think proper, in the President alone, in the Courts of Law, or in the Heads of Departments.

TREATIES

The Bible indicates treaties were discussed and agreed as early as book of Genesis. The greatest story of treaties is represented in the story of Solomon. Understand that in biblical days, many means were utilized that no longer exist. One of those dealt with the means of signifying agreement to treaties between nations. In the case of the most important treaties, the Kings would each agree by giving the other King a wife from among his family. In the case of lesser treaties, the Kings would agree by giving the other King a Concubine from his kingdom. Both Kings were expected to treat the wife as a true wife. Concubines were to be treated as a member of the family, not sexual objects.

The practice of sealing the King's agreement by giving each other a wife from among his family essentially created "brotherly nations," which suggests these treaties were more important than those agreed by means of Senatorial or Legislative concurrence.

Solomon, third king of Israel (reigned c. 968–928 B.C.E.), is said to have had a harem that included 700 wives and 300 concubines (1 Kgs 11:3). His wives were to have included the daughter of Pharaoh, as well as women of Moabite, Edomite, Sidonian, and Hittite origins (1 Kgs 7:8; 11:1). The latter group is usually understood to represent wives who were added to the harem as a means of sealing treaty agreements with these five foreign powers. Throughout human history, marriage alliance has been the most common way for rulers to secure peaceful relationships with potential enemies.

The tradition in 1 Kgs 11:1–8 about Solomon's marriage to foreign wives, whether based on historical records or not, employs the motif of the dangerous foreign woman to condemn Solomon for idolatry in his later years (see Neh.13:26).

It seems to illustrate the prohibition in Deut. 7:3 against marrying foreign women and to echo the exclusion of Moab and Edom from the congregation of the Lord in Deut.23:4–9. Foreign women were considered a potential source of trouble because they might not always adopt the culture and values of their husbands and their new place of residence. If they chose to continue to practice their native customs and cults, they would pass these on to their children and might also influence their husbands to adopt some non-Israelite practices as well. Loyalty to and identity with Israelite tradition would be threatened.

In biblical literature, foreign women, seduction, prostitution, sexual disloyalty, and fertility cults were linked together, not all foreign women were viewed as evil. Tamar (Genesis 38), Ruth (Book of Ruth), Rahab (Joshua 2), Jael (Judges 4–5) provide positive images of foreign women; each demonstrates through her behavior her adoption of Israelite or Judahite society and religion and gains acceptance in her new community. Solomon's foreign wives, by contrast, depict the negative side of foreign women. Like Potiphar's wife (Genesis 39), Samson's wife (Judges 14–16), foreign woman of Proverbs 1–9, they remain loyal to their personal or political interests, as a result, disrupt law and order in their adoptive Israelite community.

- Brenner, Athalya. *The Israelite Woman: Social Role and Literary Type in Biblical Narrative.* Sheffield, England: 1985.
- Meyers, Carol, General Editor. *Women in Scripture.* New York: 2000.
- Miller, J. Maxwell, and John H. Hayes. *A History of Ancient Israel and Judah.* Philadelphia: 1986.
- Reinhartz, Adele. "Anonymous Women, Collapse of Monarchy: A Study in Narrative Technique." In *A Feminist Companion to Samuel and Kings,* edited by Athalya Brenner, 43–65. Sheffield, England: 1994.

JUDGES AND APPOINTMENTS, agreed by the following.

"More correctly Sanhedrin (Gr. synedrion), meaning "a sitting" "together," or a "council." This word (rendered "council," A.V.)" is frequently used in the New Testament (Matt. 5:22; 26:59; Mark "15:1, etc.) to denote the supreme judicial and administrative" "council of the Jews, which, it is said, was first instituted by" "Moses, and was composed of seventy men (Num. 11:16, 17). But" that seems to have been only a temporary arrangement which Moses made. The name is first "employed by the Jewish historian Josephus. This "council" is" "referred to simply as the "chief priests and elders of the" "people" (Matt. 26:3, 47, 57, 59; 27:1, 3, 12, 20, etc.), before" whom Christ was tried on the charge of claiming to be the Messiah. "The highest levels of the Organization Chart of Moses was the Sanhedrin, (Matt. 5:22; 26:59; Mark "15:1, etc.) to denote the supreme judicial and administrative" "council of the Jews, which, it is said, was first instituted by" "Moses, and was composed of seventy men (Num. 11:16, 17). They were of three classes (1) "the chief priests, or heads of the twenty-four priestly courses" "(1 Chr. 24), (2) the scribes, and (3) the elders. As the highest" "court of judicature, "in all causes and over all persons," ecclesiastical and civil, supreme," its decrees were binding," "not only on the Jews in Palestine, but on all Jews wherever" scattered abroad. Its usual place of meeting" "was within the precincts of the temple, in the hall "Gazith," but it sometimes met also in the house of the high priest (Matt. "26:3)."

3.The President shall have Power to fill up all Vacancies that may happen during the Recess of the Senate, by granting Commissions which shall expire at the End of their next Session.

Once again we are directed to Exodus 18 20-26, wherein an "order of succession" is indicated by the method in which normal organizations perform. In the event of an unplanned succession, it was typical that a subordinate of the person retiring would become the automatic replacement, in the absence of other affirmative succession plans or appointments.

Article. 2.

Section. 3. State of the Union (and Other)

1.He shall from time to time give to the Congress Information of the State of the Union, and recommend to their Consideration such Measures as he shall judge necessary and expedient; he may, on extraordinary Occasions, convene both Houses, or either of them, and in Case of Disagreement between them, with Respect to the Time of Adjournment, he may adjourn them to such Time as he shall think proper; he shall receive Ambassadors and other public Ministers; he shall take Care that the Laws be faithfully executed, and shall Commission all the Officers of the United States.

The Hebrew people would gather for many occasions. At great Festivals, God ordered that His laws be read to all the people so that they would understand the law. The law was read at Festivals by the leading Priest. This is an early example of the great leader communicating issues of importance to the population, not just the leadership. These readings would occur at many times per year, and not just an annual basis as is the practice in America today.

Bible passages indicating reading of the law:

Exodus 18
20 And thou shalt teach them ordinances and laws, and shalt shew them the way wherein they must walk, and work that they must do.
21 Moreover thou shalt provide out of all the people able men, such as fear God, men of truth, hating covetousness; and place *such* over them, *to be* rulers of thousands, *and* rulers of hundreds, rulers of fifties, and rulers of tens:
Nehemiah 8:3 "And he read therein before the street that was before the water gate from the morning until midday, before the men and the women, and those that could understand; and the ears of all the people were attentive unto the book of the law."
Nehemiah 8:8 "So they read the law of God distinctly, and gave the sense, and caused *them* to understand the reading."

Article. 2.

Section. 4.

1.The President, Vice President, and all civil Officers of the United States, shall be removed from Office on Impeachment for, and Conviction of, Treason, Bribery, or other high Crimes and Misdemeanors.

The Biblical story of Judas gives a view of the biblical plan for Impeachment of ranking officials.

BIBLICAL ACTS OF IMPEACHMENT

Acts Chapter 1:16 Men *and* brethren, this scripture must needs have been fulfilled, which the Holy Ghost by the mouth of David spake before concerning Judas, which was guide to them that took Jesus.
17 For he was numbered with us, and obtained part of this ministry.
18 Now this man purchased a field with the reward of iniquity; and falling headlong, he burst asunder in the midst, and all his bowels gushed out.
19 And it was known unto all the dwellers at Jerusalem; insomuch as that field is called in their proper tongue, Aceldama, that is to say, The field of blood.

20 For it is written in the book of Psalms, Let his habitation be desolate, let no man dwell therein: his bishoprick let another take.
21 Wherefore of these men which have companied with us all the time that the Lord Jesus went in and out among us,
22 Beginning from the baptism of John, unto that same day that he was taken up from us, must one be ordained to be a witness with us of his resurrection.
23 They appointed two, Joseph called Barsabas, surnamed Justus, and Matthias.

CHURCH DISCIPLINE

The strongest church procedure consistent with IMPEACHMENT is the practice of "defrocking" and retraining errant Preachers who are caught in a sinful situation. All denominations have their books of procedure for this most demanding practice by which Preachers or other church leaders are removed from their positions until such time as they undergo a demanding range of biblical retraining and reproving to the elders and church membership that they are once again worthy to lead the church.

The Bibles teaching on corrective Church Discipline - - Ultimate authority resides in Christ, who authorizes the church to use it as needed. (Matthew 18:17)

Corrective discipline is for:

- Troublemakers and those who sow discord. (Romans 16:17)
- The unruly and disorderly. (1 Thessalonians 5:14)
- Those who disobey the great doctrines of the faith. (2 Thessalonians 3:13-14)
- Those who deny the great doctrines of faith. (1 Timothy 6:3-4)

Procedures in discipline

- Arrange a private meeting with the offender. (Matthew 18:15)
- If private meeting fails, meet with them and several witnesses. (Matt18:16)
- Admonish and warn them. (Titus 3:10)
- As a final resort, bring the matter up to the whole church. (Matthew 18:17)
- Remove their membership, and avoid them. (Romans 16:17)
- Be ready to forgive them when repentance occurs. (2 Corinthians 2:7)

Purpose of discipline

- To maintain standards of the church to a watching world. (Matthew 5:13-16)
- Keep sin from spreading throughout church. (Joshua 7:3); (1 Corinthians 5:6-7)
- Help the guilty find their way to God. (2nd Corinthians 2:6-8)
- To escape God's judgment on habitually sinning saints.(1 Corinthians11:30)[1]

Practice by ecclesiastical tradition   Catholic Church Discipline

The Congregation for the Doctrine of the Faith is the oldest of the nine congregations of the Roman Curia. Among the most active of these major Curial departments, which oversees Catholic doctrine. The CDF is the modern name for what used to be the Holy Office of the Inquisition.

According to Article 48 of the Apostolic Constitution on the Roman Curia, *Pastor Bonus*, promulgated by Pope John Paul II on June 28, 1988: "the duty proper to the Congregation for the Doctrine of the Faith is to promote and safeguard the doctrine on the faith and morals throughout the Catholic world: for this reason everything which in any way touches such matter falls within its competence."

The Congregation for Divine Worship and the Discipline of the Sacraments is the congregation of the Roman Curia that handles most affairs relating to liturgical practices of the Latin Catholic Church as distinct from the Eastern Catholic Churches and also some technical matters relating to the Sacraments.

In some contexts, *church discipline* may refer to the rules governing an ecclesiastical order, such as priests or monks, such as clerical celibacy.[2]

Protestant Church Discipline
Not to be confused with Church Order (Lutheran).

Along with preaching and proper administration of the sacraments, Protestants during the Reformation considered it one of the marks of a true church. Church discipline is mentioned several times in the Bible.[3]

In I Corinthians 5 and other passages, the Bible teaches that sin if not dealt with in a congregation can contaminate other members of the body of Christ, as leaven spreads through bread. This was an important doctrine in the development of different branches of the Plymouth Brethren movement. It is also an important topic of discussion in many churches today.[4]

The Westminster Confession of Faith sees the three steps of church discipline as being "admonition", "suspension from the sacrament of the Lord's Supper for a season" and then finally excommunication.[5]

Latter-day Saints Church Discipline

In the Church of Jesus Christ of Latter-day Saints, a bishop or a stake president may hold a church membership council (formerly known as a "disciplinary council) to consider restrictions on or withdrawal of church membership for members who commit crimes or otherwise violate the standards of the church.

1. Dr. H.L. Wilmington Wilmington's Guide to the Bible P. 715
2. *Herbermann, Charles, ed. (1913). "Ecclesiastical Discipline." Catholic Encyclopedia. NY: Robert Appleton Co*
3. For example in 1 Corinthians 5 and Matthew 15:15–18 and Matthew 18:15–20
4. Church Discipline, Judgment. Part 1 of 3. Digging in the Word
5. Westminster Confession of Faith, xxx.4.

Article. III

Article III can be called The Courts Establishment clause. It first establishes the Supreme Court of the United States, gives that court the power to establish lesser courts, and establishes Trial by Jury for all criminal charges. The Holy Bible provides more exacting Judicial and court procedures than our constitution. The bible mandates witnesses and evidence, and while not applying modern terms, the Bible makes clear reference to "rule of law," legal codes, "habeus corpus," and review of law by the people. The Bible does not indicate the actual physical location of courts.

Section.1.

1.The judicial Power of the United States, shall be vested in one supreme Court, and in such inferior Courts as the Congress may from time to time ordain and establish. The Judges, both of the supreme and inferior Courts, shall hold their Offices during good Behaviour, and shall, at stated Times, receive for their Services, a Compensation, which shall not be diminished during their Continuance in Office.

COURTS, JUDICIAL. There was no precise term for "court of law" in the OT (although *ḥāṣēr* occurs with great frequency for the court of the Tabernacle or Temple), at least in the sense of a specific building in which judicial proceedings were conducted. The reason for this was that cases at law were normally heard out in the open, generally in the open square near a city gate. There seems to be only one exception to this in the Heb. Scriptures (1 Kings 7:7), which states that Solomon "made the porch of judgment where he was to judge, even the porch of judgment"—which would be the nearest OT equivalent to a law court in the sense of a building. It would be natural for Solomon to erect an imposing structure of this sort for the hearing of appeals from the lower courts or for the handling of cases of major importance; his royal neighbors in Egypt and Mesopotamia maintained special courthouses or audience halls for the purpose.

Apart from this reference, court proceedings were held normally in the forum or market square which faced the principal gate of the city.

The first definite reference to this in the OT is found in Genesis 19:1 and states that "Lot was sitting in the gate of Sodom" when he noticed the two angelic visitors whom he invited to his home; v. 9 quotes the nocturnal rioters as complaining that an outsider like Lot "will needs be a judge" (ASV)—indicating that after the prestige of Abraham's victory of the Mesopotamian invaders, his nephew had been officially promoted to judicial position. Later allusions to the city gate as the place for public tribunals are Deuteronomy 16:18, "Judges and officers—*šōṭerīm*—you shall appoint in all your towns...and they shall judge the people with righteous judgment"; 21:19 (where the "elders" of the city are apparently charged with judging the case of a rebellious son); and 25:7 (where a complaint against a non-compliant *levir* is brought against him by his brother's widow "to the gate to the elders"). The "officers" associated with the judges (in Deut.16:18 above) appear to have been bailiffs who insured the appearance of litigants and witnesses at the court sessions; at least their responsibilities as assistant taskmasters or foremen in Egypt (Exod. 5:6, 10, 14, 15, 19) and as marshals for military forces (Josh 1:10; 3:2) would suggest this as their function in the judicial setting. (On the other hand, they may have functioned as court clerks, since *šāṭar*, as one knows from the Akkad. cognate, meant "to write.")

In the earliest stage of the Exodus migration Moses had the responsibility of holding court sessions in the Israelite camp, along with all his executive and military duties. At the advice of his father-in-law Jethro (Exod. 18:17-26) Moses delegated to an ascending series of petty and appellate judges (who are called "heads" or "rulers" over squads of ten soldiers, captains, or lieutenants over larger units) to hear all original cases. Only the more difficult problems for which there was no clear precedent were to be referred to Moses as the court of final appeal. During the period of the Judges, it was Deborah who figured prominently as a jurist, holding court sessions under her palm tree (Judges 4:5).

The other national leaders (who bore the title of *šōpetīm*, "judges") included court hearings with their other responsibilities as executives and military commanders. This function was taken over by the king after the Heb. monarchy was instituted; David maintained an "appellate court" for his entire kingdom (2 Sam 15:2), and Solomon as well (1 Kings 3:9), even before the erection of his aforementioned hall of justice. 1 Chronicles 23:4 states that David appointed 6,000 of the Levites as officers and judges to serve in the lower courts (see also 26:29). By the time of Jehoshaphat (2 Chron 19:5-8) it became necessary to enlarge even the central tribunal at Jerusalem into a larger complex consisting of priests, Levites, and heads of clans. Perhaps from this measure, that the Sanhedrin, or Council of Seventy, developed (although there is no specific mention of it until Hel. times), which functioned under the high priest.

Article. III.

Section. 2.

1.The judicial Power shall extend to all Cases, in Law and Equity, arising under this Constitution, the Laws of the United States, and Treaties made, or which shall be made, under their Authority;—to all Cases affecting Ambassadors, other public Ministers and Consuls;—to all Cases of admiralty and maritime Jurisdiction;—to Controversies to which the United States shall be a Party;—to Controversies between two or more States;— between a State and Citizens of another State,—between Citizens of different States,—between Citizens of the same State claiming Lands under Grants of different States, and between a State, or the Citizens thereof, and foreign States, Citizens or Subjects.

2.In all Cases affecting Ambassadors, other public Ministers and Consuls, and those in which a State shall be Party, the supreme Court shall have original Jurisdiction. In all the other Cases before mentioned, the supreme Court shall have appellate Jurisdiction, both as to Law and Fact, with such Exceptions, and under such Regulations as the Congress shall make.

3.The Trial of all Crimes, except in Cases of Impeachment, shall be by Jury; and such Trial shall be held in the State where the said Crimes shall have been committed; but when not committed within any State, the Trial shall be at such Place or Places as the Congress may by Law have directed.

The Bible on Proper levels of Administration, Legislative or Courts

"The highest levels of the Organization Chart of Moses was the Sanhedrin, (Matt. 5:22; 26:59; Mark "15:1, etc.) to denote the supreme judicial and administrative" "council of the Jews, which, it is said, was first instituted by" "Moses, and was composed of seventy men (Num. 11:16, 17). They were of three classes (1) "the chief priests, or heads of the twenty-four priestly courses" "(1 Chr. 24), (2) the scribes, and (3) the elders. As the highest" "court of judicature, "in all causes and over all persons," "ecclesiastical and civil, supreme," its decrees were binding," "not only on the Jews in Palestine, but on all Jews wherever" scattered abroad. Its usual place of meeting" "was within the precincts of the temple, in the hall "Gazith," but it sometimes met also in the house of the high priest (Matt. "26:3)."

Bible on Courts and Rulers/Judges:

- Exodus 18:20 And thou shalt teach them ordinances and laws, and shalt shew them the way wherein they must walk, and the work that they must do.
- 21 Moreover thou shalt provide out of all the people able men, such as fear God, men of truth, hating covetousness; and place *such* over them, *to be* rulers of thousands, *and* rulers of hundreds, rulers of fifties, and rulers of tens:

- 22 And let them judge the people at all seasons: and it shall be, *that* every great matter they shall bring unto thee, but every small matter they shall judge: so shall it be easier for thyself, and they shall bear *the burden* with thee.
- 1 Samuel 24:15 The LORD therefore be judge, and judge between me and thee, and see, and plead my cause, and deliver me out of thine hand.
- 1 Kings 3:9 Give thy servant an understanding heart to judge thy people, that I may discern between good and bad: for who is able to judge so great a people?
- Luke 12:58 When thou goest with thine adversary to the magistrate, as thou art in the way, give diligence that thou may be delivered from him; lest he hale thee to the judge, and judge deliver thee to the officer, the officer cast thee into prison.
- 1 Samuel 2:25 If one man sin against another, the judge shall judge him: but if a man sin against the LORD, who shall intreat for him? Notwithstanding they hearkened not unto voice of their father, because the LORD would slay them.
- Matthew 5:25 Agree with thine adversary quickly, whiles thou art in the way with him; lest at any time the adversary deliver thee to the judge, and the judge deliver thee to the officer, and thou be cast into prison.

FIRST CIRCUIT JUDGE DOCUMENTED BY THE BIBLE OR OTHER HISTORY

1 Samuel 7:15 And Samuel judged Israel all the days of his life.
16 And he went from year to year in circuit to Bethel, and Gilgal, and Mizpeh, and judged Israel in all those places.
17 And his return *was* to Ramah; for there *was* his house; and there he judged Israel; and there he built an altar unto the LORD.

BIBLE CALLS FOR WITNESSES

- Deuteronomy 17:6 At the mouth of two or three witnesses, shall he that is worthy of death be put to death; but at the mouth of one witness he shall not.

- Deuteronomy 19:15 One witness shall not rise up against a man for any iniquity, or for any sin, in any sin that he sinneth: at the mouth of two witnesses, or at the mouth of three witnesses, shall the matter be established.
- Luke 24:48 And ye are witnesses of these things.
- Acts 2:32 This Jesus hath God raised up, whereof we all are witnesses.
- Deuteronomy 19:15 One witness shall not rise up against a man for any iniquity, or for any sin, in any sin that he sinneth: at the mouth of two witnesses, or at the mouth of three witnesses, shall the matter be established.
- Luke 24:48 And ye are witnesses of these things.
- Acts 2:32 This Jesus hath God raised up, whereof we all are witnesses.
- 1 Tim 5:19 Against an elder receive not an accusation, but before 2 or 3 witness.
- Acts 2:32 This Jesus hath God raised up, whereof we all are witnesses.
- Isaiah 8:2 And I took unto me faithful witnesses to record, Uriah the priest, and Zechariah the son of Jeberechiah.
- Jeremiah 32:10 And I subscribed the evidence, sealed it, and took witnesses, and weighed him the money in the balances.

BIBLE NOW FORETELLS THE NEED FOR EVIDENCE

- Jeremiah 32:14 Thus saith the LORD, the God of Israel; Take these evidences, this evidence of the purchase, both which is sealed, and this evidence which is open; and put them in an earthen vessel, that they may continue many days.
- Hebrews 11:1 **F**aith is substance of things hoped for, evidence of things not seen.
- Jeremiah 32:16 Now when I had delivered the evidence of the purchase unto Baruch the son of Neriah, I prayed unto the LORD, saying,
- Jeremiah 32:10 And I subscribed the evidence, and sealed it, took witnesses, and weighed him the money in the balances.

- Jeremiah 32:11 So I took the evidence of the purchase, both that which was sealed according to the law and custom, and that which was open:
- Jeremiah 32:12 And I gave the evidence of the purchase unto Baruch the son of Neriah, the son of Maaseiah, in the sight of Hanameel mine uncle's son, and in the presence of the witnesses that subscribed the book of the purchase, before all the Jews that sat in the court of the prison.

TRIAL BY JURY

During biblical days, the population was tiny compared to today. There is no biblical requirement for a jury of one's peers. We see cases in the Bible in which wrong doers were placed before a crowd of people for judgment, yet that was never established as a practice. As early as 500 BC in Greece and Rome, the Jury becomes fully established, yet utilized differently than is practiced today. These were neither biblical nor court practices. Sanhedrin provided a court plan for any requirement.

Article. III.

Section. 3.

1.Treason against the United States, shall consist only in levying War against them, or in adhering to their Enemies, giving them Aid and Comfort. No Person shall be convicted of Treason unless on the Testimony of two Witnesses to the same overt Act, or on Confession in open Court.

2.The Congress shall have Power to declare the Punishment of Treason, but no Attainder of Treason shall work Corruption of Blood, or Forfeiture except during the Life of the Person attainted.

The Bible documents one huge case of TREASON that is closely matched to non-biblical stories, typically from royal residences in which family members incapacitate the rightful rulers and then do terrible things. The biblical books of Kings and Chronicles document Athaliah and wickedness resulting in her removal and execution, rightful ruler being restored.

Athaliah, in the Old Testament, the daughter of Ahab and Jezebel and wife of Jeham, king of Judah. After the death of Ahaziah, her son, Athaliah usurped the throne and reigned for seven years. She massacred all the members of the royal house of Judah (II Kings 11:1–3), except Joash. A successful revolution was organized in favour of Joash, and she was killed.

2 Chronicles 22 And the inhabitants of Jerusalem made Ahaziah his youngest son king in his stead: for the band of men that came with the Arabians to the camp had slain all the eldest. So Ahaziah the son of Jehoram king of Judah reigned.
2 Forty and two years old *was* Ahaziah when he began to reign, and he reigned one year in Jerusalem. His mother's name also Athaliah the daughter of Omri.
3 He walked in ways of house of Ahab: his mother was his counsellor to do wickedly.
4 Wherefore he did evil in sight of the LORD like the house of Ahab: they were his counsellors after death of his father to his destruction.
5 He walked after their counsel, went with Jehoram the son of Ahab king of Israel to war against Hazael king of Syria at Ramoth Gilead: the Syrians smote Joram.
6 And he returned to be healed in Jezreel because of the wounds which were given him at Ramah, when he fought with Hazael king of Syria. And Azariah the son of Jehoram king of Judah went down to see Jehoram the son of Ahab at Jezreel, because he was sick.
7 And the destruction of Ahaziah was of God by coming to Joram: for when he was come, he went out with Jehoram against Jehu the son of Nimshi, whom the LORD anointed to cut off house of Ahab.
8 And it came to pass, when Jehu was executing judgment upon the house of Ahab, and found the princes of Judah, and sons of the brethren of Ahaziah, that ministered to Ahaziah, he slew them.

9 And he sought Ahaziah: and they caught him, (for he was hid in Samaria,) and brought him to Jehu: and when they had slain him, they buried him: Because, said they, he *is* the son of Jehoshaphat, who sought the LORD with all his heart. So the house of Ahaziah had no power to keep still the kingdom.
10 But when Athaliah the mother of Ahaziah saw that her son was dead, she arose and destroyed all seed of the house of Judah.
11 Jehoshabeath, daughter of the king, took Joash the son of Ahaziah, stole him from among the king's sons that were slain, put him and his nurse in a bedchamber. So Jehoshabeath, the daughter of king Jehoram, the wife of Jehoiada the priest, (she was sister of Ahaziah,) hid him from Athaliah, so that she slew him not.
12 And he was with them hid in the house of God six years: and Athaliah reigned.

2 Chronicles 23 And in the seventh year Jehoiada strengthened himself, and took the captains of hundreds, Azariah the son of Jeroham, and Ishmael, son of Jehohanan, and Azariah, son of Obed, and Maaseiah the son of Adaiah, and Elishaphat the son of Zichri, into covenant with him.
2 And they went about in Judah, and gathered the Levites out of all the cities of Judah, and the chief of the fathers of Israel, and they came to Jerusalem.
3 And the congregation made a covenant with the king in house of God. And he said, Behold, the king's son shall reign, as the LORD hath said of the sons of David.
4 This *is* the thing that ye shall do; A third part of you entering on the sabbath, of priests and of Levites, *shall be* porters of the doors;
5 And a third part *shall be* at the king's house; and a third part at the gate of the foundation: and all the people *shall be* in the courts of the house of the LORD.
6 Let none come into house of the LORD, save the priests, and they that minister of the Levites; shall go in, they *are* holy: all the people shall keep watch of the LORD.
7 And the Levites shall compass the king round about, every man with his weapons in his hand; and whosoever *else* cometh into the house, he shall be put to death: but be ye with the king when he cometh in, and when he goeth out.

8 The Levites and all Judah did all things that Jehoiada the priest
had commanded, took every man his men that were to come in on
the sabbath, with them that were to go *out* on the sabbath: for
Jehoiada the priest dismissed not the courses.
9 Moreover Jehoiada the priest delivered to the captains of
hundreds spears, and bucklers, and shields, that *had been* king
David's, which *were* in the house of God.
10 He set all the people, every man having weapon in hand, from
right side of the temple to left side of the temple, along by the altar
and the temple, round about.
11 They brought out the king's son, put upon him the crown, *gave
him* the testimony, made him king. Jehoiada and his sons anointed
him, and said, God save the king.
12 Now when Athaliah heard the noise of the people praising the
king, she came to the people into the house of the LORD:
13 And she looked, and behold, the king stood at his pillar at the
entering in, and the princes and the trumpets by the king: and all
the people of the land rejoiced, and sounded with trumpets, also
the singers with instruments of music, and such as taught to sing
praise. Then Athaliah rent her clothes, and said, Treason, Treason.
14 Jehoiada the priest brought out the captains of hundreds that
were set over the host, and said unto them, Have her forth of the
ranges: and whoso followeth her, let him be slain with the sword.
The priest said, Slay her not in the house of the LORD.
15 So they laid hands on her; and when she was come to the
entering of the horse gate by the king's house, they slew her there.
16 And Jehoiada made a covenant between him, between all the
people, between the king, that they should be the LORD'S people.
17 Then all the people went to the house of Baal, and brake it
down, and brake his altars and his images in pieces, and slew
Mattan the priest of Baal before the altars.
18 Also Jehoiada appointed the offices of the house of the LORD
by the hand of the priests the Levites, whom David had distributed
in the house of the LORD, to offer the burnt offerings of the LORD,
as *it is* written in the law of Moses, with rejoicing and with singing,
as it was ordained by David.

19 And he set the porters at the gates of the house of the LORD, that none *which was* unclean in any thing should enter in.
20 And he took the captains of hundreds, the nobles, the governors of the people, all the people of the land, and brought down the king from the house of the LORD: and they came through the high gate into the king's house, and set the king upon the throne.
21 And all the people of the land rejoiced: and the city was quiet, after that they had slain Athaliah with the sword.

Article. IV.

Section. 1.

1.Full Faith and Credit shall be given in each State to the public Acts, Records, and judicial Proceedings of every other State. And the Congress may by general Laws prescribe the Manner in which such Acts, Records and Proceedings shall be proved, and the Effect thereof.

Now we arrive at issues that seem missing in action in The Bible. These issues are simply stated differently than we are accustomed to seeing in our modern language. You should recall that the concept of states is in infancy, albeit the Bible recognizes and addresses how those of other lands are to be treated.

The Bible makes clear that all, both Hebrews and Gentiles must follow the laws and procedures set forth in the Bible. In the event of a point of misunderstanding or misinterpretation, then those involved were expected to take the matter to the next higher level of Mosaic organization chart mentioned many times herein. The affected parties would continue to move the matter up the organization of Judges and Elders until a resolution was reached.

Numbers 15:13-16
13 All born of the country shall do these things after this manner, in offering an offering made by fire, of a sweet savour unto the LORD.

[14] If a stranger sojourn with you, or whosoever be among you in your generations, and offer an offering made by fire, of sweet savour to the LORD; as ye do, so he shall do.
[15] One ordinance shall be both for you of the congregation, and for the stranger that sojourneth with you, an ordinance for ever in your generations: as ye are, so shall the stranger be before the LORD.
[16] One law, one manner shall be for you, and the stranger that sojourneth with you.

Exodus 12:49 One law shall be to him that is homeborn, and unto the stranger that sojourneth among you.

<u>Article. IV.</u>

<u>Section. 2.</u>

<u>1.The Citizens of each State shall be entitled to all Privileges and Immunities of Citizens in the several States</u>.

<u>2.A Person charged in any State with Treason, Felony, or other Crime, who shall flee from Justice, and be found in another State, shall on Demand of the executive Authority of the State from which he fled, be delivered up, to be removed to the State having Jurisdiction of the Crime.</u>

<u>3.No Person held to Service or Labour in one State, under the Laws thereof, escaping into another, shall, in Consequence of any Law or Regulation therein, be discharged from such Service or Labour, but shall be delivered up on Claim of the Party to whom such Service or Labour may be due.</u>

Numbers 15:13-16 King James Version

[13] All that are born of the country shall do these things after this manner, in offering an offering made by fire, of a sweet savour unto the LORD.

14 If a stranger sojourn with you, or whosoever be among you in your generations, and offer an offering by fire, of sweet savour unto the LORD; as ye do, so shall he.
15 One ordinance shall be for you of the congregation, and also for the stranger that sojourneth with you, an ordinance for ever in your generations: as ye are, so shall the stranger be before the LORD.
16 One law, for you, and the stranger that sojourneth with you.

Exodus 12:49 One law shall be to him that is homeborn, and unto the stranger that sojourneth among you.

Section 2 makes it illegal to attempt to escape the law. The Biblical plan called BIBLICAL CITIES OF REFUGE WAS ESTABLISHED as a means of providing a civilized domicile for those falsely accused, or possibly sometimes prior to court trial.

NUMBERS CHAPTER 35

The LORD spake unto Moses in the plains of Moab by Jordan *near* Jericho, saying,
2Command the children of Israel, that they give unto the Levites of the inheritance of their possession cities to dwell in; and ye shall give *also* unto the Levites suburbs for the cities round about them.
3And the cities shall they have to dwell in; and the suburbs of them shall be for their cattle, and for their goods, and for all their beasts.
4And the suburbs of the cities, which ye shall give unto the Levites, *shall reach* from the wall of the city and outward a thousand cubits round about.
5And ye shall measure from without the city on the east side two thousand cubits, and on the south side two thousand cubits, and on the west side two thousand cubits, and on the north side two thousand cubits; and the city *shall be* in the midst: this shall be to them the suburbs of the cities.
6And among the cities which ye shall give unto the Levites *there shall be* six cities for refuge, which ye shall appoint for the manslayer, that he may flee thither: and to them ye shall add forty and two cities.

7*So* all the cities which ye shall give to the Levites *shall be* forty
and eight cities: them *shall ye give* with their suburbs.
8And the cities which ye shall give *shall be* of the possession of the
children of Israel: from *them that have* many ye shall give many;
but from *them that have* few ye shall give few: every one shall give
of his cities unto the Levites according to his inheritance.
9And the LORD spake unto Moses, saying,
10Speak unto the children of Israel, and say unto them, When ye
be come over Jordan into the land of Canaan;
11Then ye shall appoint you cities to be cities of refuge; that the
slayer may flee thither, which killeth any person at unawares.
12And they shall be unto you cities for refuge from the avenger;
that the manslayer die not, until he stand before the congregation
in judgment.
13Of these cities which ye shall give, six cities shall ye have for
refuge.
14Ye shall give three cities on this side Jordan, and three cities
shall ye give in the land of Canaan, *which* shall be cities of refuge.
15These six cities shall be a refuge, *both* for the children of Israel,
and for the stranger, and for the sojourner among them: that every
one that killeth any person unawares may flee thither.
16If he smite him with an instrument of iron, so that he die, he *is* a
murderer: the murderer shall surely be put to death.
17If he smite him with throwing a stone, wherewith he may die, and
he die, he *is* a murderer: the murderer shall surely be put to death.
18Or *if* he smite him with an hand weapon of wood, and he die,
he *is* a murderer: the murderer shall surely be put to death.
19The revenger of blood himself shall slay the murderer: when he
meeteth him, he shall slay him.
20But if he thrust him of hatred, or hurl at him by laying of wait, that
he die;
21Or in enmity smite him with his hand, that he die: he that
smote *him* shall surely be put to death; *for* he *is* a murderer: the
revenger of blood shall slay the murderer, when he meeteth him.
22But if he thrust him suddenly without enmity, or have cast upon
him any thing without laying of wait,

23Or with any stone, wherewith a man may die, seeing *him* not,
and cast *it* upon him, that he die, and *was* not his enemy, neither
sought his harm:
24Then the congregation shall judge between the slayer and the
revenger of blood according to these judgments:
25The congregation shall deliver the slayer out of the hand of the
revenger of blood, the congregation shall restore him to the city of
his refuge, whither he was fled: and he shall abide in it unto death
of the high priest, which was anointed with holy oil.
26But if the slayer shall at any time come without the border of the
city of his refuge, whither he was fled;
27And the revenger of blood find him without the borders of the city
of his refuge, and the revenger of blood kill the slayer; he shall not
be guilty of blood:
28Because he should've remained in city of his refuge until death
of the high priest: but after death of the high priest, slayer shall
return into the land of his possession.
29So these *things* shall be for a statute of judgment unto you
throughout your generations in all your dwellings.
30Whoso killeth any person, the murderer shall be put to death by
the mouth of witnesses: but one witness shall not testify against
any person *to cause him* to die.
31Moreover ye shall take no satisfaction for the life of a murderer,
which *is* guilty of death: but he shall be surely put to death.
32And ye shall take no satisfaction for him that is fled to the city of
his refuge, that he should come again to dwell in the land, until the
death of the priest.
33So ye shall not pollute the land wherein ye *are*: for blood it
defileth the land: and land cannot be cleansed of blood that is shed,
but by the blood of him that shed it.
34Defile not therefore the land which ye shall inhabit, wherein I
dwell: for I the LORD dwell among the children of Israel.

Article. IV.

Section. 3.

1.New States may be admitted by the Congress into this Union; but no new State shall be formed or erected within the Jurisdiction of any other State; nor any State be formed by the Junction of two or more States, or Parts of States, without the Consent of the Legislatures of the States concerned as well as of the Congress.

We established in a previous section, a discussion detailing the manner in which the 12 tribes of Israel were allotted geographic specifically defined lands within their nation. A review of modern and ancient maps of the middle east demonstrate little change in the “geo/political land” features that define the national and territorial borders. This point documents the biblical reasoning behind establishment of National borders or subdivision thereof.

2.The Congress shall have Power to dispose of and make all needful Rules and Regulations respecting the Territory or other Property belonging to the United States; and nothing in this Constitution shall be so construed as to Prejudice any Claims of the United States, or of any particular State.

The Bible provides a procedure for correct level of judges to review and adjudicate the weightiest matters. In the Moses organization, we learn that the people were to bring lesser matters to the lower level leaders, and the heavier matters should go before Moses, or the person atop the organization. In this manner, the Bible provides precedence for the weighty matters in the Constitution.

"The highest levels of the Organization Chart of Moses was the Sanhedrin, (Matt. 5:22; 26:59; Mark "15:1, etc.) to denote the supreme judicial and administrative" "council of the Jews, which, it is said, was first instituted by" "Moses, and was composed of seventy men (Num. 11:16, 17).

They were of three classes (1) "the chief priests, or heads of the twenty-four priestly courses" as elaborated fully within "(1 Chr. 24), (2) the scribes, and (3) the elders. As the highest" "court of judicature, "in all causes and over all persons," "ecclesiastical and civil, supreme," its decrees were binding," "not only on the Jews in Palestine, but on all Jews wherever" scattered abroad. Its usual place of meeting" "was within the precincts of the temple, in the hall "Gazith," but it sometimes met also in the house of the high priest (Matt. "26:3)."

Article. IV.

Section. 4.

1.The United States shall guarantee to every State in this Union a Republican Form of Government, and shall protect each of them against Invasion; and on Application of the Legislature, or of the Executive (when the Legislature cannot be convened) against domestic Violence.

It is clear that the Moses Organization provided a government closely resembling what is called a Republic Form of Government. In that republic form of government, the people elect representatives to the nations capitol and representatives handle all the business and voting. The Bible provides the same methodology, absent specific rules of voting. Within the Moses organization, lower and mid level leaders surely required election, thus the republic form of government.

In the Bible form of government, the Sanhedrin would take added responsibility to ensure conformance to the Will of God.

Article. V.

1.The Congress, whenever two thirds of both Houses shall deem it necessary, shall propose Amendments to this Constitution, or, on the Application of the Legislatures of two thirds of the several States, shall call a Convention for proposing Amendments, which, in either Case, shall be valid to all Intents and Purposes, as Part of this Constitution, when ratified by the Legislatures of three fourths of the several States, or by Conventions in three fourths thereof, as the one or the other Mode of Ratification may be proposed by the Congress; Provided that no Amendment which may be made prior to the Year One thousand eight hundred and eight shall in any Manner affect the first and fourth Clauses in the Ninth Section of the first Article; and that no State, without its Consent, shall be deprived of its equal Suffrage in the Senate.

God made no specific allowance for changes to His laws. However, the famous Moses organization indicates that the weighty matters may be taken before Moses or the leader of the Hebrews. Any change in laws is indeed a weighty matter. Those matters that could be decided in full obeisance to the Word of God would be allowed and cast into law. Those not in concert with Laws of God would be in trouble. "The highest levels of the Organization Chart of Moses was the Sanhedrin, (Matt. 5:22; 26:59; Mark "15:1, etc.) to denote the supreme judicial and administrative" "council of the Jews, which, it is said, was first instituted by" "Moses, and was composed of seventy men (Num. 11:16, 17). They were of three classes (1) "the chief priests, or heads of the twenty-four priestly courses" "(1 Chr. 24), (2) the scribes, and (3) the elders. As the highest" "court of judicature, "in all causes and over all persons," "ecclesiastical and civil, supreme," its decrees were binding," "not only on the Jews in Palestine, but on all Jews wherever" scattered abroad. Its usual place of meeting" "was within the precincts of the temple, in the hall "Gazith," but it sometimes met in the house of the high priest (Matt. "26:3)."

There are instances in the Bible during which God told key leaders to LISTEN TO THE VOICE OF THE PEOPLE. These were instances in which the people desired a major change, sometimes against the wishes or commandments of God. God essentially tells the people that prophets should show them the error of what they desire and then to listen to their voices. (1 Samuel 8:9) This should indicate God fully expects us to remain within His word at all times, or else to suffer possible punishment for your sins.

Article. VI.

1.All Debts contracted and Engagements entered into, before the Adoption of this Constitution, shall be as valid against the United States under this Constitution, as under the Confederation.

The Founders included this clause to make sure any debts entered into during the period at which America was governed by the ARTICLES OF CONFEDERATION, would continue to be valid under our new US Constitution.

SEE BANKRUPTCY SECTION ON CONTRACTS

God provided laws for loaning money or goods. These laws were based upon the concept of "usury" which is today called "interest rate loans." Please see the 613 laws chapter.

The bible provides evidence of a legal code in the Book of Nahum 1:12. The contract phrase, "quiet and likewise many," now defined by many professionals to represent our modern contract terms: Joint And Several Responsibility.

2.This Constitution, and the Laws of the United States which shall be made in Pursuance thereof; and all Treaties made, or which shall be made, under the Authority of the United States, shall be the supreme Law of the Land; and the Judges in every State shall be bound thereby, any Thing in the Constitution or Laws of any State to the Contrary notwithstanding.

This explanation has been described in sections above.

Now we arrive at issues that seem missing in action in The Bible. These issues are stated far differently than we are accustomed to seeing in our modern language. You are urged to recall that the concept of states is in infancy, albeit the Bible recognizes and addresses how those of other lands are to be treated.

Numbers 15:13-16

13 All that are born of the country shall do these things after this
manner, in offering an offering made by fire, of a sweet savour unto
the LORD.
14 And if a stranger sojourn with you, or whosoever be among you
in your generations, and will offer an offering made by fire, of a
sweet savour unto the LORD; as ye do, so he shall do.
15 One ordinance shall be both for you of the congregation, and also
for the stranger that sojourneth with you, an ordinance for ever in
your generations: as ye are, so shall the stranger be before
the LORD.
16 One law and one manner shall be for you, and the sojourner.

Exodus 12:49 One law shall be to him that is homeborn, and unto the stranger that sojourneth among you.

God made no specific allowance for changes to His laws. However, the Moses organization indicates that the weighty matters may be taken before Moses or the leader of the Hebrews. Any change in laws is indeed weighty. Those matters decided in full obeisance to the Word of God would be allowed and cast into law. Those not in concert with Laws of God would be in trouble.

Biblical Sanhedrin would review any and all changes, or challenges to any law to ensure correlation with the Will of God. US Constitution makes no reference to ensuring the Will of God.

3.The Senators and Representatives before mentioned, and the Members of the several State Legislatures, and all executive and judicial Officers, both of the United States and of the several States, shall be bound by Oath or Affirmation, to support this Constitution; but no religious Test shall ever be required as a Qualification to any Office or public Trust under the United States.

In nearly all published statements for "Oath of Office," the person taking the oath is asked to Vow, Swear, or Affirm. God speaks against any acts of Oath or Swearing, as God expects us to Vow your Oath to God only. Therefore, the word Affirm or Affirmation is included to differentiate the concept so that Swearing does not take the form of cursing. Affirmation to support and uphold all requirements of your office, while supporting and defending the US Constitution is acceptable.

Article. VII

1.The Ratification of the Conventions of nine States, shall be sufficient for the Establishment of this Constitution between the States so ratifying the Same.

God made no specific allowance for changes to His laws. However, the famous Moses organization indicates the weighty matters may be taken before Moses or leader of the Hebrews. Any change in laws is weighty matter. Matters that could be decided in full obeisance to the Word of God would be allowed and cast into law. Those not in concert with Laws of God would be in trouble.

US Constitution established a super-majority was required, representing 9 of the original 12 states to change the constitution. Moses needed to hear from a heavy majority of elders and group of 24 in order to consider any change to Gods law, any change or amendment must be in full accord with the Word of God.

ASSEMBLY OF MAJOR DECISION MAKERS, SANHEDRIN:

Sanhedrin (Gr. synedrion), meaning "a sitting" "together," or a "council." This word (rendered "council,")" is frequently used in the New Testament (Matt. 5:22; 26:59; Mark "15:1, etc.) to denote the supreme judicial and administrative" "council of the Jews, which, it is said, was first instituted by" "Moses, composed of seventy men (Num. 11:16, 17). But" that seems to have been only a temporary arrangement which Moses made. The name is first "employed by the Jewish historian Josephus. This "council" is" "referred to simply as the "chief priests and elders of the" "people" (Matt. 26:3, 47, 57, 59; 27:1, 3, 12, 20, etc.), before" whom Christ was tried on the charge of claiming to be the Messiah. "The Sanhedrin is said to have consisted of seventy-one members. They were of three classes (1) "the chief priests, or heads of the twenty-four priestly courses" "(1 Chr. 24), (2) the scribes, and (3) the elders. The highest" "court of judicature, "in all causes, over all persons," "ecclesiastical and civil, supreme," its decrees were binding," "not only on Jews in Palestine, but on Jews wherever" scattered. Its jurisdiction was curtailed by "Herod, and Romans. Its place of meeting" "was the temple, in the hall "Gazith," sometimes in the home of the high priest (Matt. 26).

Chapter 17. NATURAL LAW, UNALIENABLE RIGHTS, LIFE, LIBERTY, HAPPINESS

Not just clever words written by Thomas Jefferson to add power to our DECLARATION OF INDEPENDENCE.

The concept of Natural Rights has been articulated by mankind since the earliest days of our Holy Bible. By the time of The Crusades, natural rights was established in the 1100s and 1200s by European medieval Christian lawyers dealing with property law in the Catholic Christian church, making God's law an important part of Man's Law. These lawyers viewed property or dominium as a natural right based on Genesis 1 in which God creates mankind in His image and gives man dominion of the earth.

The American, Bible-Based Defense of Unalienable Rights

THE BIBLE everywhere assumes, and in some places explicitly appeals to, natural law. The written book of God constantly bears witness to God's other book, the book of nature. To prove this, we will walk through chapters of The Bible, noting some important rights along the way.

On the seventh day, he rested, having pronounced his work good. This is the first proclamation of the doctrine of natural law. Anything that would destroy or corrupt this good-created order, logic would dictate, would be bad or evil.

GENESIS 1: In the beginning, God created the heavens and the earth. At the end of the seventh day, he rested, having pronounced his work good. This is the first proclamation of the doctrine of natural law. Anything that would destroy or corrupt this good created order, logic would dictate, would be bad or evil.

Genesis 2 gives us evidence. God saw lonely Adam and said this was "not good" (Gen. 2:18). What could this mean? It must communicate something like, "Given the nature of Adam, given his intrinsic properties, his remaining without a complement[1], - - God evaluated the kind of being Adam was and judged he was not in a good situation. Adam's male form was intrinsically directed toward a female companion that he lacked and needed for his fulfillment.

Within first two chapters of the Bible, we see natural law.

The idea of natural rights was articulated in the 1100s and 1200s by European medieval Christian lawyers dealing with property law in the Catholic Christian church. These lawyers viewed property or *dominium* as a natural right based on Genesis 1 where God creates mankind in His image and gives him dominion over the earth.

Genesis 1:26-27 says, "Then God said, 'Let us make man in Our image, according to Our likeness. Let them have dominion...over all the earth.' So God created man in His *own* image, male and female [bold emphasis Mine]."[1] Yet the lawyers thought that while a person's material property is transferrable or alienable, the property of his personhood such as his life is non-transferrable or unalienable. In the 1400s, liberty was also articulated as a natural right. French scholar and theologian Jean Charlier de Gerson articulated liberty as a natural right in his 1402 *De Vita Spirituali Animae* or *The Life of Spiritual Souls*. Soon after, Dominican theologians classified liberty as unalienable. Life and liberty thus came to be theologically expressed as sacred, unalienable rights of mankind.

Christian thinkers of the Reformation era of the 1500s indirectly supported natural rights due to their belief that human beings, as created by God, have certain duties to God. John Calvin asserted in his 1536 *Institutes of the Christian Religion* that human beings have duties to God because they are God's "workmanship" or masterpiece. Calvin draws this idea from Ephesians 2:10 in which the Apostle Paul expresses, "We are God's **workmanship**, created in Christ Jesus unto good works, which God hath ordained, that we should walk in them."

American Founder, lawyer professor, and U. S. Supreme Court Justice James Wilson also supported the principle of natural and unalienable rights in his 1790-1791 *Lectures on Law* and in his 1793 court decision *Chisholm vs. Georgia*. In his *Lectures*, he observed that all human beings possess natural rights which are upheld by the universal moral law of God and Nature.

He writes, ... In US Supreme Court Case *Chisholm vs. Georgia*, Wilson, like Locke, referenced ideas from Genesis 1, Ephesians 2:10, and Psalm 139:14 (in which the individual is described as "fearfully and wonderfully made"). He thus defended from the Bible a person's God-given rights that should be protected by civil government. Likewise expressing the idea of man as God's workmanship found in Ephesians 2:10, Wilson expounds, "MAN, fearfully and wonderfully made, is the workmanship of his all perfect CREATOR. A State, as useful and valuable as the contrivance is, is the inferior contrivance of man and from man's native dignity derives all its acquired importance [bold emphasis mine]."[11] Because the state consists of the people, Wilson essentially asserted, if the state diminishes the rights and dignity of the individual citizen, it basically also diminishes rights of the state itself.

The principle of God-given natural, unalienable rights of "life, liberty, and the pursuit of happiness" is a key philosophical principle expressed in the U. S. Declaration of Independence and reflected in the U. S. Constitution. Taking up Locke's worldview and arguments, the American Founders grounded man's natural rights in the "Creator God" and the "Law of Nature and Nature's God." They considered these rights to be a gift from God granted to humanity as God's image-bearing masterpiece, His workmanship. Such rights allowed mankind to fulfill their God-ordained duties in life. The Founders were acutely aware that removing God or moral law as the grounding of natural rights would place those rights in jeopardy. For if one could separate these rights from the divine source, one could justify taking them away for any reason. Jefferson pressed the point in his 1781 *Notes on the State of Virginia*: "Can the liberties of a nation be thought secure when we have removed their only firm basis, a conviction in the minds of the people that these liberties are the gift of God? That they are not to be violated but with His wrath?" The principle of natural, unalienable rights in America's founding philosophy is, affirms Waldman in his 2008 *Founding Faith: Providence, Politics, and the Birth of Religious Freedom in America*, "best argument that Judeo-Christian tradition created our nation."

THE DOCTRINE of natural law can be found not only in the Bible, but also in the writings of Plato, Aristotle, Cicero and the other Stoics, St. Augustine and most of the church fathers, Thomas Aquinas, and most pre-Kantian Reformed thinkers. Arthur F. Holmes suggests, rightly, that natural law theories depend, for their truth, upon the metaphysical theories which undergird them. Two forms of natural law theory, founded on two quite different ontologies, have been popular in the history of Christian moral thought: that of the Stoics and that of Aristotle. The Stoic system finds the foundation for moral laws in reason alone, whereas the Aristotelian system finds the foundation for moral laws in the very nature of being (i.e., in human nature itself). In this section, we will consider the philosophical foundations of what we take to be a consistent Christian natural law theory—that which flows out of Aristotelian metaphysics. We will begin with distinctions and definitions. We will then go into greater detail concerning the two metaphysical foundations of natural law, and, finally, some epistemological elements of natural law, which flow out of the metaphysical foundations. We hope to show that a coherent natural law theory depends upon a particular philosophical position, and, secondly, that this philosophical position and the natural law theory which it supports are defensible.

Because the bulk of this chapter will be considering the biblical perspective of natural law, we will not belabor the point here. However, it is worth noting that Romans 2:14-15 has been traditionally understood as teaching natural law:

> For when Gentiles, who do not have the law, by nature do what the law requires, they are a law to themselves, even though they do not have the law. They show that the work of the law is written on their hearts, while their conscience also bears witness, and their conflicting thoughts accuse or even excuse them. (Rom. 2:14-15)

THE HEBREW SCRIPTURES

THE WEALTH of evidence for natural law in Scripture surpasses the ability to catalogue it, at least in a brief period. What follows is only small sampling of what the Scriptures contain. It is however representative, and, by the end of the chapter, I trust readers will be able to readily detect other evidence themselves. GENESIS In the beginning, God created the heavens and the earth. At the end of the seventh day, he rested, having pronounced his work good. This is the first proclamation of the doctrine of natural law. Anything that would destroy or corrupt this good created order, logic would dictate, would be bad or evil.[1]

Genesis 2 gives us another piece of evidence. God saw lonely Adam and said this was "not good" (Gen. 2:18). What could this statement mean? It must communicate something like, "Given the nature of Adam, given his intrinsic properties, his remaining without a complement[1], woman will harm him." God evaluated the kind of being Adam was and judged he was not in a good situation. Adam's male form was intrinsically directed toward a female companion that he lacked and needed for his fulfillment. So already, after the first two chapters of the Bible, we see an affirmation of an objective order, a natural law.

EXODUS

Bockmuehl mentions the case of Jethro in Exodus 18. During his visit with Moses, Jethro noticed people bringing cases to be judged consumed all Moses time. He responded: "What you are doing is not good.... For the thing is too heavy for you. You are not able to do it alone" (vs. 17-18). Jethro's basic criticism was that Moses was failing to steward his time: in this regard, his actions were "not good." Here we have an example of someone outside of the visible assembly of God's people (though most likely a God-fearer of some kind), who offers moral wisdom to God's lawgiver himself, Moses. Jethro's suggestion could not have been derived from the Torah, or else he would not have needed to give it. His advice is simple common sense. Moses needed to delegate and divide the labor; his time and energy simply could not handle the workload. And he was certainly able to delegate. Jethro perceived the problem and solution where no explicit divine law addressed the issue. Now of course, one could say that Jethro's advice is derived by extension from some more basic Mosaic principle, but just as obviously, this advice is common sense.[1] It surely strains credulity to suggest that only someone who had read Moses' law could produce this suggestion. And yet it benefitted Moses, and so fulfilled the natural law, which points people toward their own good.

DEUTERONOMY

Collins highlights[1] Deuteronomy 4:5-6, where God tells Moses:

> See, I have taught you statutes and rules, as the Lord my God commanded me, that you should do them in the land you are entering to take possession of it. Keep them and do them, for that will be your wisdom and your understanding in the sight of the peoples, who, when they hear all these statutes, will say, 'Surely this nation is a wise and understanding people.'

If Israel keeps the law, God says the nations will conclude it is a wise and understanding people. What is the logic of this promise? It must be that the nations will look on and see how obeying this law leads to flourishing, to human good. But this assumes several things. Firstly, it assumes there is an objective human good. The contrary assertion would be that good is whatever the law says it is and nothing more. But then, the peoples' statement would mean nothing more than: "Surely this is a nation that lives according to its laws." Obviously, this is nonsense. Rather, it must assume, secondly, that pagans know what human flourishing is, and that they see that obeying God's law leads to it.

When the American Founders wrote the U. S. Declaration of Independence, they set down important philosophical principles to defend and justify freedom from British rule and their formation of a new, independent nation, the United States of America. One key principle asserted by the Founders was the unalienable rights of mankind—the "self-evident truth" that all men "are endowed by their Creator with certain unalienable Rights, that among these are Life, Liberty, and the pursuit of Happiness."

Not often recognized today is that influential European philosophers and the American Founders grounded, articulated, and affirmed the idea of unalienable rights, in large part, based on the Law of Nature and God, the Bible, and Judeo-Christian thought.

Unalienable rights are natural rights. What exactly are natural rights and unalienable rights? Natural rights are God-given or inherent birthrights or properties of all mankind due to our nature and dignity as human beings. These rights are grounded in the Law of Nature and God, the universal moral law. These rights include, as John Locke describes in his 1689 *Second Treatise of Civil Government*, one's personhood, means, and possessions—his life, body and health, liberty, labor and industry, and goods and estates. Natural rights can be classified specifically in two ways—as "alienable" or "unalienable." "Alienable" rights or properties include an individual's means, labor, and possessions that can be transferred–bought, sold, or given–and thus removed or alienated from the owner as he sees fit, for example, in order to make a living or to better his own or another's life. "Unalienable" or "inalienable" rights are those properties of personhood that cannot be transferred, removed, or alienated from an individual by any person, power, or civil law without just cause. Doing so would violate the Law of Nature and God. For mankind does not have total control or authority over these properties. Unalienable rights, as recognized in the Declaration, include life, liberty, and the pursuit of happiness.

Natural Rights / Properties
God-given or inherent birthrights of all mankind
Due to our nature and dignity as human beings

Alienable Rights / Properties Transferable (by owner)	Unalienable Rights / Non-transferable
Means of living (labor & industry)	Life (includes body & health)
Material & intellectual possessions	Liberty (includes religious)
(goods, estates, research, creative)	Pursuit of happiness

The idea of natural rights was articulated in the 1100s and 1200s by European medieval Christian lawyers dealing with property law in the Catholic Christian church. These lawyers viewed property or *dominium* as a natural right based on Genesis 1 where God creates mankind in His image and gives him dominion over the earth. Genesis 1:26-27 says, "Then God said, 'Let us make man in Our image, according to Our likeness. Let them have **dominion**...over all the earth.' So God created man in His *own* image, male and female [bold emphasis mine]."[1] Yet the lawyers thought that while a person's material property is transferrable or alienable, the property of his personhood such as his life is non-transferrable or unalienable. In the 1400s, liberty was also articulated as a natural right. French scholar and theologian Jean Charlier de Gerson articulated liberty as a natural right in his 1402 *De Vita Spirituali Animae* or *The Life of Spiritual Souls*. Soon after, Dominican theologians classified liberty as unalienable. Life and liberty thus came to be theologically expressed as sacred, unalienable rights of mankind.

Christian thinkers of the 1500s Reformation era indirectly supported natural rights due to their belief that human beings, as created by God, have certain duties to God. John Calvin asserted in his 1536 *Institutes of the Christian Religion* that human beings have duties to God because they are God's "workmanship" or masterpiece. Calvin draws this idea from Ephesians 2:10 in which the Apostle Paul expresses, "We are God's **workmanship**, created in Christ Jesus unto good works, which God hath ordained, that we should walk in them [emphasis mine]." (KJV, GNV)[2] Calvin thus writes, "How can the idea of God enter your mind without instantly giving rise to the thought that since you are His **workmanship**, you are bound, by the very law of creation, to submit to His authority?—that your life is due to Him?—that whatever you do ought to have reference to Him [emphasis mine]?"[3] The idea that human beings have natural rights because of their duties to God, was asserted by reformed political writers including John Ponet in his 1556 *Short Treatise on Political Power* and Stephen Junius Brutus in his 1579 *Vindiciae Contra Tyrannos*.

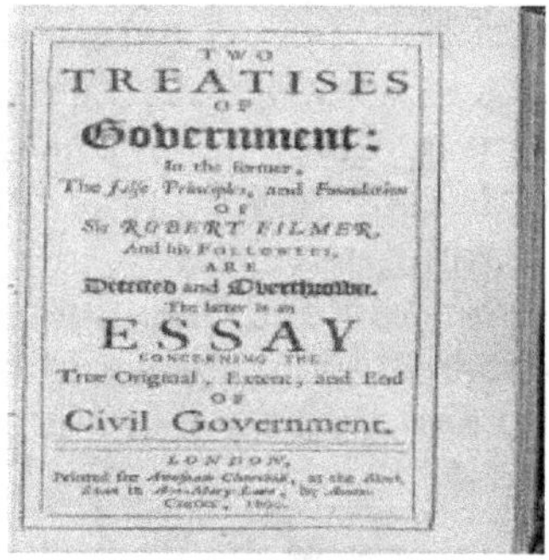

TWO
TREATISES
OF
Government:

ESSAY

True Original, Extent, and End
OF
Civil Government.

LONDON,

Cover Page of *Two Treatises of Civil Government* by John Locke, 1689.

Enlightenment-era British philosopher John Locke, in his 1689 *Second Treatise*, introduced a clear, modern explanation of natural rights which became very influential to early Americans and American founding political thought. Locke shared the view of Christian thinkers like Calvin that because human beings are created by God, they have certain duties to God. Locke went on to assert that individuals, as created by and owing duties to God, possess certain natural rights including "life, liberty, and estate" which are necessary to preserve humanity, maintain order, and perform such duties in the world. Reflecting Calvin, Locke expressed the idea found in Ephesians 2:10 that man is God's workmanship to ground the principle of natural rights. He reasons, . . .

> As such, Locke asserted that man is God's property, created for God's and not another's purpose and use. As a result, human beings have natural rights which they are bound to uphold. Locke was saying that natural rights allow human beings—who possess a unique identity and relationship with God—to freely worship and follow God, serve as stewards for God, and fulfill their God-ordained duties and purposes on earth.

The American Founders' understanding of natural rights was influenced by Locke. They believed that natural rights are the inherent gift of <u>God, the Creator</u>, for mankind. Civil governments may secure these rights, but they do not originally grant them. As such, governments cannot take away these rights without just cause, and men may justly defend their rights for self-preservation. Importantly, the Founders recognized that removing God as the source of natural or human rights would endanger these rights and freedoms.

Portrait of Samuel Adams by John Singleton Copley, 1772.

American Founder and revolutionary leader Samuel Adams, addressed the American colonists' natural rights to life, liberty (including religious liberty), and estate in his 1772 revolutionary pamphlet, *Report on the Rights of Colonists*. Because God gives man life and dignity, Adams argued, man has a natural right to life. And as God gives man reason and free will to reflect and choose, man has a natural right to liberty—including political and religious liberty. Man also has a God-given right to his labor and possessions for his survival. Adams, like Locke, defended these rights by their origin in the Law of Nature and God. He writes of liberty, for example, "'Just and true liberty, equal and impartial liberty' in matters spiritual and temporal is a thing that all men are clearly entitled to by the eternal and immutable laws of God and Nature, as well as by the law of Nations & all well-grounded municipal laws which must have their foundation in the former."[5] Adams further recognized that the Bible supports these rights, that they "may be best understood by reading and carefully studying the institutes of the great Lawgiver and head of the Christian Church [Jesus Christ] which are to be found closely promulgated in the *New Testament*."[6]

Portrait of Thomas Jefferson by Rembrandt Peale, 1800.

American Founder and primary author of the Declaration, Thomas Jefferson shared the long-held view that life and liberty were natural, unalienable rights. He acknowledged that such rights were the gift of God, stating in his 1774 *Summary View of the Rights of British America*, "The God who gave us life, gave us liberty at the same time. The hand of force may destroy, but cannot disjoin them."[7] However, unlike many Calvinists in America and England, Jefferson did not classify man's "estate" as unalienable. Rather, in line with the moral-sense thinkers of the Scottish Enlightenment—including Francis Hutcheson, David Hume, and Jean-Jacques Burlamaqui—Jefferson defined man's goods, possessions, and fruits of labor as transferrable or alienable property. As such, he did not list "estate" as an unalienable right in the Declaration but instead listed the "pursuit of happiness."

Portrait of James Madison by John Vanderlyn, 1816.

American Founder, *Federalist Papers* author, and architect of the U. S. Constitution and Bill of Rights, James Madison shared Locke's idea that natural rights were granted to mankind based on their duties to God. In speaking of religious liberty, Madison wrote in the Virginia Declaration of Rights of 1776, "Religion, the duty we owe to our Creator and the manner of discharging it, can be directed by reason and conviction, not by force or violence. Therefore, all men are equally entitled to the free exercise of religion according to conscience. It is the mutual duty of all to practice Christian forbearance, love, and charity towards each other [emphasis mine]."[8] Madison reasserted in his 1785 *Memorial and Remonstrance* this idea that inherent, unalienable rights such as religious liberty are based on mankind's natural duties to God, which exist before civil society: "Religion must be left to the conviction and conscience of every man. [This right] is unalienable because the opinions of men...cannot follow the dictates of other men. What is here a right towards men is a duty towards the Creator. This duty is precedent to claims of civil society."[9]

Portrait of U. S. Supreme Court Justice James Wilson

American Founder, lawyer professor, and U. S. Supreme Court Justice James Wilson also supported the principle of natural and unalienable rights in his 1790-1791 *Lectures on Law* and in his 1793 court decision *Chisholm vs. Georgia*. In his *Lectures*, he observed that all human beings possess natural rights which are upheld by the universal moral law of God and Nature. He writes,

> In *Chisholm vs. Georgia*, Wilson, like Locke, referenced ideas from Genesis 1, Ephesians 2:10, and Psalm 139:14 (in which the individual is described as "fearfully and wonderfully made"). He defended from the Bible a person's God-given rights to be protected by civil government. Likewise expressing man as God's workmanship found in Ephesians 2:10. Wilson says, "MAN, fearfully and wonderfully made, is workmanship of his perfect CREATOR. A State, as useful and valuable as the contrivance is, is the inferior contrivance of man and from man's native dignity derives acquired importance." Because the state consists of the people, Wilson asserted, if the state diminishes rights and dignity of individual citizens, it diminishes rights of the state.[10]

The principle of God-given natural, unalienable rights of "life, liberty, and the pursuit of happiness" is a key philosophical principle expressed in the U. S. Declaration of Independence and reflected in the U. S. Constitution. Taking up Locke's worldview arguments, the American Founders grounded man's natural rights in the "Creator God" and "Law of Nature and Nature's God." They considered these rights a gift from God granted to humanity as God's image-bearing masterpiece, His workmanship. Such rights allowed mankind to fulfill their God-ordained duties in life. The Founders were acutely aware that removing God or moral law as the grounding of natural rights would place those rights in jeopardy. For if one could separate these rights from the divine source, one could justify taking them away for any reason. Jefferson pressed the point in his 1781 *Notes on the State of Virginia*: "Can the liberties of a nation be thought secure when we have removed their only firm basis, a conviction in the minds of the people that these liberties are the gift of God? That they are not to be violated but with His wrath?"

[1] King James Version (KJV)

[2] 1599 Geneva Bible (GNV); King James Version (KJV)

[3] John Calvin, Institutes of Christian Religion: A New Translation, vol. 1, trans. Henry Beveridge (Edinburgh, Scotland: for Calvin Translation Society, 1845), book 1, 52-53.

[4] John Locke, Second Treatise of Civil Government, 1690, in Two Treatises on Government (London: George Routledge and Sons, 1884), chapter 2, 194.

[5] Samuel Adams, "A State of the Rights of Colonists," 1772, in Tracts of the American Revolution, 1763-1776, ed. Merrill Jensen (Indianapolis, IN: Bobbs-Merrill Co., 1967), 236.

[6] Adams, "Rights of Colonists," 238.

[7] Thomas Jefferson, Summary View of Rights of British America Set Forth in Resolutions, 1774 (Williamsburg: Printed by Clementina Rind; London: Reprinted G. Kearsly, 1774), 43.

[8] Virginia Declaration of Rights, 1776, in Documents of American Democracy: A Collection of Essential Works, ed. Roger L. Kemp (Jefferson, NC: McFarland & Co., 2010), 54.

[9] James Madison, Memorial and Remonstrance Against Religious Assessments, 1785, The Writings of James Madison: 1783-1787, vol. 2, ed. Gaillard Hunt (New York: G. P. Putnam's Sons, 1901), 184-185.

[10] J. Wilson, Lectures on Law, Part 1, 1790-1791, Works of Honorable James Wilson, vol. 1, ed. Bird Wilson (Phil, PA: Lorenzo Press, Printed for Bronson and Chauncey, 1804), 308.

thefounding.net/the-american-bible-based-defense-of-unalienable-rights-life-liberty-

Chapter 18. MAJOR STATUTES OF LAW FROM THE BIBLE

THE FOLLOWING IS A NICELY CONSTRUCTED BIBLICAL GUIDE FOR SOURCES OF THE LAW, BY UNIVERSITY OF WISCONSIN-WHITEWATER
https://users.ssc.wisc.edu/~rkeyser/?page_id=540

The Bible does not focus primarily on matters of secular (i.e., non-religious) law, but what it does say about law had a great influence on later legal systems in many parts of the world. The excerpts below also show that ancient Hebrews took the existence of a sophisticated legal system for granted. They also suggest that the Bible's lessons for social norms are complex. On the one hand, many passages emphasize respect for authority and acceptance of traditional social hierarchies that kept slaves, servants, the poor, and women in subordinate roles. On the other hand, other passages recognize the need for treating all people fairly and for avoiding corruption that wealth and power make possible. A few passages also point to an underlying equality among all people.

1. The Ten Commandments are the most well-known legal rules found in the Bible (see Exodus 20:1-17 and Deuteronomy 5:6-21). Four of these mandates became enduring features of most secular law, namely those that prohibit murder, adultery, theft, and the giving of false testimony against one's neighbor. Four others are purely religious mandates (worship no other gods; do not make or bow down to any idols; do not misuse God's name; keep the Sabbath holy); and two state social ideals more than precise legal rules (honor your father and mother; do not covet your neighbor's house, wife, servant, ox, or donkey).
2. *The First Judges*: "Moses' father-in-law said to him: …You should also look for able men among all the people, men who fear God, are trustworthy, and hate dishonest gain; set such men over them as officers… Let them sit as judges for the people at all times; let them bring every important case to you, but decide every minor case themselves… So Moses…chose able men from all Israel" (*Exodus* 18:17-24).

3. *Truthful & Just Testimony*: "Do not spread false reports. Do not help a guilty person by being a malicious witness... When you give testimony in a lawsuit, do not pervert justice by siding with the crowd, and do not show favoritism to a poor person in a lawsuit... Do not deny justice to your poor people in their lawsuits. Have nothing to do with a false charge... Do not accept a bribe, for a bribe blinds those who see and twists the words of the innocent. Do not oppress a foreigner" (*Exodus* 23:1-9).
4. *Judging Fairly*: "Do not pervert justice; do not show partiality to the poor or favoritism to the great but judge your neighbor fairly" (*Leviticus* 19:15). "Appoint judges and officials...[who] shall judge the people fairly. Do not pervert justice or show partiality. Do not accept a bribe, for a bribe blinds the eyes of the wise and twists the words of the innocent. Follow justice and justice alone" (*Deuteronomy* 16:18-20). "The wicked accept bribes in secret to pervert the course of justice" (*Proverbs* 17:23).
5. *Number of Witnesses*: "One witness is not enough to convict anyone accused of any crime or offense they may have committed. A matter must be established by the testimony of two or three witnesses" (*Deut.* 19:15). "But if they will not listen, take one or two others along, so 'every matter may be established by testimony of two or three witnesses'" (*Matt* 18:16).
6. *Avoiding Lawsuits & False Testimony (Old Testament)*: "Do not go hastily to court, for what will you do in the end, if your neighbor puts you to shame? If you take your neighbor to court, do not betray another's confidence, or the one who hears it may shame you and the charge against you will stand. Like apples of gold in settings of silver is a ruling rightly given. Like an earring of gold or an ornament of fine gold is the rebuke of a wise judge to a listening ear... Like a club or a sword or a sharp arrow is one who gives false testimony against a neighbor" (*Proverbs* 25:8-12, 18).

7. *Avoiding Lawsuits (New Testament)*: "If any of you has a dispute with another, do you dare to take it before the ungodly for judgment instead of before the Lord's people? Or do you not know that the Lord's people will judge the world? ...But instead, one brother takes another to court—and this in front of unbelievers! The very fact that you have lawsuits among you means you have been completely defeated already. Why not rather be wronged? Why not rather be cheated? Instead, you yourselves cheat and do wrong, and you do this to your brothers and sisters.
8. Or do you not know that wrongdoers will not inherit the kingdom of God?" (*1 Corinthians* 6:1-9).
9. *God Appoints Rulers*: "Samuel took the horn of oil and anointed him in the midst of his brothers; and the Spirit of the Lord came mightily upon David from that day forward" (*1 Samuel* 16:3). "When all the elders of Israel had come to King David at Hebron, the king made a covenant with them at Hebron before the Lord, and they anointed David king over Israel" (*2 Samuel* 5:3). "I have found David my servant; with my holy oil I have anointed him" (*Psalm* 89.20). "By me kings reign and rulers issue decrees that are just; by me princes govern, and nobles—all who rule on earth" (*Proverbs* 8:15-16).
10. *Subjection to Authority*: "Let everyone be subject to the governing authorities, for there is no authority except that which God has established. The authorities that exist have been established by God. Consequently, whoever rebels against the authority is rebelling against what God has instituted... For rulers hold no terror for those who do right, but for those who do wrong... For the one in authority is God's servant for your good. But if you do wrong, be afraid, for rulers do not bear the sword for no reason. They are God's servants, agents of wrath to bring punishment on the wrongdoer. Therefore, it is necessary to submit to authorities, not only because of possible punishment but also as a matter of conscience. This is also why you pay taxes, for the authorities are God's servants" (*Romans* 13:1-6).

11. *Law is for Lawbreakers*: "We know that the law is good if one uses it properly. We also know that the law is made not for the righteous but for lawbreakers and rebels, the ungodly and sinful, the unholy and irreligious, for those who kill their fathers or mothers, for murderers, for the sexually immoral, for those practicing homosexuality, for slave traders, liars and perjurers—and for whatever else is contrary to sound doctrine" (*1 Timothy* 1:8-10).
12. *Men and Women: The Curse*: "To the woman [the Lord] said, 'I will greatly multiply your pain in childbirth; in pain you will bring forth children; yet your desire will be for your husband, and he will rule over you.' Then to Adam He said, 'Because you have listened to the voice of your wife, and have eaten from the tree..., cursed is the ground because of you; in toil you will eat of it all the days of your life'" (*Genesis* 3:16-17).
13. *Women Subordinate to Men (New Testament)*: "But I want you to understand that Christ is the head of every man, and the man is the head of a woman..." (*1 Corinthians* 11:3). "The women are to keep silent in the churches; for they are not permitted to speak, but are to subject themselves... If they desire to learn anything, let them ask their own husbands at home; for it is improper for a woman to speak in church" (*1 Corinthians* 14:34-35). "Wives, be subject to your own husbands, as to the Lord. For the husband is the head of the wife, as Christ also is the head of the church... But as the church is subject to Christ, so also the wives ought to be to their husbands in everything" (*Ephesians* 5:22-24). "A woman should learn in quietness and full submission. I do not permit a woman to teach or to assume authority over a man; she must be quiet. For Adam was formed first, then Eve. And Adam was not the one deceived; it was the woman who was deceived and became a sinner. But women will be saved through childbearing—if they continue in faith, love, and holiness with propriety" (*1 Timothy* 2:11-15). "You husbands..., live with your wives in an understanding way, as with someone weaker, since she is a woman; and show her honor as a fellow heir of the grace of life" (*1 Peter* 3:7).

14. "For by one Spirit we were all baptized into one body, whether Jews or Greeks, whether slaves or free, and we were all made to drink of one Spirit" (*1 Corinthians* 12:13). "So in Christ Jesus you are all children of God through faith... There is neither Jew nor Greek, there is neither slave nor free man, there is neither male nor female; for you are all one in Christ Jesus" (*Galatians* 3:26-28). "There is no distinction between Greek and Jew, circumcised and uncircumcised, barbarian, Scythian, slave and freeman, but Christ is all, and in all" (*Colossians* 3:11).

Our Authors respectfully add the following points to those outlined by an established Law School.

EVIDENCE

King James Bible holds several verses regarding EVIDENCE. Jeremiah Chapter 32 being the strongest authority.

Hebrews 11:1
Now faith is the substance of things hoped for, the evidence of things not seen.

Jeremiah Chapter 32
10And I subscribed the evidence, and sealed *it*, and took witnesses, and weighed *him* the money in the balances.
11So I took the evidence of the purchase, *both* that which was sealed *according* to the law and custom, and that which was open:
12And I gave the evidence of the purchase unto Baruch the son of Neriah, the son of Maaseiah, in the sight of Hanameel mine uncle's *son*, and in the presence of the witnesses that subscribed the book of the purchase, before all the Jews that sat in the court of the prison.
13And I charged Baruch before them, saying,
14Thus saith the LORD of hosts, the God of Israel; Take these evidences, this evidence of the purchase, both which is sealed, and this evidence which is open; and put them in an earthen vessel, that they may continue many days.

15For thus saith the LORD of hosts, the God of Israel; Houses and fields and vineyards shall be possessed again in this land.
16Now when I had delivered the evidence of the purchase unto Baruch the son of Neriah, I prayed unto the LORD, saying,

CITIES OF REFUGE, PROVISION FOR FALSELY ACCUSED

Cities of refuge (Hebrew: המקלט ערי *'ārê ha-miqlāṭ*) were six Levitical towns in the Kingdom of Israel and the Kingdom of Judah in which the perpetrators of accidental manslaughter could claim the right of asylum. Maimonides, invoking talmudic literature, expands the city of refuge count to all 48 Levitical cities. Outside of these cities, blood vengeance against such perpetrators was allowed by law. The Bible names six cities as being cities of refuge: Golan, Ramoth, and Bosor, on the east (left bank) of the Jordan River, and Kedesh, Shechem, and Hebron on western side. (Joshua 20:7)

In Numbers

In the Book of Numbers, laws concerning cities of refuge state that, once he had claimed asylum, a perpetrator had to be taken from the city and put on trial; (Numbers 35:11–24) if the trial found the perpetrator was innocent of murder, then the perpetrator had to be returned under guard (for their own protection) to the city in which they claimed asylum. (Numbers 35:25) This law code treats blood money as an unacceptable device that would compound the crime, insisting that atonement can only be made by the murderer's blood. (Numbers 35:31–34)

Numbers states that no harm was allowed to come to the perpetrator once the Jewish high priest had died, at which point the perpetrator was free to leave the city without fear. (Num. 35:25-28)

In Deuteronomy

In the setting of the Book of Deuteronomy, the Israelites have conquered several kingdoms on the east side of the Jordan river and are about to enter the land of Canaan. At this point, Moses separated three cities of refuge on the east side. (Deut. 4:41–43)

Later, it is prescribed that three cities of refuge be set aside in Canaan once it is conquered, (Deuteronomy 19:2–3) and three additional cities to be set aside 'if the Lord your God enlarges your territory'. (Deuteronomy 19:8–9) Thus, the total number of cities could be as high as nine. Albert Barnes Commentary on Deuteronomy 19, stated that the additional three cities allowed for "the anticipated enlargement of the borders of Israel to the utmost limits promised by God, from the river of Egypt to the Euphrates" (Genesis 15:8) and the King James Version refers in Deuteronomy 19:8 to the enlargement of the *coast* of the promised land.

While the Book of Numbers describes the perpetrator being put on trial, Deuteronomy merely states that if the perpetrator is guilty of murder, the elders of the town in which the crime was committed should demand the perpetrator's return and hand him over without pity to the avenger of blood to be killed. (Deuteronomy 19:11–13) Deuteronomy does not give any role to the high priest or mention the terms on which the perpetrator could return home but does state that roads should be built to cities of refuge to ease the escape of the perpetrator to them. (Deuteronomy 19:3)

In Joshua

A chapter in the Book of Joshua also reiterates the regulations for the cities of refuge, adding that when a perpetrator arrived at the city, he had to disclose the events that had occurred to the city elders, after which they had to find him a place to live within the city. (Joshua 20) Modern biblical critics regard the chapter as being written by the Deuteronomist. (Peake's commentary on the Bible) Though the masoretic text for this chapter includes a role for death of the high priest, the Septuagint's version of the chapter does not mention it.

CITIZENSHIP AND IMMIGRATION

The Bible provides several orders intended to control immigration so as to prevent resultant hostilities. God's major intent is that we treat all people as brothers and to be kind to all the world. However, God never intended that we allow enemies into our nations. God places a THIRD-GENERATION standard in "friendly cases" along with a TENTH GENERATION standard for those leaving enemy nations.

Deuteronomy 23 CITIZENSHIP FOR MIGRANTS, THIRD TO TENTH GENERATION

1He that is wounded in the stones, or hath his privy member cut
off, shall not enter into the congregation of the LORD.
2 A bastard shall not enter into the congregation of the LORD; even
to his tenth generation shall he not enter into the congregation of
the LORD.
3 An Ammonite or Moabite shall not enter the congregation of the
LORD; even to their tenth generation shall they not enter the
congregation of the LORD for ever:
4 Because they met you not with bread and with water in the way,
when ye came forth out of Egypt; and because they hired against
thee Balaam the son of Beor of Pethor of Mesopotamia.
5 The LORD thy God would not hearken unto Balaam; but the
LORD thy God turned the curse into a blessing to thee, because
the LORD thy God loved thee.
6 Thou shalt not seek their peace nor their prosperity all thy days.
7 Thou shalt not abhor an Edomite; for he *is* thy brother: thou shalt
not abhor an Egyptian; because thou wast a stranger in his land.
8 The children that are begotten of them shall enter into the
congregation of the LORD in their third generation.

BIBLE PROHIBITS SOME FROM CITIZENSHIP - - God's forgiveness extends even to enemies once they embrace the word of God.

Deuteronomy 7:1-4
[1] When the LORD they God shall bring thee into the land whither
thou goest to possess it, and hath cast out many nations before
thee, the Hittites, and the Girgashites, and the Amorites, and the
Canaanites, and the Perizzites, and the Hivites, and the Jebusites,
seven nations greater and mightier than thou;[2] And when the LORD
thy God shall deliver them before thee; thou shalt smite
them, *and* utterly destroy them; thou shalt make no covenant with
them, nor shew mercy unto them: [3]
Neither shalt thou make marriages with them; thy daughter thou
shalt not give unto his son, nor his daughter shalt thou take unto
thy son. [4]For they will turn away thy son from following me, that
they may serve other gods: so will the anger of the LORD be
kindled against you, and destroy thee suddenly.

Joshua 6:1-20
Yes, God won the battles, which He let the Hebrew army then mop up. For example, in the battle for Jericho, God miraculously blew out the city's protective wall, which ended the battle before it began. In Verse 22, you see the forgiveness of God by bringing out the Harlot that assisted the spies of Joshua.

Now Jericho was straitly shut up because of the children of Israel:
none went out, and none came in. 2And the LORD said unto
Joshua, See, I have given into thine hand Jericho, and the king
thereof, *and* the mighty men of valour.
3And ye shall compass the city, all *ye* men of war, *and* go round
about the city once. Thus shalt thou do six days.
4And seven priests shall bear before the ark seven trumpets of
rams' horns: the seventh day ye shall compass the city seven
times, the priests shall blow trumpets.
5And it shall come to pass, that when they make a long *blast* with
the ram's horn, *and* when ye hear the sound of the trumpet, all the
people shall shout with a great shout; and the wall of the city shall

fall down flat, and the people shall ascend up every man straight before him.
6And Joshua called the priests, and said unto them, Take up the ark of the covenant, and let seven priests bear seven trumpets of rams' horns before the ark of the LORD.
7And he said unto the people, Pass on, and compass the city, and let him that is armed pass on before the ark of the LORD.
8And it came to pass, when Joshua had spoken unto the people, that the seven priests bearing the seven trumpets of rams' horns passed on before the LORD, and blew with the trumpets: and the ark of the covenant of the LORD followed them.
9And the armed men went before the priests that blew with the trumpets, and the rereward came after the ark, *the priests* going on, and blowing with the trumpets.
10And Joshua had commanded the people, saying, Ye shall not shout, nor make any noise with your voice, neither shall *any* word proceed out of your mouth, until the day I bid you shout; then shall ye shout.
11So the ark of the LORD compassed the city, going about *it* once: and they came into the camp, and lodged in the camp.
12Joshua rose early in the morning, and the priests took up the ark of the LORD.
13And seven priests bearing seven trumpets of rams' horns before the ark of the LORD went on continually, and blew with the trumpets: and the armed men went before them; but the rereward came after the ark of the LORD, *the priests* going on, and blowing with the trumpets.
14Second day they compassed the city once, returned to camp: they did six days.
15And it came to pass on the seventh day, that they rose early about the dawning of the day, and compassed the city after the same manner seven times: only on that day they compassed the city seven times.
16And it came to pass at the seventh time, when the priests blew with the trumpets, Joshua said unto the people, Shout; for the LORD hath given you the city.
17And the city shall be accursed, *even* it, and all that *are* therein, to the LORD: only Rahab the harlot shall live, she and all

that *are* with her in the house, because she hid the messengers
that we sent.
18And ye, in any wise keep *yourselves* from the accursed thing,
lest ye make *yourselves* accursed, when ye take of the accursed
thing, and make the camp of Israel a curse, and trouble it.
19But all the silver, and gold, and vessels of brass and
iron, *are* consecrated unto the LORD: they shall come into the
treasury of the LORD.
20So the people shouted when *the priests* blew with the trumpets:
and it came to pass, when the people heard the sound of the
trumpet, and the people shouted with a great shout, that the wall
fell down flat, so that the people went up into the city, every man
straight before him, and they took the city.
21And they utterly destroyed all that *was* in the city, both man and
woman, young and old, and ox, and sheep, and ass, with the edge
of the sword.
22Joshua had said unto the two men that had spied out the
country, Go into the harlot's house, bring out the woman, and all
that she hath, as ye sware unto her.
23And the young men that were spies went in, and brought out
Rahab, and her father, and her mother, and her brethren, and all
that she had; and they brought out all her kindred, and left them
without the camp of Israel.
24They burnt the city with fire, and all that *was* therein: only the
silver, the gold, the vessels of brass and of iron, they put into the
treasury of the house of the LORD.
25And Joshua saved Rahab the harlot alive, and her father's
household, and all that she had; and she dwelleth in
Israel *even* unto this day; because she hid the messengers,
which Joshua sent to spy out Jericho.
27So the LORD was with Joshua; and his fame *noised* throughout
all the country.

Chapter 19. MOSAIC ORGANIZATION CHART

Our Author first learned of this original, very first organization chart in a collegiate Management case study course. This great work of Moses continues to be the form of organization chart that drives all organizations today, from church to government, military, business, industrial, automotive, insurance, etc. Most importantly today, the very same chart is perfectly scalable - - a business organization intellectual asset, scalability, demanded by the major money markets and major corporations.

Within this great advice, we learn it is designed to simplify daily management tasks; to teach the various requirements of the organization, we learn the virtues required of leaders within the organization, along with the establishment of Judges. The term "leaders" in sometimes rendered Judge, Captain, Priest, or leader.

EXODUS 18:18-23

Now having survived the Red Sea crossing, Moses finds himself the sole leader of 1.5 million people. He must seek a method by which he can "share" his work load.

18Thou wilt surely wear away, both thou, and this people
that *is* with thee: for this thing *is* too heavy for thee; thou art not
able to perform it thyself alone.
19Hearken now unto my voice, I will give thee counsel, and God
shall be with thee: Be thou for the people to God-ward, that thou
mayest bring the causes unto God:
20And thou shalt teach them ordinances and laws, and shalt shew
them the way wherein they must walk, the work that they must do.
21Moreover thou shalt provide out of all the people able men, such
as fear God, men of truth, hating covetousness; and
place *such* over them, *to be* rulers of thousands, and rulers of
hundreds, rulers of fifties, and rulers of tens:
22And let them judge the people at all seasons: and it shall
be, *that* every great matter they shall bring unto thee, but every
small matter they shall judge: so shall it be easier for thyself, and
they shall bear *the burden* with thee.

23If thou shalt do this thing, and God command thee *so*, then thou shalt be able to endure, and all this people shall also go to their place in peace.

Deuteronomy Chapter 5 can be considered a companion rendering of THE TEN COMMANDMENTS. This chapter provides the perfect closing statement for our book. It can only be clear that in this chapter, God commands that we continue to practice and live by ALL THE LAWS AND FORMS OF GOVERNMENT HE PROVIDES AND OUTLINES FOR FUTURE DAYS.

1Moses called Israel, and said unto them, Hear, O Israel, the statutes, and judgments which I speak in your ears this day, that ye may learn them, keep, and do them.
2The LORD our God made a covenant with us in Horeb. (covenant = contract)
3The LORD made not this covenant with our fathers, but with us, here alive this day.
4The LORD talked with you face to face in the mount out of the midst of the fire,
6I *am* the LORD thy God, which brought thee out of land of Egypt, from bondage.
31But as for thee, stand thou here by me, and I will speak unto thee all the commandments, and the statutes, and the judgments, which thou shalt teach them, that they may do *them* in the land which I give them to possess it.
32Ye shall observe to do therefore as the LORD your God hath commanded you: ye shall not turn aside to the right hand or the left.
33Ye shall walk in all the ways which the LORD your God hath commanded you, that ye may live, and *that it may be* well with you, and *that* ye may prolong *your* days in the land which ye shall possess.

Sanhedrin (Gr. synedrion), meaning "a sitting" "together," or a "council." This word (rendered "council,")" is often used in the New Testament (Matt. 5:22; 26:59; Mark "15:1, etc.) to denote the supreme judicial and administrative" "council of the Jews, which, it is said, was first instituted by" "Moses, composed of seventy men (Num. 11:16, 17). But" that seems to have been only a temporary arrangement which Moses made. The name is first "employed by the Jewish historian Josephus. This "council" is" "referred to simply as the "chief priests and elders of the" "people" (Matt. 26:3, 47, 57, 59; 27:1, 3, 12, 20, etc.), before" whom Christ was tried on the charge of claiming to be the Messiah. "The Sanhedrin is said to have consisted of seventy-one members. They were of three classes (1) "the chief priests, or heads of the twenty-four priestly courses" "(1 Chr. 24), (2) the scribes, and (3) the elders. As the highest" "court of judicature, "in all causes and over all persons," "ecclesiastical and civil, supreme," its decrees were binding," "not only on the Jews in Palestine, but on all Jews wherever" scattered abroad. Its jurisdiction was greatly curtailed by "Herod, and afterwards by the Romans. Its usual place of meeting" "was within the precincts of the temple, in the hall "Gazith," but it sometimes met also in the house of the high priest (Matt. "26:3)."

Halakhah: Jewish Law הֲלָכָה

Judaism is not just a set of beliefs about God, man, and the universe. Judaism is a comprehensive way of life, filled with rules and practices that affect every aspect of life: what you do when you wake up in the morning, what you can and cannot eat, what you can and cannot wear, how to groom yourself, how to conduct business, who you can marry, how to observe the holidays and Shabbat, and perhaps most important, how to treat God, other people, and animals. This set of rules and practices is known as halakhah.

The word "halakhah" is usually translated as "Jewish Law," although a more literal translation might be "the path that one walks." The word is derived from the Hebrew root Hei-Lamed-Kaf (הלך), meaning to go, walk or to travel.

Sources of Halakhah

Halakhah comes from three sources: from the Torah, from laws instituted by the rabbis and from long-standing customs. Halakhah from any of these sources can be referred to as a mitzvah (מִצְוָה, commandment; plural: mitzvot מִצְוֹת). The word "mitzvah" is also commonly used in a casual way to refer to any good deed. Because of this imprecise usage, sophisticated halakhic discussions are careful to identify mitzvot as being mitzvot d'oraita (an Aramaic word meaning "from the Torah") or mitzvot d'rabbanan (Aramaic for "from the rabbis"). A mitzvah that arises from custom is referred to as a minhag.

Positive and Negative Law

Positive mitzvot are commandments to do something, such as the commandment to honor your mother and father. In Hebrew, these are called mitzvot aseh commandments to do. Negative mitzvot are commandments not to do something, such as the commandment not to murder.

Mitzvot D'Rabbanan: Laws Instituted by the Rabbis

This section will connect the concept of Amendment of laws built into the Holy Bible. Any law added by the Rabbinic group would have been required to be submitted to the highest level of the Moses Organization Chart, that being the group of 24 church leaders reporting to Aaron and the Elders of the 1 Tribes of Israel. They were expected to review the proposed law and determine that it was in keeping with the Word of God. If they agreed the law was in keeping with God's law, it could be submitted to Moses, Aaron, and Joshua to become new law. Those involved with the review process became known as The Sanhedrin and ultimately The United States Congress and Tripartite organizations of government.

In addition to laws that come directly from Torah (d'oraita), halakhah includes laws enacted by the rabbis (d'rabbanan). These rabbinic laws are still referred to as mitzvot (commandments), even though they are not part of the original 613 mitzvot d'oraita. Mitzvot d'rabbanan are considered to be as binding as Torah laws, but there are differences in the way we apply laws that are d'oraita and laws that are d'rabbanan (see below).

Mitzvot d'rabbanan are divided into three categories: gezeirah, takkanah, minhag.

Gezeirah גְּזֵרָה

A gezeirah is a law instituted by the rabbis to prevent people from accidentally violating a Torah mitzvah. We commonly speak of a gezeirah as a "fence" around the Torah. For example, the tTorah commands us not to work on Shabbat, but a gezeirah commands us not to even handle an implement that you would use to perform prohibited work (such as a pencil, money, a hammer), because someone holding the implement might forget it was Shabbat and perform prohibited work. The word is derived from the root Gimel-Zayin-Reish (גזר), meaning cut off or separate.

Takkanah תַּקָּנָה

A takkanah is a rule unrelated to biblical laws that was created by the rabbis for the public welfare. For example, the practice of public Torah readings every Monday and Thursday is a takkanah instituted by Ezra. The "mitzvah" to light candles on Chanukah, a post-biblical holiday, is also a takkanah. The word is derived from the Hebrew root Tav-Qof-Nun (תקן), meaning to fix, to remedy or to repair. It is the same root as in "tikkun olam," repairing the world, or making the world a better place, an important concept in all branches of Judaism.

Some takkanot vary by community or from region to region. Around the year 1000 C.E., Rabbeinu Gershom Me'or Ha-Golah instituted a takkanah prohibiting polygyny (polygamy, multiple wives), said to be permitted by the Torah and the Talmud. This takkanah was accepted by Ashkenazic Jews, who lived in Christian countries where polygyny was not permitted, but not accepted by Sephardic Jews, who lived in Islamic countries where men were permitted four wives.

Minhag: Customs

Minhag is treated as a category of mitzvot d'rabbanan (from the rabbis), mostly because it is clearly not d'oraita (from the Torah), but minhag is generally not the sort of rule that is created by reasoned decision-making. A minhag is a custom that developed for worthy religious reasons and has continued long enough to become a binding religious practice. For example, the second, extra day of holidays was originally instituted as a gezeirah, so that people outside of Israel, not certain of the day of a holiday, would not accidentally violate the holiday's mitzvot. After the mathematical calendar was instituted and there was no doubt about the days, the added second day was not necessary. The rabbis considered ending the practice at that time, but decided to continue it as a minhag: the practice of observing an extra day had developed for worthy religious reasons, and became customary. It is important to note that these "customs" are a binding part of halakhah, just like a mitzvah, a takkanah or a gezeirah.

The word "minhag" is also used in a looser sense, to indicate a community or an individual's customary way of doing some religious thing. For example, it may be the minhag in one synagogue to stand while reciting a certain prayer, while in another synagogue it is the minhag to sit during that prayer. It may become an individual's minhag to sit in a certain location in synagogue, or to walk to synagogue in a certain way, and under appropriate circumstances these too may become minhag. Even in this looser sense, these customs can become binding on the individual, it is recommended that a person follow his own personal or community minhag as much as possible, even when visiting another community, unless that minhag would cause the other community discomfort or embarrassment.

The Difference Between Torah Law and Rabbinic Law

As we have seen, Jewish law includes both laws that come directly from the Torah and laws that were enacted by the rabbis. In a sense, however, even laws enacted by the rabbis can be considered derived from the Torah: the Torah gives certain people authority to teach and make judgments about the law (Deut. 17:11), so these rabbinical laws should not be casually dismissed as the "laws of man" (as opposed to the laws of God). Rabbinical laws are considered to be as binding as Torah laws, but there are differences in the way we apply laws that are "d'oraita" (from the Torah) and laws that are "d'rabbanan" (from the rabbis).

The first major difference is a matter of precedence: d'oraita takes precedence over d'rabbanan. If two d'oraita rules come into conflict in a particular situation, rules of precedence are applied to determine which rule is followed; however, if a d'oraita rule comes into conflict with a d'rabbanan rule, the d'oraita rule (Torah rule) always takes precedence. Do we fast on Yom Kippur when it falls on Shabbat? These are both d'oraita, so rules of precedence must apply. Specific rules take precedence over general rules, so the specific rules of Yom Kippur fasting takes precedence over the general rule of Shabbat joy, and yes, we fast on Yom Kippur on Shabbat. However, the other fasts on the Jewish calendar are d'rabbanan, so the d'oraita rule of Shabbat joy takes precedence, and other fasts that fall on Shabbat are moved to another day.

The second major difference is the strictness of observance. If there is doubt (in Hebrew: safek) in a matter that is d'oraita, we take the strict position (in Hebrew: machmir) regarding the rule; if there is doubt in a matter that is d'rabbanan, we take the lenient position (in Hebrew: makil) regarding the rule. In Hebrew, this rule is stated: safek d'oraita l'humra; safek d'rabbanan l'kula. This is easier to understand with an example: suppose you are reading the morning prayers and you cannot remember whether you read Bar'khu and Shema (two important prayers). You are in doubt, safek. The recitation of Shema in the morning is a mitzvah d'oraita, a biblical commandment (Deut. 6:7), so you must be machmir, you must go back and recite Shema if you are not sure whether you did.

Chapter 20. **THE DECLARATION OF INDEPENDENCE**

In Congress, July 4, 1776

The unanimous Declaration of the thirteen
United States of America

When in the Course of human events it becomes necessary for one people to dissolve the political bands which have connected them with another and to assume among the powers of the earth, the separate and equal station to which the Laws of Nature and of Nature's God entitle them, a decent respect to the opinions of mankind requires that they should declare the causes which impel them to the separation.

We hold these truths to be self-evident, that all men are created equal, that they are endowed by their Creator with certain unalienable Rights, that among these are Life, Liberty, and the pursuit of Happiness. — That to secure these rights, Governments are instituted among Men, deriving their just powers from the consent of the governed, —That whenever any Form of Government becomes destructive of these ends, it is the Right of the People to alter or to abolish it, and to institute new Government, laying its foundation on such principles and organizing its powers in such form, as to them shall seem most likely to effect their Safety and Happiness. Prudence, indeed, will dictate that Governments long established should not be changed for light and transient causes; and accordingly, all experience hath shewn that mankind are more disposed to suffer, while evils are sufferable than to right themselves by abolishing the forms to which they are accustomed. But when a long train of abuses and usurpations, pursuing invariably the same Object evinces a design to reduce them under absolute Despotism, it is their right, it is their duty, to throw off such Government, and to provide new Guards for their future security. —Such has been the patient sufferance of these Colonies; and such is now the necessity which constrains them to alter their former Systems of Government. The history of the present King of Great Britain is a history of repeated injuries and usurpations, all having in direct object the establishment of an absolute Tyranny over these States. To prove this, let Facts be submitted to a candid world.

He has refused his Assent to Laws, most wholesome and necessary for public good.

He has forbidden his Governors to pass Laws of immediate and pressing importance, unless suspended in their operation till his Assent should be obtained; and when so suspended, he has utterly neglected to attend to them.

He has refused to pass other Laws for the accommodation of large districts of people, unless those people would relinquish the right of Representation in the Legislature, a right inestimable to them and formidable to tyrants only.

He has called together legislative bodies at places unusual, uncomfortable, and distant from the depository of their Public Records, for the sole purpose of fatiguing them into compliance with his measures.

He has dissolved Representative Houses repeatedly, for opposing with manly firmness his invasions on the rights of the people.
He has refused for a long time, after such dissolutions, to cause others to be elected, whereby the Legislative Powers, incapable of Annihilation, have returned to the People at large for their exercise; the State remaining in the meantime exposed to all the dangers of invasion from without, and convulsions within.

He has endeavoured to prevent the population of these States; for that purpose obstructing the Laws for Naturalization of Foreigners; refusing to pass others to encourage their migrations, and raising conditions of new Appropriations of Lands.

He has obstructed the Administration of Justice by refusing his Assent to Laws for establishing Judiciary Powers.

He has made Judges dependent on his Will alone for the tenure of their offices, and the amount an payment of their salaries.

He has erected a multitude of New Offices, and sent hither swarms of Officers to harass our people and eat out their substance.

He has kept among us, in times of peace, Standing Armies without the Consent of our legislatures.

He has affected to render the Military independent of and superior to the Civil Power.

He has combined with others to subject us to a jurisdiction foreign to our constitution, and unacknowledged by our laws, giving his Assent to their Acts of pretended Legislation:

For quartering large bodies of armed troops among us:

For protecting them, by a mock Trial from punishment for any Murders which they should commit on the Inhabitants of these States:

For cutting off our Trade with all parts of the world:

For imposing Taxes on us without our Consent:

For depriving us in many cases, of the benefit of Trial by Jury:

For transporting us beyond Seas to be tried for pretended offences:

For abolishing the free System of English Laws in a neighbouring Province, establishing therein an Arbitrary government, and enlarging its Boundaries so as to render it at once an example and fit instrument for introducing the same absolute rule into these Colonies:

For taking away our Charters, abolishing our most valuable Laws and altering fundamentally the Forms of our Governments:

For suspending our own Legislatures, and declaring themselves invested with power to legislate for us in all cases whatsoever.

He has abdicated Government here, by declaring us out of his Protection and waging War against us.

He has plundered our seas, ravaged our Coasts burnt our towns, and destroyed the lives of our people.

He is at this time transporting large Armies of foreign Mercenaries to complete the works of death, desolation, and tyranny, already begun with circumstances of Cruelty & Perfidy scarcely paralleled in the most barbarous ages, and unworthy of the Head of a civilized nation.

He has constrained our fellow Citizens taken Captive on the high Seas to bear Arms against their Country, to become the executioners of their friends and Brethren, or to fall themselves by their Hands.

He has excited domestic insurrections amongst us, and has endeavoured to bring on the inhabitants of our frontiers, the merciless Indian Savages whose known rule of warfare, is an undistinguished destruction of all ages, sexes, and conditions.

In every stage of these Oppressions We have Petitioned for Redress in the most humble terms: Our repeated Petitions have been answered only by repeated injury. A Prince, whose character is thus marked by every act which may define a Tyrant, is unfit to be the ruler of a free people.

Nor have We been wanting in attentions to our British brethren. We have warned them from time to time of attempts by their legislature to extend an unwarrantable jurisdiction over us. We have reminded them of the circumstances of our emigration and settlement here. We have appealed to their native justice and magnanimity, and we have conjured them by the ties of our common kindred. to disavow these usurpations, which would inevitably interrupt our connections and correspondence. They too have been deaf to the voice of justice and of consanguinity. We must, therefore, acquiesce in the necessity, which denounces our Separation, and hold them, as we hold the rest of mankind, Enemies in War, in Peace Friends.

We, therefore, the Representatives of the United States of America, in General Congress, Assembled, appealing to the Supreme Judge of the world for the rectitude of our intentions, do, in the Name, and by Authority of the good People of these Colonies, solemnly publish and declare, That these United Colonies are, and of Right ought to be Free and Independent States, that they are Absolved from all Allegiance to the British Crown, and that all political connection between them and the State of Great Britain, is and ought to be totally dissolved; and that as Free and Independent States, they have full Power to levy War, conclude Peace contract Alliances, establish Commerce, and to do all other Acts and Things which Independent States may of right do. — And for the support of this Declaration, with a firm reliance on the protection of Divine Providence, we mutually pledge to each other our Lives, our Fortunes, and our sacred Honor.

—John Hancock

New Hampshire: Josiah Bartlett, William Whipple, Matthew Thornton

Massachusetts: J. Hancock, Sam Adams, John Adams, Rob Treat Paine, Elbridge Gerry

Rhode Island: Stephen Hopkins, William Ellery

Connecticut: Roger Sherman, Samuel Huntington, William Williams, Oliver Wolcott

New York: William Floyd, Philip Livingston, Francis Lewis, Lewis Morris

New Jersey: Richard Stockton, J. Witherspoon, Francis Hopkinson, J. Hart, Abr. Clark

Pennsylvania: Robert Morris, Benjamin Rush, Benjamin Franklin, John Morton, G. Clymer, James Smith, G. Taylor, James Wilson, G. Ross

Delaware: Caesar Rodney, George Read, Thomas McKean

Maryland: Sam Chase, Will Paca, Thomas Stone, Charles Carroll of Carrollton

Virginia: George Wythe, Richard Henry Lee, Thomas Jefferson, Benjamin Harrison, Thomas Nelson, Jr., Francis Lightfoot Lee, Carter Braxton

North Carolina: William Hooper, Joseph Hewes, John Penn

So Carolina: Ed Rutledge, T. Heyward, Jr., T. Lynch, Jr., Arthur Middleton

Georgia: Button Gwinnett, Lyman Hall, George Walton

Chapter 21. **CONSTITUTION OF THE UNITED STATES**

We the People of the United States, in Order to form a more perfect Union, establish Justice, insure domestic Tranquility, provide for the common defence, promote the general Welfare, and secure the Blessings of Liberty to ourselves and our Posterity, do ordain and establish this Constitution for the United States of America.

Article. I.

Section. 1.

All legislative Powers herein granted shall be vested in a Congress of the United States, which shall consist of a Senate and House of Representatives.

Section. 2.

The House of Representatives shall be composed of Members chosen every second Year by the People of the several States, and the Electors in each State shall have the Qualifications requisite for Electors of the most numerous Branch of the State Legislature.

No Person shall be a Representative who shall not have attained to the Age of twenty five Years, and been seven Years a Citizen of the United States, and who shall not, when elected, be an Inhabitant of that State in which he shall be chosen.

Representatives and direct Taxes shall be apportioned among the several States which may be included within this Union, according to their respective Numbers, which shall be determined by adding to the whole Number of free Persons, including those bound to Service for a Term of Years, and excluding Indians not taxed, three fifths of all other Persons. The actual Enumeration shall be made within three Years after the first Meeting of the Congress of the

United States, and within every subsequent Term of ten Years, in such Manner as they shall by Law direct. The Number of Representatives shall not exceed one for every thirty Thousand, but each State shall have at Least one Representative; and until such enumeration shall be made, the State of New Hampshire shall be entitled to chuse three, Massachusetts eight, Rhode-Island and Providence Plantations one, Connecticut five, New-York six, New Jersey four, Pennsylvania eight, Delaware one, Maryland six, Virginia ten, North Carolina five, South Carolina five, and Georgia three.

When vacancies happen in the Representation from any State, the Executive Authority thereof shall issue Writs of Election to fill such Vacancies.

The House of Representatives shall choose their Speaker and other Officers; and shall have the sole Power of Impeachment.

Section. 3.

The Senate of the United States shall be composed of two Senators from each State, chosen by the Legislature thereof, for six Years; and each Senator shall have one Vote.

Immediately after they shall be assembled in Consequence of the first Election, they shall be divided as equally as may be into three Classes. The Seats of the Senators of the first Class shall be vacated at the Expiration of the second Year, of the second Class at the Expiration of the fourth Year, and of the third Class at the Expiration of the sixth Year, so that one third may be chosen every second Year; and if Vacancies happen by Resignation, or otherwise, during the Recess of the Legislature of any State, the Executive thereof may make temporary Appointments until the next Meeting of the Legislature, which shall then fill such Vacancies.

No Person shall be a Senator who shall not have attained to the Age of thirty Years, and been nine Years a Citizen of the United States, and who shall not, when elected, be an Inhabitant of that State for which he shall be chosen.

The Vice President of the United States shall be President of the Senate, but shall have no Vote, unless they be equally divided.

The Senate shall chuse their other Officers, and also a President pro tempore, in the Absence of the Vice President, or when he shall exercise the Office of President of the United States.

The Senate shall have the sole Power to try all Impeachments. When sitting for that Purpose, they shall be on Oath or Affirmation. When the President of the United States is tried, the Chief Justice shall preside: And no Person shall be convicted without the Concurrence of two thirds of the Members present.

Judgment in Cases of Impeachment shall not extend further than to removal from Office, and disqualification to hold and enjoy any Office of honor, Trust, or Profit under the United States: but the Party convicted shall nevertheless be liable and subject to Indictment, Trial, Judgment and Punishment, according to Law.

Section. 4.

The Times, Places and Manner of holding Elections for Senators and Representatives, shall be prescribed in each State by the Legislature thereof; but the Congress may at any time by Law make or alter such Regulations, except as to the Places of choosing Senators.

The Congress shall assemble at least once in every Year, and such Meeting shall be on the first Monday in December, unless they by Law appoint a different Day.

Section. 5.

Each House shall be the Judge of the Elections, Returns and Qualifications of its own Members, and a Majority of each shall constitute a Quorum to do Business; but a smaller Number may adjourn from day to day, and be authorized to compel Attendance of absent Members, in such Manner, and under such Penalties as each House may provide.

Each House may determine the Rules of its Proceedings, punish its Members for disorderly Behaviour, and, with the Concurrence of two thirds, expel a Member.

Each House shall keep a Journal of its Proceedings, and from time to time publish the same, excepting such Parts as may in their Judgment require Secrecy; and the Yeas and Nays of the Members of either House on any question shall, at the Desire of one fifth of those Present, be entered on the Journal.

Neither House, during the Session of Congress, shall, without the Consent of the other, adjourn for more than three days, nor to any other Place than that in which the two Houses shall be sitting.

Section. 6.

The Senators and Representatives shall receive a Compensation for their Services, to be ascertained by Law, and paid out of the Treasury of the United States. They shall in all Cases, except Treason, Felony and Breach of the Peace, be privileged from Arrest during their Attendance at the Session of their respective Houses, and in going to and returning from the same; and for any Speech or Debate in either House, they shall not be questioned in any other Place.

No Senator or Representative shall, during the Time for which he was elected, be appointed to any civil Office under the Authority of the United States, which shall have been created, or the Emoluments whereof shall have been encreased during such time;

and no Person holding any Office under the United States, shall be a Member of either House during his Continuance in Office.

Section. 7.

All Bills for raising Revenue shall originate in the House of Representatives; but the Senate may propose or concur with Amendments as on other Bills.

.Every Bill which shall have passed the House of Representatives and the Senate, shall, before it become a Law, be presented to the President of the United States; If he approve he shall sign it, but if not he shall return it, with his Objections to that House in which it shall have originated, who shall enter the Objections at large on their Journal, and proceed to reconsider it. If after such Reconsideration two thirds of that House shall agree to pass the Bill, it shall be sent, together with the Objections, to the other House, by which it shall likewise be reconsidered, and if approved by two thirds of that House, it shall become a Law. But in all such Cases the Votes of both Houses shall be determined by yeas and Nays, and the Names of the Persons voting for and against the Bill shall be entered on the Journal of each House respectively. If any Bill shall not be returned by the President within ten Days (Sundays excepted) after it shall have been presented to him, the Same shall be a Law, in like Manner as if he had signed it, unless the Congress by their Adjournment prevent its Return, in which Case it shall not be a Law.

Every Order, Resolution, or Vote to which the Concurrence of the Senate and House of Representatives may be necessary (except on a question of Adjournment) shall be presented to the President of the United States; and before the Same shall take Effect, shall be approved by him, or being disapproved by him, shall be repassed by two thirds of the Senate and House of Representatives, according to the Rules and Limitations prescribed in the Case of a Bill.

Section. 8.

The Congress shall have Power To lay and collect Taxes, Duties, Imposts and Excises, to pay the Debts and provide for the common Defence and general Welfare of the United States; but all Duties, Imposts and Excises shall be uniform throughout the United States;

To borrow Money on the credit of the United States;

To regulate Commerce with foreign Nations, and among the several States, and with the Indian Tribes;

To establish an uniform Rule of Naturalization, and uniform Laws on the subject of Bankruptcies throughout the United States;

To coin Money, regulate the Value thereof, and of foreign Coin, and fix the Standard of Weights and Measures;

To provide for the Punishment of counterfeiting the Securities and current Coin of the United States;

To establish Post Offices and post Roads;

To promote the Progress of Science and useful Arts, by securing for limited Times to Authors and Inventors the exclusive Right to their respective Writings and Discoveries;

To constitute Tribunals inferior to the supreme Court;

To define and punish Piracies and Felonies committed on the high Seas, and Offences against the Law of Nations;

To declare War, grant Letters of Marque and Reprisal, and make Rules concerning Captures on Land and Water;

To raise and support Armies, but no Appropriation of Money to that Use shall be for a longer Term than two Years;

To provide and maintain a Navy;

To make Rules for the Government and Regulation of the land and naval Forces;

To provide for calling forth the Militia to execute the Laws of the Union, suppress Insurrections and repel Invasions;

To provide for organizing, arming, and disciplining, the Militia, and for governing such Part of them as may be employed in the Service of the United States, reserving to the States respectively, the Appointment of the Officers, and the Authority of training the Militia according to the discipline prescribed by Congress;

To exercise exclusive Legislation in all Cases whatsoever, over such District (not exceeding ten Miles square) as may, by Cession of particular States, and the Acceptance of Congress, become the Seat of the Government of the United States, and to exercise like Authority over all Places purchased by the Consent of the Legislature of the State in which the Same shall be, for the Erection of Forts, Magazines, Arsenals, dock-Yards, and other needful Buildings;—And

To make all Laws which shall be necessary and proper for carrying into Execution the foregoing Powers, and all other Powers vested by this Constitution in the Government of the United States, or in any Department or Officer thereof.

Section. 9.

The Migration or Importation of such Persons as any of the States now existing shall think proper to admit, shall not be prohibited by the Congress prior to the Year one thousand eight hundred and eight, but a Tax or duty may be imposed on such Importation, not exceeding ten dollars for each Person.

The Privilege of the Writ of Habeas Corpus shall not be suspended, unless when in Cases of Rebellion or Invasion the public Safety may require it.

No Bill of Attainder or ex post facto Law shall be passed.

No Capitation, or other direct Tax shall be laid, unless in Proportion to the Census or enumeration herein before directed to be taken.

No Tax or Duty shall be laid on Articles exported from any State.

No Preference shall be given by any Regulation of Commerce or Revenue to the Ports of one State over those of another: nor shall Vessels bound to, or from, one State, be obliged to enter, clear, or pay Duties in another.

No Money shall be drawn from the Treasury, but in Consequence of Appropriations made by Law; and a regular Statement and Account of the Receipts and Expenditures of all public Money shall be published from time to time.

No Title of Nobility shall be granted by the United States: And no Person holding any Office of Profit or Trust under them, shall, without the Consent of the Congress, accept of any present, Emolument, Office, or Title, of any kind whatever, from any King, Prince, or foreign State.

Section. 10.

No State shall enter into any Treaty, Alliance, or Confederation; grant Letters of Marque and Reprisal; coin Money; emit Bills of Credit; make any Thing but gold and silver Coin a Tender in Payment of Debts; pass any Bill of Attainder, ex post facto Law, or Law impairing the Obligation of Contracts, or grant any Title of Nobility.

No State shall, without the Consent of the Congress, lay any Imposts or Duties on Imports or Exports, except what may be absolutely necessary for executing it's inspection Laws: and the net Produce of all Duties and Imposts, laid by any State on Imports or Exports, shall be for the Use of the Treasury of the United States; and all such Laws shall be subject to the Revision and Control of the Congress.

No State shall, without the Consent of Congress, lay any Duty of Tonnage, keep Troops, or Ships of War in time of Peace, enter into any Agreement or Compact with another State, or with a foreign Power, or engage in War, unless actually invaded, or in such imminent Danger as will not admit of delay.

Article. II

Section. 1.

The executive Power shall be vested in a President of the United States of America. He shall hold his Office during the Term of four Years, and, together with the Vice President, chosen for the same Term, be elected, as follows:

Each State shall appoint, in such Manner as the Legislature thereof may direct, a Number of Electors, equal to the whole Number of Senators and Representatives to which the State may be entitled in the Congress: but no Senator or Representative, or Person holding an Office of Trust or Profit under the United States, shall be appointed an Elector.

The Electors shall meet in their respective States, and vote by Ballot for two Persons, of whom one at least shall not be an Inhabitant of the same State with themselves. And they shall make a List of all the Persons voted for, and of the Number of Votes for each; which List they shall sign and certify, and transmit sealed to the Seat of the Government of the United States, directed to the President of the Senate. The President of the Senate shall, in the Presence of the Senate and House of Representatives, open all the Certificates, and the Votes shall then be counted.

The Person having the greatest Number of Votes shall be the President, if such Number be a Majority of the whole Number of Electors appointed; and if there be more than one who have such Majority, and have an equal Number of Votes, then the House of Representatives shall immediately chuse by Ballot one of them for President; and if no Person have a Majority, then from the five highest on the List the said House shall in like Manner chuse the President. But in chusing the President, the Votes shall be taken by States, the Representation from each State having one Vote; A quorum for this Purpose shall consist of a Member or Members from two thirds of the States, and a Majority of all the States shall be necessary to a Choice. In every Case, after the Choice of the President, the Person having the greatest Number of Votes of the Electors shall be the Vice President. But if there should remain two or more who have equal Votes, the Senate shall chuse from them by Ballot the Vice President.

The Congress may determine the Time of chusing Electors, and the Day on which they shall give their Votes; which Day shall be the same throughout the U.S.

No Person except a natural born Citizen, or a Citizen of the United States, at the time of the Adoption of this Constitution, shall be eligible to the Office of President; neither shall any Person be eligible to that Office who shall not have attained to the Age of thirty five Years, and been fourteen Years a Resident within the United States.

In Case of the Removal of the President from Office, or of his Death, Resignation, or Inability to discharge the Powers and Duties of the said Office, the Same shall devolve on the Vice President, and the Congress may by Law provide for the Case of Removal, Death, Resignation or Inability, both of the President and Vice President, declaring what Officer shall then act as President, and such Officer shall act accordingly, until the Disability be removed, or a President shall be elected.

The President shall, at stated Times, receive for his Services, a Compensation, which shall neither be encreased nor diminished during the Period for which he shall have been elected, and he shall not receive within that Period any other Emolument from the United States, or any of them.

Before he enter on the Execution of his Office, he shall take the following Oath or Affirmation:—"I do solemnly swear (or affirm) that I will faithfully execute the Office of President of the United States, and will to the best of my Ability, preserve, protect and defend the Constitution of the United States."

Section. 2.

The President shall be Commander in Chief of the Army and Navy of the United States, and of the Militia of the several States, when called into the actual Service of the United States; he may require the Opinion, in writing, of the principal Officer in each of the executive Departments, upon any Subject relating to the Duties of their respective Offices, and he shall have Power to grant Reprieves and Pardons for Offences against the United States, except in Cases of Impeachment.

He shall have Power, by and with the Advice and Consent of the Senate, to make Treaties, provided two thirds of the Senators present concur; and he shall nominate, and by and with the Advice and Consent of the Senate, shall appoint Ambassadors, other public Ministers and Consuls, Judges of the supreme Court, and all other Officers of the United States, whose Appointments are not herein otherwise provided for, and which shall be established by Law: but the Congress may by Law vest the Appointment of such inferior Officers, as they think proper, in the President alone, in the Courts of Law, or in the Heads of Departments.

The President shall have Power to fill up all Vacancies that may happen during the Recess of the Senate, by granting Commissions which shall expire at the End of their next Session.

Section. 3.

He shall from time to time give to the Congress Information of the State of the Union, and recommend to their Consideration such Measures as he shall judge necessary and expedient; he may, on extraordinary Occasions, convene both Houses, or either of them, and in Case of Disagreement between them, with Respect to the Time of Adjournment, he may adjourn them to such Time as he shall think proper; he shall receive Ambassadors and other public Ministers; he shall take Care that the Laws be faithfully executed, and shall Commission all the Officers of the United States.

Section. 4.

The President, Vice President, and all civil Officers of the United States, shall be removed from Office on Impeachment for, and Conviction of, Treason, Bribery, or other high Crimes and Misdemeanors.

Article. III.

Section. 1.

The judicial Power of the United States, shall be vested in one supreme Court, and in such inferior Courts as the Congress may from time to time ordain and establish. The Judges, both supreme and inferior Courts, shall hold their Offices during good Behaviour, and shall, at stated Times, receive for their Services, a Compensation, which shall not be diminished during their Continuance in Office.

Section. 2.

The judicial Power shall extend to all Cases, in Law and Equity, arising under this Constitution, the Laws of the United States, and Treaties made, or which shall be made, under their Authority;—to all Cases affecting Ambassadors, other public Ministers and Consuls;—to all Cases of admiralty and maritime Jurisdiction;—to Controversies to which the United States shall be a Party;—to Controversies between two or more States;— between a State and Citizens of another State,—between Citizens of different States,—between Citizens of the same State claiming Lands under Grants of different States, and between a State, or the Citizens thereof, and foreign States, Citizens or Subjects.

In all Cases affecting Ambassadors, other public Ministers, and Consuls, and those in which a State shall be Party, the supreme Court shall have original Jurisdiction. In all the other Cases before mentioned, the supreme Court shall have appellate Jurisdiction, both as to Law and Fact, with such Exceptions, and under such Regulations as the Congress shall make.

The Trial of all Crimes, except in Cases of Impeachment, shall be by Jury; and such Trial shall be held in the State where the said Crimes shall have been committed; but when not committed within any State, the Trial shall be at such Place or Places as the Congress may by Law have directed.

Section. 3.

Treason against the United States, shall consist only in levying War against them, or in adhering to their Enemies, giving them Aid and Comfort. No Person shall be convicted of Treason unless on the Testimony of two Witnesses to the same overt Act, or on Confession in open Court.

The Congress shall have Power to declare the Punishment of Treason, but no Attainder of Treason shall work Corruption of Blood, or Forfeiture except during the Life of the Person attainted.

Article. IV.

Section. 1.

Full Faith and Credit shall be given in each State to the public Acts, Records, and judicial Proceedings of every other State. And the Congress may by general Laws prescribe the Manner in which such Acts, Records and Proceedings shall be proved, and the Effect thereof.

Section. 2.

The Citizens of each State shall be entitled to all Privileges and Immunities of Citizens in the several States.
A Person charged in any State with Treason, Felony, or other Crime, who shall flee from Justice, and be found in another State, shall on Demand of the executive Authority of the State from which he fled, be delivered up, to be removed to the State having Jurisdiction of the Crime.

No Person held to Service or Labour in one State, under the Laws thereof, escaping into another, shall, in Consequence of any Law or Regulation therein, be discharged from such Service or Labour, but shall be delivered up on Claim of the Party to whom such Service or Labour may be due.

Section. 3.

New States may be admitted by the Congress into this Union; but no new State shall be formed or erected within the Jurisdiction of any other State; nor any State be formed by the Junction of two or more States, or Parts of States, without the Consent of the Legislatures of the States concerned as well as of the Congress.
The Congress shall have Power to dispose of and make all needful Rules and Regulations respecting the Territory or other Property belonging to the United States; and nothing in this Constitution shall be so construed as to Prejudice any Claims of the United States, or of any particular State.

Section. 4.

The United States shall guarantee to every State in this Union a Republican Form of Government, and shall protect each of them against Invasion; and on Application of the Legislature, or of the Executive (when the Legislature cannot be convened) against domestic Violence.

Article. V.

The Congress, whenever two thirds of both Houses shall deem it necessary, shall propose Amendments to this Constitution, or, on the Application of the Legislatures of two thirds of the several States, shall call a Convention for proposing Amendments, which, in either Case, shall be valid to all Intents and Purposes, as Part of this Constitution, when ratified by the Legislatures of three fourths of the several States, or by Conventions in three fourths thereof, as the one or the other Mode of Ratification may be proposed by the Congress; Provided that no Amendment which may be made prior to the Year One thousand eight hundred and eight shall in any Manner affect the first and fourth Clauses in the Ninth Section of the first Article; and that no State, without its Consent, shall be deprived of its equal Suffrage in the Senate.

Article. VI.

All Debts contracted and Engagements entered into, before the Adoption of this Constitution, shall be as valid against the United States under this Constitution, as under the Confederation.

This Constitution, and the Laws of the United States which shall be made in Pursuance thereof; and all Treaties made, or which shall be made, under the Authority of the United States, shall be the supreme Law of the Land; and the Judges in every State shall be bound thereby, any Thing in the Constitution or Laws of any State to the Contrary notwithstanding.

The Senators and Representatives before mentioned, and the Members of the several State Legislatures, and all executive and judicial Officers, both of the United States and of the several States, shall be bound by Oath or Affirmation, to support this Constitution; but no religious Test shall ever be required as a Qualification to any Office or public Trust under the United States.

Article. VII.

The Ratification of the Conventions of nine States, shall be sufficient for the Establishment of this Constitution between the States so ratifying the Same.

The Word, "the," being interlined between the seventh and eighth Lines of the first Page, The Word "Thirty" being partly written on an Erasures in the fifteenth Line of the first Page, The Words "is tried" being interlined between the thirty second and thirty third Lines of the first Page and the Word "the" being interlined between the forty third and forty fourth Lines of the second Page.

Attest William Jackson Secretary

done in Convention by the Unanimous Consent of the States present the Seventeenth Day of September in the Year of our Lord one thousand seven hundred and Eighty seven and of the Independence of the United States of America the Twelfth In witness whereof We have hereunto subscribed our Names,

G°. Washington
Presiding and deputy from Virginia

Delaware
Geo: Read, Gunning Bedford jun, John Dickinson, Richard Bassett, Jaco: Broom

Maryland James McHenry, Dan of St Thos. Jenifer, Danl. Carroll

Virginia John Blair, James Madison Jr.

North Carolina Wm. Blount, Richard D. Spaight, Hu Williamson

South Carolina
J. Rutledge, Charles Cotesworth Pinckney, Charles Pinckney, Pierce Butler

Georgia William Few, Abraham Baldwin

New Hampshire John Langdon, Nicholas Gilman

Massachusetts Nathaniel Gorham, Rufus King

Connecticut Wm. Saml. Johnson, Roger Sherman

New York Alexander Hamilton

New Jersey
Wil Livingston, David Brearley, Wm. Paterson, Jonathan Dayton

Pennsylvania
B. Franklin, Thomas Mifflin, Robert Morris, Geo. Clymer, Thomas Fitzsimons, Jared Ingersoll, James Wilson, Gouvernour Morris

Chapter 22. THE 613 MITZVOT (Cross Reference)

God	Employees	The Firstborn
Torah	Vows	Priests & Levites
Signs & Symbols	Sabbatical & Jubilee	Tithes & Taxes
Prayer & Blessings	Court	The Temple
Love & Brotherhood	Injuries & Damages	Sacrifices&Offering
The Poor	Property	Ritual Purity
Gentiles	Criminal Laws	Leprosy
Family	Punishment & Restitution	The King
Forbidden Sex	Prophecy	Wars
Times	Idolatry	Business Practices
Dietary Laws	Agriculture	Clothing

Codes associated with each law. (Ex. 20:2; Deut. 5:6) (CCA1).

For each Biblical law or commandment, we have provided a citation to the biblical passage or passages from which it is derived. We added an addendum following the Index that provides much information beyond the actual Verse. For commandments that can be observed today, we have also provided citations to the Chafetz Chayim's Concise Book of Mitzvot (CCA refers to affirmative commandments; CCN refers to negative commandments; CCI refers to commandments that only apply in Israel).

God

1. (Ex. 20:2; Deut. 5:6) (CCA1)
2. (Ex. 20:3) (CCN8).
3. (Ex. 22:27; Ex. 22:28), penalty is death (Lev. 24:16) (neg).
4. (Lev. 22:32) (CCA5). See The Name of God.
5. (Lev . 22:32) (CCN155). See The Name of God.
6. (Deut. 6:4) (CCA2). See What Do Jews Believe?.
7. (Deut. 6:5) (CCA3). See What Do Jews Believe?.
8. (Deut. 6:13; 10:20) (CCA4).
9. (Deut. 6:16) (negative).
10. (Deut. 28:9) (CCA6).

Torah
11. (Lev. 19:32) (CCA17).
12. (Deut. 6:7) (CCA14). See Torah.
13. (Deut. 10:20)) (CCA16).
14. (Deut. 13:1) (CCN159). See Torah.
15. (Deut. 13:1) (CCN160). See Torah.
16. (CCA15). See Torah. (Deut.17:18)

Signs and Symbols
17. (Gen. 17:12; Lev. 12:3) (CCA47) Brit Milah: Circumcision.
18. (Num. 15:38) (CCA10). Tzitzit and Tallit. (decorative fringe)
19. (Deut. 6:8) (CCA9). See Tefillin.
20. (Deut. 6:8) (CCA8). See Tefillin.
21. (Deut. 6:9) (CCA12). See Mezuzah.

Prayer and Blessings
22. (Ex. 23:25; Deut. 6:13) (CCA7). Prayers and Blessings;
23. (Deut. 6:7) (CCA11). Shema, Jewish Liturgy.
24. (Deut. 8:10) (CCA13). Birkat Ha-Mazon: Grace After Meals
25. (Lev. 26:1) (CCN161).

Love and Brotherhood
26. (Lev. 19:18) (CCA60). See Love and Brotherhood.
27. (Lev. 19:16) (CCN82). See Love and Brotherhood.
28. (Lev. 25:17) (CCN48). See Speech and Lashon Ha-Ra.
29. (Lev. 19:16) (CCN77). See Speech and Lashon Ha-Ra.
30. (Lev. 19:17) (CCN78). See Love and Brotherhood.
31. (Lev. 19:18) (CCN80).
32. (Lev. 19:18) (CCN81).
33. (Lev. 19:17) (CCN79).
34. (Lev. 19:14) (CCN45).
35. (Lev. 19:14) (anything that cause another to sin) (CCN76).
36. (Lev. 19:17) (CCA72).
37. (Ex. 23:5) (CCA70). See Love and Brotherhood.
38. (Deut. 22:4) (CCA71). See Love and Brotherhood.
39. (Deut. 22:4) (CCN183). See Love and Brotherhood.

The Poor and Unfortunate
40. (Ex. 22:21) (CCN51).
41. (Lev. 19:9; Lev. 23:22) (negative) (CCI6).
42. (Lev. 19:9) (affirmative) (CCI1).
43. (Lev. 19:9) (negative) (CCI7).
44. (Lev. 19:9) (affirmative) (CCI2).

45. (Lev. 19:10) (negative) (CCI8).
46. (Lev. 19:10; Deut. 24:21) (affirmative) (CCI3).
47. (Lev. 19:10) (negative) (CCI9).
48. (Lev. 19:10) (affirmative) (CCI4).
49. (Deut. 24:19) Applies all fruit trees (Deut. 24:20) (CC10).
50. (Deut. 24:19-20) (affirmative) (CCI5).
51. (Deut. 15:7) (CCN62). See Tzedakah: Charity.
52. (Deut. 15:11) (CCA38). See Tzedakah: Charity.

Treatment of Gentiles

53. (Deut. 10:19) (CCA61). See Love and Brotherhood.
54. (Ex. 22:20) (CCN49).
55. (Ex. 22:20) (CCN50).
56. (Deut. 7:3) (CCN19). See Interfaith Marriages.
57. (Deut. 15:3) (affirmative).
58. (Deut. 23:21) According to tradition, is mandatory (affirm).

Marriage, Divorce and Family

59. (Ex. 20:12) (CCA41).
60. (Ex. 21:15) (CCN44).
61. (Ex. 21:17) (CCN46).
62. (Lev. 19:3) (CCA42).
63. (Gen. 1:28) (CCA43).
64. (Deut. 23:2) (CCN136).
65. (Deut. 23:3)(CCN137)Prohibited Marriages, Illegitimate child
66. (Deut. 23:4) (negative).
67. (Deut. 23:8-9) (negative).
68. (Deut. 23:8-9) (negative).
69. (Deut. 23:18) (CCN133). See Marriage.
70. (Deut. 24:1) (CCA44). Process of Marriage: Kiddushin, Nisuin.
71. (Deut. 24:5) (affirmative).
72. (Deut. 24:5) (negative).
73. (Ex. 21:10) (CCN42). See The Marital Relationship.
74. (Num. 5:30) (affirmative).
75. (Deut. 22:19) (affirmative).
76. (Deut. 22:19) (negative).
77. (Deut. 24:1) (affirmative). Process of Obtaining a Divorce.
78. (Deut. 24:4) (CCN134). See Divorce.
79. (Deut. 25:5) (CCN135
80. (Deut. 25:5) (CCA45).
81. (Deut. 25:7-9) (CCA46).

Forbidden Sexual Relations
82. (Lev. 18:6) (CCN110).
83. (Lev. 18:7) (CCN112). Prohibited Marriages Illegitimate Child
84. (Lev. 18:7) (CCN111).
85. (Lev. 18:8) (CCN113). Prohibited Marriages Illegitimate Child
86. (Lev. 18:9) (CCN127). Prohibited Marriages Illegitimate Child
87. (Lev. 18:11) (CCN128)Prohibited Marriages Illegitimate Child
88. (Lev. 18:10) (CCN119)Prohibited Marriages Illegitimate Child
89. (Lev. 18:10) (CCN119)Prohibited Marriages Illegitimate Child
90. (CCN120). See Prohibited Marriages and Illegitimate Children.
91. (Lev. 18:12) (CCN129)Prohibited Marriages Illegitimate Child
92. (Lev. 18:13) (CCN130)Prohibited Marriages Illegitimate Child
93. (Lev. 18:14) (CCN125)Prohibited Marriages Illegitimate Child
94. (Lev. 18:14) (CCN114).
95. (Lev. 18:15) (CCN115)Prohibited Marriages Illegitimate Child
96. (Lev. 18:16) (CCN126)Prohibited Marriages Illegitimate Child
97. (Lev. 18:17) (CCN121)Prohibited Marriages Illegitimate Child
98. (Lev. 18:17) (CCN122)Prohibited Marriages Illegitimate Child
99. (Lev. 18:17) (CCN123)Prohibited Marriages Illegitimate Child
100. (Lev. 18:18) (CCN131)Prohibited Marriages Illegitimate Child
101. (Lev. 18:19) (CCN132).
102. (Lev. 18:20) (CCN124).
103. (Lev. 18:22) (CCN116).
104. (Lev. 18:23) (CCN117).
105. (Lev. 18:23) (CCN118).
106. (Lev. 22:24) (CCN143).

Times and Seasons
107. (Ex. 12:2) (affirmative
108. (Ex. 16:29) (CCN7). See Shabbat.
109. (Ex. 20:8) (CCA19). See Shabbat.
110. (Ex. 20:10) (CCN6). See Shabbat.
111. (Ex. 23:12; 34:21) (CCA20). See Shabbat.
112. [Passover, Shavu'ot and Sukkot] (Ex. 23:14) (affirmative).
113. (Deut. 16:14) (CCA21).
114. (Deut. 16:16) (affirmative).
115. (Ex. 12:15) (CCA22). See Passover.
116. (Ex. 12:16; Lev. 23:7) (CCA25). See Passover.
117. (Ex. 12:16; Lev. 23:6-7) (CCN147). See Passover.
118. (Ex. 12:16; Lev. 23:8) (CCA27). See Passover.
119. (Ex. 12:16; Lev. 23:8) (CCN148). See Passover.
120. (Ex. 12:18) (CCA23). See Passover.
121. (Ex. 12:19) (CCN3). See Passover.

122. (Ex. 12:20) (CCN5). See Passover.
123. (Ex. 13:3) (CCN4). See Passover.
124. (Ex. 13:7) (CCN2). See Passover.
125. (Ex. 13:8) (CCA24). See The Passover Seder.
126. (Deut. 16:3) (CCN104). See Passover.
127. (Lev. 23:15) (CCA26). See The Counting of the Omer.
128. (Lev. 23:21) (CCA28). See Shavu'ot.
129. (Lev. 23:21) (CCN149). See Shavu'ot.
130. (Lev. 23:24) (CCA29). See Rosh Hashanah.
131. (Lev. 23:25) (CCN150). See Rosh Hashanah.
132. (Num. 29:1) (CCA30). See Rosh Hashanah.
133. (Lev. 23:27) (CCA32). See Yom Kippur.
134. (Lev. 23:29) (CCN152). See Yom Kippur.
135. (Lev. 23:31) (CCN151). See Yom Kippur.
136. (Lev. 23:32) (CCA31). See Yom Kippur.
137. (Lev. 23:35) (CCA34). See Sukkot.
138. (Lev. 23:35) (CCN153). See Sukkot.
139. (Shemini Atzeret)(Lev.23:36) (CCA37). Simchat Torah
140. (Lev. 23:36) (CCN154). Shemini Atzeret and Simchat Torah.
141. (Lev. 23:40) (CCA36). See Sukkot.
142. (Lev. 23:42) (CCA35). See Sukkot.

Dietary Laws

143. (Lev. 11:2) (affirmative). See Animals that may not be eaten.
144. (Lev. 11:4) (CCN93). See Animals that may not be eaten.
145. (Lev. 11:9) (affirmative). See Animals that may not be eaten.
146. (Lev. 11:11) (CCN95). See Animals that may not be eaten.
147. (Deut. 14:11) (affirmative). See Animals that may not be eaten.
148. (Lev. 11:13) (CCN94). See Animals that may not be eaten.
149. (Lev. 11:21) (affirmative). See Animals that may not be eaten.
150. (Lev. 11:41) (CCN98). See Animals that may not be eaten.
151. (Lev. 11:41-42) (CCN97). See Animals that may not be eaten.
152. (Lev. 11:44) (CCN100). See Animals that may not be eaten.
153. (Lev. 11:43 and 46) (CCN99). Animals that may not be eaten.
154. (Deut. 14:19) (CCN96). See Animals that may not be eaten.
155. (Ex. 22:30) (CCN87). See Kosher slaughtering.
156. (Deut. 14:21) (CCN86). See Kosher slaughtering.
157. (Deut. 12:21) (CCA48). See Kosher slaughtering.
158. (Deut. 12:23) (CCN90). See Kosher slaughtering.
159. (Lev. 22:28) (CCN108).
160. (Deut. 22:6) (CCN189). See Treatment of Animals.
161. (Deut. 22:6-7) (CCA74). See Treatment of Animals.
162. (Ex. 21:28) (negative).

163. (Ex. 23:19) (CCN91). See Separation of Meat and Dairy.
164. (Ex. 34:26, Ex. 23:19) (CCN92). Separation of Meat and Dairy.
165. (Gen. 32:33) (CCN1). See Forbidden Fats and Nerves.
166. (Lev. 7:23) (CCN88). See Forbidden Fats and Nerves.
167. (Lev. 7:26) (CCN89). See Draining of Blood.
168. (Lev. 17:13) (CCA49).
169. (Lev. 19:26; Deut. 21:20) (CCN106).

Business Practices

170. (Lev. 25:14) (CCN47).
171. (Lev. 25:37) (CCN54).
172. (Deut. 23:20) (CCN55).
173. (Ex. 22:24) (CCN53).
174. (Ex. 22:24) (CCA62).
175. (Ex. 22:24) (CCN52).
176. (Deut. 24:6) (CCN58).
177. (Deut. 24:10) (CCN59).
178. (Deut. 24:12) (CCN61).
179. (Deut. 24:13) (CCA63).
180. (Deut. 24:17) (CCN60).
181. (Lev. 19:35) (CCN83).
182. (Lev. 19:36) (affirmative).
183. (Deut. 25:13-14) (CCN84).

Employees, Servants, and Slaves

184. (Lev. 19:13) (CCN38).
185. (Deut. 23:25-26) (CCA65).
186. (Deut. 23:25) (CCN187).
187. (Deut. 23:26) (CCN186).
188. (Deut. 24:15) (CCA66).
189. (Ex. 21:2-6) (affirmative).
190. (Lev. 25:39) (negative).
191. (Lev. 25:42) (negative).
192. (Lev. 25:43) (negative).
193. (Lev. 25:53) (negative).
194. (Deut. 15:13) (negative).
195. (Deut. 15:14) (affirmative).
196. (Ex. 21:8) (affirmative).
197. (Ex. 21:8) (negative).
198. (Ex. 21:8-9) (affirmative).
199. (Lev. 25:46) (affirmative).
200. (Deut. 23:16) (negative).
201. (Deut. 23:17) (negative).
202. (Deut. 25:4) (CCN188).

Vows, Oaths and Swearing
203. (Deut. 23:24) (CCA39).
204. (Ex. 20:7) (CCN29).
205. (Lev. 19:12) (CCN31).
206. (Num. 30:2-17) (CCA40).
207. (Num. 30:3) (CCN184).
208. (Deut. 10:20) (affirmative).
209. (Deut. 23:22) (CCN185).

The Sabbatical and Jubilee Years
210. (Ex. 23:11; Lev. 25:2) (affirmative) (CCI20).
211. (Ex. 23:11) (affirmative) (Lev. 25:2) (CCI21).
212. (Lev. 25:4) (negative) (CCI22).
213. (Lev. 25:4) (negative) (CCI23).
214. (Lev. 25:5) (negative) (CCI24).
215. (Lev. 25:5) (negative) (CCI25).
216. (Lev. 25:9) (affirmative).
217. (Deut. 15:2) (CCA64).
218. (Deut. 15:2) (CCN57).
219. (Deut. 15:9) (CCN56).
220. (Deut. 31:12) (affirmative)
221. (Lev. 25:8) (affirmative).
222. (Lev. 25:10) (affirmative).
223. (Lev. 25:11) (negative).
224. (Lev. 25:11) (negative).
225. No Cross Reference
226. (Lev. 25:24) (affirmative).

The Court and Judicial Procedure
227. (Deut. 16:18) (affirmative).
228. (Deut. 1:17) (CCN64).
229. (Lev. 25:14) (CCA67).
230. (Ex. 22:9) (affirmative).
231. (Ex. 22:13-14) (affirmative).
232. (Num. 27:8-11) (CCA73).
233. (Ex. 21:33-34) (affirmative).
234. (Ex. 21:35-36) (affirmative).
235. (Ex. 22:4) (affirmative).
236. (Ex. 22:5) (affirmative).
237. (Ex. 22:6-7) (affirmative).
238. (Ex. 22:8) (affirmative).
239. (Ex. 22:27) (CCN63).
240. (Lev. 5:1) (affirmative).
241. (Ex. 20:13) (CCN39).

242. (Num. 35:30) (negative).
243. (Ex. 23:1) (CCN75).
244. (Deut. 24:16) (CCN74).
245. (Ex. 23:1) (CCN65).
246. (Deut. 13:15) (affirmative).
247. (Deut. 19:15) (CCN73).
248. (Ex. 23:2) (affirmative).
249. (Ex. 23:2) (negative).
250. (Ex. 23:2) (negative).
251. (Lev. 19:15) (affirmative).
252. (Lev. 19:15) (CCN69).
253. (Lev. 19:15) (CCN70).
254. (Ex. 23:8) (CCN71).
255. (Deut. 1:17) (CCN72).
256. (Ex. 23:3; Lev. 19:15) (CCN66).
257. (Deut. 24:17) (CCN68).
258. (Ex. 23:6) (CCN67).
259. (Ex. 23:7) (negative).
260. (Num. 35:12) (negative).
261. (Deut. 17:11) (affirmative).
262. (Deut. 17:11) (CCN158).

Injuries and Damages

263. (Deut. 22:8) (CCA75). See Love and Brotherhood.
264. (Deut. 22:8) (CCN190). See Love and Brotherhood.
265. (Deut. 25:12) (affirmative). See Life.
266. (Deut. 25:12) (negative).

Property and Property Rights

267. (Lev. 25:23) (negative).
268. (Lev. 25:34) (negative). See Levi.
269. (Lev. 25:29) (affirmative).
270. (Deut. 19:14) (CCN85).
271. (Lev. 19:11) (CCN30).
272. (Lev. 19:11) (CCN36).
273. (Deut. 17:16) (CCN192).
274. (Lev. 19:11) (CCN34).
275. (Lev. 5:23) (CCA68).
276. (Deut. 22:1) (CCA69).
277. (Deut. 22:3) (CCN182).

Criminal Laws
278. (Ex. 20:13) (CCN32). See Life.
279. (Lev. 19:11, regarding the taking of property) (CCN33).
280. (Lev. 19:13) (CCN35).
281. (Lev. 19:13) (CCN37).
282. (Ex. 20:14) (CCN40).
283. (Deut. 5:18) (CCN41).
284. (Num. 15:39) (CCN156).

Punishment and Restitution
285. (Ex. 21:20; Lev. 26:25) (affirmative).
286. (Lev. 20:10) (affirmative).
287. (Lev. 20:14) (affirmative).
288. Court pass sentence, death by stoning (Deut. 22:24) affirmative)
289. Hang body of one who incurred penalty(Deut. 21:22) affirmative)
290. (Deut. 21:23) (affirmative)
291. No Cross Reference
292. (Num. 35:31) (negative).
293. (Num. 35:25) (affirmative).
294. (Deut. 19:3) (affirmative).
295. (Num. 35:32) (negative).
296. (Deut. 21:4) (affirmative).
297. (Deut. 21:4) (negative).
298. (Ex. 21:16; Ex. 21:37; Ex. 22:1) (affirmative).
299. (Ex. 21:18-19) (affirmative).
300. (Ex. 22:15-16) (affirmative).
301. (Deut. 22:28-29) (affirmative).
302. (Deut. 22:29) (negative).
303. (Ex. 35:3) (negative). See Shabbat.
304. (Deut. 25:2) (affirmative).
305. (Deut. 25:3) (and by implication, not to strike anyone) (CCN43).
306. (Deut. 19:13) (negative).
307. (Deut. 19:19) (affirmative).
308. (Deut. 22:26) (negative).

Prophecy
309. (Deut. 18:15) (affirmative).
310. (Deut. 18:20) (CCN175).
311. (Deut. 18:22) (negative).

Idolatry, Idolaters, and Idolatrous Practices

312. (Ex. 20:4) (CCN9).
313. (Ex. 20:20) (CCN144).
314. (Ex. 34:17; Lev. 19:4) (CCN10).
315. (Deut. 7:25) (CCN17).
316. (Deut. 7:26) (CCN18). See Grape Products.
317. (Deut. 32:38) (CCN15). See Grape Products.
318. (Ex. 20:5) (CCN12).
319. (Ex. 20:5) (CCN11).
320. (Ex. 23:13; Deut. 18:20) (CCN27).
321. (Deut. 13:4) (CCN22).
322. (Ex. 23:13) (CCN14).
323. No Cross Reference
324. No Cross Reference
325. (Deut. 13:9) (CCN24).
326. (Deut. 13:9) (CCN25).
327. (Deut. 13:9) (negative).
328. (Deut. 13:9) (CCN26).
329. (Deut. 13:9) (negative).
330. (Ex. 23:13) (CCN13).
331. (Lev. 19:4) (CCN16).
332. (Lev. 18:3; Lev. 20:23) (CCN21).
333. (Lev. 18:21) (negative).
334. (Ex. 22:17) (negative).
335. (Lev. 19:26) (CCN166).
336. (Lev. 19:26) (CCN165).
337. (Lev. 19:31) (CCN170).
338. (Lev. 19:31) (CCN171).
339. (Deut. 18:10) (CCN168).
340. (Deut. 18:10) (CCN167).
341. (Deut. 18:11) (CCN169).
342. (Deut. 18:11) (CCN172).
343. (Deut. 18:11) (CCN174).
344. (Deut. 18:11) (CCN173).
345. (Lev. 19:27) (CCN177).
346. (Lev. 19:27) (CCN176).
347. (Lev. 19:28; Deut. 14:1) (CCN28).
348. (Lev. 19:28) (CCN163).
349. (Deut. 14:1) (CCN164).
350. (Deut. 16:21) (negative).
351. (Deut. 16:22) (CCN162).
352. (Deut. 7:2) (CCN20).
353. (Ex. 23:32; Deut. 7:2) (negative).
354. (Ex. 23:33) (negative) (CCI26).

355. (Deut. 13:16-17) (affirmative).
356. (Deut. 13:17) (negative).
357. (Deut. 13:18) (negative).

Agriculture and Animal Husbandry
358. (CCN142).
359. (Lev. 19:19) (CCN107).
360. (Lev. 19:23) (CCN105). See Tu B'Shevat.
361. (Lev. 19:24) (affirmative) (CCI16). See Tu B'Shevat.
362. (Deut. 22:9) (negative).
363. (Deut. 22:9) (negative).
364. (Deut. 22:10) (CCN180).

Clothing
365. (Deut. 22:5) (CCN179).
366. (Deut. 22:5) (CCN178).
367. (Deut. 22:11) (CCN181).

The Firstborn
368. (Ex. 13:13; Ex. 34:20; Num. 18:15) (CCA54). See
369. (Ex. 13:13; Ex. 34:20) (CCA55).
370. (Ex. 13:13; Ex. 34:20) (CCA56).
371. (Num. 18:17) (CCN109).

Kohanim and Levites (See Kohein for all entries) (child or children)
372. (Ex. 28:2) (affirmative). See Kohein.
373. (Ex. 28:32) (negative). See Kohein.
374. (Lev. 16:2) (negative). See Kohein.
375. (Lev. 21:1-3) (CCN141). Kohein, Care for the Dead.
376. (Lev. 21:3) (CCA59). Care for the Dead; Mourning.
377. (Lev. 21:6) (negative). See Kohein.
378. (Lev. 21:7) (CCN140).Prohibited Marriage, Illegitimate Children
379. (Lev. 21:7) (CCN138).Prohibited Marriage, Illegitimate Children
380. (Lev. 21:7) (CCN139).Prohibited Marriage, Illegitimate Children
381. (Lev. 21:8) (CCA50). See Kohein.
382. (Lev. 21:11) (negative). See Kohein, Care for the Dead.
383. (Lev. 21:11) (negative). See Kohein, Care for the Dead.
384. (Lev. 21:13) (affirmative) Prohibited Marriage, Illegitimate Child
385. (Lev. 21:14) (negative). Prohibited Marriages, Illegitimate Child
386. (Lev. 21:15) (negative). Prohibited Marriages, Illegitimate Child
387. (Lev. 21:17) (negative).
388. (Lev. 21:21) (negative). See Kohein.
389. No cross reference
390. (Lev. 22:2-3) (negative). See Kohein.
391. (Num. 5:2) (affirmative).

392. (Num. 5:2-3) Refers to the Camp of the Shechinah (negative).
393. (Num. 6:23) (CCA58). See Kohein.
394. (Num. 15:20) (CCA57). See Kohein.
395. (Num. 18:3) (negative). See Kohein, Levi.
396. (In the Sanctuary) (Num. 18:4-7) (negative).
397. (Num. 18:23) (affirmative). See Levi.
398. (Num. 35:2) (affirmative). See Levi.
399. (Deut. 18:1) (negative). See Levi.
400. (Deut. 18:1) (negative). See Levi.
401. (Deut. 18:6-8) (affirmative). See Kohein.

T'rumah, Tithes and Taxes (each involves Kohein or Levi)

402. (Ex. 12:44-45 Lev. 22:10) (negative). Brit Milah: Circumcision
403. (Ex. 22:28) (negative) (CCI19).
404. (Ex. 30:13) (affirmative). See Shabbat Sheqalim
405. (Lev. 22:3-4) (negative). See Kohein.
406. (Lev. 22:10) (negative). See Kohein.
407. (Lev. 22:10) (negative). See Kohein.
408. (Lev. 22:15) (negative) (CCI18).
409. (Lev. 27:30; Num. 18:24) (affirmative) (CCI12). See Levi.
410. (Lev. 27:32) (affirmative).
411. (Lev. 27:32-33) (negative).
412. (Called t'rumah of the tithe)(Num. 18:26)(affirmative)(CCI13).
413. (Deut. 12:17) (negative).
414. (Deut. 12:17) (negative).
415. (Deut. 12:17) (negative).
416. (Deut. 12:19); (negative). See Levi.
417. (Deut. 14:22) (affirmative) (CCI14)
418. (Deut. 14:28-29) (affirmative) (CCI15)
419. (Deut. 18:3) (CCA51). See Kohein.
420. (Deut. 18:4) (CCA52). See Kohein.
421. (Deut. 18:4) (affirmative) (CCI11). See Kohein.
422. (Deut. 26:14) Outside necessary sustenance. Given for dead.
423. (Deut. 26:14) (negative).
424. (Deut. 26:14) (negative).
425. (Deut. 26:13) (affirmative) (CCI17).

The Temple, the Sanctuary and Sacred Objects

426. (Ex. 20:22) (negative).
427. (Ex. 20:23) (negative).
428. (Ex. 25:8) (affirmative).
429. (Ex. 25:15) (negative).
430. (Ex. 25:30) (affirmative). Shabbat
431. (Ex. 27:21) (affirmative).
432. (Ex. 28:28) (negative).

433. (Ex. 30:7) (affirmative).
434. (Ex. 30:9) (negative).
435. (Ex. 30:19) (affirmative). See Kohein.
436. (Ex. 30:31) (affirmative). See Kohein.
437. (Ex. 30:32-33) (CCN145).
438. (Ex. 30:32) (negative).
439. (Ex. 30:37) (CCN146).
440. (Lev. 5:16) (affirmative).
441. (Lev. 6:3) (affirmative).
442. (Lev. 6:6) (affirmative).
443. (Lev. 6:6) (negative).
444. (Lev. 10:6) (negative). See Kohein.
445. (Lev. 10:6) (negative). See Kohein.
446. (Lev. 10:7) (negative). See Kohein.
447. (Lev. 10:9-11) (negative).
448. (CCA18). See Synagogues, Shuls and Temples.
449. (Num. 7:9) (affirmative).
450. (Num. 9:11) (affirmative).
451. (Num. 9:11) (affirmative).
452. (Num. 9:12) (negative).
453. (Num. 9:12) (negative).
454. (Num. 10:9-10) (affirmative).
455. (Num. 18:2) (affirmative).
456. (Num. 18:5) (negative).
457. (affirmative). See Asham: Guilt Offering.
458. (Deut. 12:2-4) (CCN157). See The Name of God.

Sacrifices and Offerings

459. (Ex. 13:2; Deut. 15:19) (at present, not offered up) (CCA53).
460. (Ex. 12:6) (affirmative).
461. (Ex. 12:8) (affirmative).
462. (Ex. 12:9) (negative).
463. (Ex. 12:10) (negative).
464. No cross reference
465. (Ex. 12:45) (negative).
466. (Ex. 12:46) (negative).
467. (Ex. 12:46) (negative).
468. (Ex. 12:48) (negative). See Brit Milah: Circumcision
469. (Ex. 23:18; Ex. 24:25) (negative).
470. (Ex. 23:18; Ex. 24:25) (negative).
471. (Ex. 23:15) (negative).
472. (Ex. 23:19) (affirmative).
473. (Ex. 29:33) (affirmative). See Qorbanot: Sacrifices and Offerings
474. (Ex. 29:33) (negative).
475. (Lev. 1:3) (affirmative). See Olah: Burnt Offering.

476. (Lev. 2:1) (affirmative). See Food and Drink Offerings.
477. (Lev. 2:11) (negative).
478. (Lev. 2:13) (affirmative).
479. (Lev. 2:13) (negative).
480. (Lev. 4:13) (affirmative).
481. (Lev. 4:27-28) (affirmative). See Chatat: Sin Offering.
482. (Lev. 5:7) (affirmative).
483. (Lev. 5:8) (negative).
484. (Lev. 5:11) (negative).
485. (Lev. 5:11) (negative).
486. (Lev. 5:17-19) (affirmative). See Asham: Guilt Offering.
487. (Lev. 6:9) (affirmative).
488. (Lev. 6:10) (negative).
489. (Lev. 6:13) (affirmative).
490. (Lev. 6:16) (negative).
491. (Lev. 6:18) (affirmative). See Chatat: Sin Offering.
492. (Lev. 6:23) (negative).
493. (Lev. 7:1) (affirmative).See Asham: Guilt Offering.
494. (Lev. 7:11) (affirmative). See Zebach Sh'lamim: Peace Offering.
495. (Lev. 7:17) (affirmative).
496. (Lev. 7:18) The penalty is excision (negative).
497. (Lev. 7:19) (negative).
498. (Lev. 7:19) (affirmative).
499. (Lev. 7:20) (negative).
500. (Lev. 10:14, Lev. 22:12) (negative). See Kohein.
501. (Lev. 12:6) (affirmative). See Birth.
502. (Lev. 14:10) (affirmative).
503. (Lev. 15:13-15) (affirmative).
504. (Lev. 15:28-30) (affirmative).
505. (Lev. 16:3-34) (affirmative).
506. (Lev. 17:3-4) (negative).
507. (Lev. 19:8) (negative).
508. (negative).
509. (Lev. 22:21) (affirmative).
510. (Lev. 22:21) (negative).
511. (Lev. 22:22) (negative).
512. (Lev. 22:22) (negative).
513. (Lev. 22:24) (negative).
514. (Lev. 22:25) (negative).
515. (Lev. 22:27) (affirmative).
516. (Lev. 22:30) (negative).
517. (Lev. 23:10) (affirmative). See The Counting of the Omer.
518. (Lev. 23:14) (CCN101). See The Counting of the Omer.
519. (Lev. 23:14) (CCN102). See The Counting of the Omer.
520. (Lev. 23:14) (CCN103). See The Counting of the Omer.

521. (Lev. 23:17-20) (affirmative).
522. (Lev. 23:36) (affirmative).
523. (Lev. 27:2-8) (affirmative).
524. (Lev. 27:10) (affirmative).
525. (Lev. 27:10) (negative).
526. (Lev. 27:11-13) (affirmative).
527. (Lev. 27:11-13) (affirmative). See Kohein.
528. (Lev. 27:16-24) (affirmative).
529. (Lev. 27:26) (negative).
530. (Lev. 27:28) (affirmative). See Kohein.
531. (Lev. 27:28) (negative).
532. (Lev. 27:28) (negative).
533. (Num. 5:6-7) (CCA33).
534. (Num. 5:15) (negative).
535. (Num. 5:15) (negative).
536. (Num. 28:3) (affirmative).
537. (Num. 28:9) (affirmative).
538. (Num. 28:11) (affirmative).
539. (Num. 28:26-27) (affirmative).
540. (Num. 29:1-6) (affirmative).
541. (Num. 29:7-8) (affirmative).
542. (Num. 29:12-34) (affirmative).
543. (Num. 29:35-38) (affirmative).
544. (Deut. 12:5-6) (affirmative).
545. (Deut. 12:13) (negative).
546. (Deut. 12:14) (affirmative).
547. (Deut. 12:15) (affirmative).
548. (Deut. 12:17) (negative).
549. (Deut. 12:17) (negative).
550. (Deut. 12:17) (negative).
551. (Deut. 12:17) (negative).
552. (Deut. 14:3) (negative).
553. No cross reference
554. No cross reference
555. (Deut. 15:19) (negative).
556. (Deut. 15:19) (negative).
557. (Deut. 16:4) (negative).
558. (Deut. 17:1) (negative).
559. (Deut. 23:19) (negative).
560. (Deut. 26:5-10) (affirmative).

Ritual Purity and Impurity
561. (Lev. 11:29-30) (affirmative).
562. (Lev. 11:34) (affirmative).
563. (Lev. 11:39) (affirmative).
564. No cross reference
565. (Lev. 13:2-46) (affirmative).
566. (Lev. 13:45) (affirmative).
567. (Lev. 13:47-49) (affirmative).
568. (Lev. 14:34-46) (affirmative).
569. (Lev. 15:1-15) (affirmative).
570. (Lev. 15:16) (affirmative).
571. (Lev. 15:16) (affirmative).
572. (Lev. 15:19-24) (affirmative).
573. (Lev. 15:25-27) (affirmative).
574. (Num. 19:9) (affirmative). Parah Adumah: Red Heifer, Shabbat
575. (Num. 19:11-16) (affirmative). See Care for the Dead.
576. (Num. 19:19-22) (affirmative).

Lepers and Leprosy
577. (Lev. 13:33) (negative).
578. (Lev. 14:1-7) (affirmative).
579. (Lev. 14:9) (affirmative).
580. (Deut. 24:8) (negative).

The King
581. (Ex. 22:27) (negative).
582. (Deut. 17:15) (affirmative).
583. (Deut. 17:15) (negative).
584. No cross reference
585. (Deut. 17:17) (negative).
586. No cross reference
587. (Deut. 17:18) (affirmative). See Torah.

Nazarites
588. (Num. 6:3) (negative).
589. (Num. 6:3) (negative).
590. (Num. 6:3) (negative).
591. (Num. 6:4) (negative).
592. (Num. 6:4) (negative).
593. (Num. 6:5) (affirmative).
594. (Num. 6:5) (negative).
595. (Num. 6:6) (negative).
596. (Num. 6:7) (negative).
597. (Num. 6:9) (affirmative).

Wars

598. (Deut. 3:22, 7:21, 20:3) (negative).
599. (Deut. 20:2) (affirmative). See Kohein.
600. (Deut. 20:10) (affirmative).
601. (Deut. 20:16) (negative).
602. (Deut. 20:17) (affirmative).
603. (Deut. 20:19-20) (CCN191).
604. (Deut. 21:10-14) (affirmative).
605. (Deut. 21:14) (negative).
606. (Deut. 21:14) (negative).
607. (Deut. 23:7) (negative).
608. (Deut. 23:11) (CCN193).
609. (Deut. 23:13) (affirmative).
610. (Deut. 23:14-15) (affirmative).
611. (Deut. 25:17) (CCA76). See Shabbat Zakhor.
612. (Deut. 25:19) (CCN194). See Shabbat Zakhor.
613. (Deut. 25:19) (CCA77). See Shabbat Zakhor.

Chapter 23. FOUNDING FATHERS COMPLIANCE WITH GOD

Deuteronomy Chapter 5 can be considered a companion rendering of THE TEN COMMANDMENTS. This chapter provides the perfect closing statement for this book. It can only be clear, God commands that we continue to practice and live by ALL THE LAWS AND FORMS OF GOVERNMENT HE PROVIDES AND OUTLINES FOR FUTURE GENERATIONS.

DEUTERONOMY CHAPTER 5

1And Moses called all Israel, and said unto them, Hear, O Israel,
the statutes and judgments which I speak in your ears this day,
that ye may learn them, and keep, and do them.
2The LORD our God made a covenant with us in Horeb.
(covenant = contract)
3The LORD made not this covenant with our fathers, but with
us, *even* us, who *are* all of us here alive this day.
4The LORD talked with you face to face in the mount out of the
midst of the fire,
6 I *am* the LORD thy God, which brought thee out of the land of
Egypt, from the house of bondage.
31But as for thee, stand thou here by me, and I will speak unto
thee all the commandments, and the statutes, and the judgments,
which thou shalt teach them, that they may do *them* in the land
which I give them to possess it.
32Ye shall observe to do therefore as the LORD your God hath
commanded: ye shall not turn aside to the right hand or to the left.
33Ye shall walk in the ways which the LORD your God hath
commanded you, that ye may live, and *that it may be* well with
you, *that* ye may prolong *your* days in the land which ye shall
possess.
33Ye shall walk in all the ways which the LORD your God hath
commanded you, that ye may live, and *that it may be* well with
you, *that* ye may prolong *your* days in land which ye shall possess.

In the opening pages, we noted that Benjamin Franklin opened debate one morning with the following statement: "we can save much argument and debate by simply agreeing to implement 'The Laws of Moses' as the initial legal code of our constitution . . ."

> Benjamin Franklin, in 1788, saw the difficulties some of the newly independent American states were having forming a government, and proposed that until a new code of laws could be agreed to, they should be governed by "the laws of Moses", as contained in the Old Testament. He justified his proposal by explaining that the laws had worked in biblical times:
>
> > "The Supreme Being ... having rescued them from bondage by many miracles, performed by his servant Moses, he personally delivered to that chosen servant, in the presence of the whole nation, a constitution and code of laws for their observance." (Franklin 1834, p. 211. Franklin, Benjamin (1834), Franklin, William Temple (ed.), Memoirs (eBook), vol. 2, Philadelphia: McCarty & Davis.)

The rendering of knowledge and cross reference contained in this writing makes it clear, our Founding Fathers did in fact continue to observe and include "all the commandments, and the statutes, and the judgments, as included in The Holy Bible.

Chapter 24. BIO OF CO AUTHORS

George McCarley's Executive career began with degrees in Management, Business Administration, Economics, Military Science and Engineering, becoming the G.O.A.T. of Corporate Turnaround leaders, with 48 wins and 0 losses, including Fortune 500 and Harvard MBA owned corporations in the Industrial, Mining, Metals, Retail, Automotive, Hardware/Software and Corporate Services sectors. The turnaround background included leadership of Mergers and Acquisitions of 22 "deals." This career activity is often referred to as "Masters of the Universe."

While the turnaround/M&A effort was ongoing, he led Congressional Campaigns and was a force on Presidential Campaigns. Drawn to Religion, he began Preaching in Jails and rehab/ Homeless ministry and has Preached to over 20,000 men. He has Docketed a legal case at Supreme Court of the United States, his personal work product.

The Army Veteran has been in four war zones since military exit, including Albania/Kosovo as a Missionary during the terrible Kosovo war, along with two wars you never heard about.

The McCarley background and career closely reproduces the lifetime of America's Founding Fathers, thus the perfect and rare background required to Coauthor this epic book linking The Holy Bible to every Article/Section/Clause of the US Constitution.

McCarley Authored and published DEMOKRATIA TO DEMOCRACY, THE REQUIEM, The 7000 year development of Democracy, available at 40,000 bookstore websites, in several languages. Google the title and be taken to many sources.

Ben Hand is the founding partner of Hand Law Firm, LLC. as well as a partner in Hand & Hand Mediation, LLC. Ben was admitted to the Bar in Alabama in 1990 after earning his Juris Doctor from Cumberland School of Law at Samford University. Ben completed his undergraduate degree in Business Administration from Auburn University in 1987.

Ben was born in Valley, Alabama and travelled as a child to Nicaragua, Guatemala and Mexico with his parents who worked as missionaries and teachers. It was during his childhood travels that he learned to love the Central American culture and learned to speak fluent Spanish. After high school, Ben returned to Auburn and has remained a citizen of Lee County for thirty-five years.

In 1990, Ben founded Hand Law Firm, LLC. He has been practicing for over twenty five years. Ben focuses his practice on criminal defense, civil litigation, social security, family law, and probate law. In addition to his duties at Hand Law Firm, Ben is also a state registered mediator and has served as a Municipal Judge for over twenty years. Ben has served the cities of Roanoke, Wedowee, Camp Hill and Opelika during his tenure as Municipal Judge and Prosecutor and thus has a unique perspective in criminal defense.

Ben established and is currently the Vice President of the Legal and Contracting with Emergency Response Training Systems, the only company to run military style software (jcats/acats) for training of civilian law enforcement (ERTS Opelika, Alabama). This also provides homeland security training for the Auburn University Homeland Security department.

Ben Hand is the winner of various Who's-Who awards, the Republican of the year for 2001, and a Republican Nominee for the U.S. House in 1994. He is licensed to practice law in Alabama and Georgia. Ben founded Hand, Fellows and Associates law firm and is the founding member of the board of directors of Beacon University in Columbus, Georgia.

Ben represents thirty-two different non-profit organizations in Alabama, Texas, Georgia, and Tennessee. He is a legal adviser to seventy-five different small business and corporations.

In 2006, charges were brought for an article Justice Parker, Alabama Supreme Court Judge, wrote critical of his colleagues. Parker asked Ben to represent him during the investigation. The Judicial inquiry commission found that Justice Parker had not violated any ethics codes.

Ben is a Gideon speaker and member since 1992.

Ben lives in Opelika with his wife Elizabeth Hand, together they are raising their ten children.

MOST SIGNIFICANT LEGAL INDUSTRY AWARDS

SECRETARY OF THE ARMY PROFESSIONAL RECOGNITION – 2009

TOP LAWYERS IN ALABAMA – 2013
Awarded By: The Legal Network

BEST IN CRIMINAL DEFENSE - ALABAMA -- 2015
Awarded By: The Corporate America Legalelite

10 BEST AWARD IN CLIENT SATISFACTION – 2016
Awarded By: American Institute of Criminal Law Attorneys

TOP LAWYERS IN ALABAMA – 2017
Awarded By: The Legal Network

10 BEST ATTORNEYS -- 2018
Awarded By: American Institute of Criminal Law Attorneys

LAWYERS OF DISTINCTION -- 2020
Awarded By: The National Trial Lawyers

TOP 10 CRIMINAL DEFENSE ATTORNEY -- 2021
Awarded By: Attorney And Practice Magazine's

NATIONS TOP ONE PERCENT (NADC) -- 2021
Awarded By: National Association of Distinguished Counsel

AV PREEMINENT PEER RATED FOR HIGHEST LEVEL -- 2023
OF PROFESSIONAL EXCELLENCE
Awarded By: Martindale-Hubbell

Chapter 25 INDEX and ILLUSTRATIONS

Pictorial Display

CROSS REFERENCE, CONSTITUTION - -BIBLE PARALLEL

The following is a cross reference chart so that you may quickly locate a clause of the US Constitution and go to the pages discussing Biblical roots of that clause.

You are most strongly cautioned to read the entire book prior to seeking individual clause comparisons

15TH Century BC, God gave Moses a set of Laws that our Founding Fathers utilized as the basis for the United States Constitution. We document in this book, that every clause of our United States Constitution is contained in our Holy Bible.

Contained in the US Constitution are the following highlights:
1. What Biblical Patriarch was architect of the first Pyramid?
2. Why was Moses The Lawgiver and Great Legislator?
3. What was the famous Moses Organization Plan?
4. Who was Maimonides, how does he proclaim Bible Law? (613)
5. How many men did God number of the Hebrews?
6. How did God number the men for war or battle?
7. How did God number the men for defense?
8. Why did God order the very first Signal Instrument?
9. What was the Signal Instrument?
10. Of what material was the Signal Instrument ordered by God?
11. Why did Joshua send spies into the Holy Land?
12. How many battles did Joshua fight to retake the Holy Land?
13. Who provided the battle plan for Joshua?
14. What was Gods harshest penalty for Hebrew enemies?
15. Why did God order such a harsh penalty?
16. What was Gods immigration plan?
17. What was Gods 3 part Citizenship plan?
18. What are the primary books of the law in our Holy Bible?
19. Which nation did David defeat and send off the Mainland?
20. How did King Solomon develop such vast wealth?
21. What Biblical figure was first in history named PRESIDENT?
22. What prominent member of our Founding Fathers demanded we apply the Laws of Moses within United States Constitution?
23. What mysterious verse of the Holy Bible became a standard feature of Contract Law, before writing the US Constitution?

The reader will discover all these answers within the Moses Wisdom book, as all apply to Constitutional law. You will also learn that America has "backslid" on very important biblical lessons that Founding Fathers expected to remain sacrosanct? The Co-Authors Pray that our book will help to restore America.

WHY THIS BOOK on MOSES WISDOM?

Across many generations, American schoolchildren grew up in schools that had them sing THE NATIONAL ANTHEM and often other songs, such as THIS IS GODS COUNTRY.

America of today seems to have lost much of that patriotic spirit. While reflecting on our faded American spirit, it became clear to this author that the American fading likely commenced in the aftermath of World War One. It was the outcome of that most terrible war that began to place America in the position of Greatest Among Nations. Why - - We remained on the sidelines for the first few years of WWI, and within 14 months of entry, we had won that most terrible war.

America's prowess then began to grow. Within a few years, we had sunset the League of Nations and christened The United Nations. Then we sat out WWII too long, yet our entry allowed the free world to win WWII after our entry.

Next came an economic Iconic act that made the American Dollar $ the primary currency of Planet Earth.

In the past 50 years, we have seen such a burst of new issues such as technology that we are in process of consciously amending education curriculum, shortchanging the knowledge that has made America great for 250 years.

The impact of these and other activities and triumphs of America led to a growing demise of interest in the most basic tenets of education that allowed us to gain world prominence.

While Jail Preaching for many years, we discovered a sermon approach that won many rebirths within the jailhouse. First discovery was the power of a "SONS OF THUNDER" sermon delivery. Second, anytime a sermon centered on our Bibles impact on the US Constitution and Government, inmates audience grew, weekly.

It was during Jail Preaching years, that we discovered the unison between the wording and intent of the Bible and the US Constitution, that this book was birthed.

www.ingramcontent.com/pod-product-compliance
Lightning Source LLC
La Vergne TN
LVHW022033200926
848481LV00007B/2673